Postmodernity and Univocity

Postmodernity and Univocity

A Critical Account of Radical Orthodoxy and John Duns Scotus

Daniel P. Horan, OFM

Fortress Press
Minneapolis

POSTMODERNITY AND UNIVOCITY

A Critical Account of Radical Orthodoxy and John Duns Scotus

Cover image: John Duns Scotus. Ghent, Joos (Justus) van (c.1435–c.1480). Galleria Nazionale delle Marche, Urbino (Palazzo Ducale), Ital. Photo Credit: Scala / Art Resource, NY

Cover design: Alisha Lofgren

Library of Congress Cataloging-in-Publication Data

Print ISBN: 978-1-4514-6572-3

eBook ISBN: 978-1-4514-6965-3

The paper used in this publication meets the minimum requirements of American National Standard for Information Sciences — Permanence of Paper for Printed Library Materials, ANSI Z329.48-1984.

Manufactured in the U.S.A.

This book was produced using Pressbooks.com, and PDF rendering was done by PrinceXML.

Contents

Acknowledgements

A book with an audacious subtitle the likes of "a critical account" might be seen as offering a final word or the definitive take on the subject about which it is concerned. However, that is not the case here. I do not feign to be a Scotus expert in the way that many of the insightful medievalists I cite in this text surely are, nor do I lay claim to having the apodictic interpretation of his thought and legacy. Rather, I present the following project in an effort to offer an alternative accounting of the "Scotus Story" and encourage other scholars and students to explore more critically and deeply the theological narratives that cast the medieval Franciscan philosopher and theologian John Duns Scotus in such inauspicious light. I am grateful for religious and intellectual communities that have fostered such an interest on my part, and hope that this initial "critical account" might lead others along similar paths. I wish to acknowledge a number of people who have been helpful and encouraging along this particular journey.

I extend a sincere note of gratitude to those who have offered scholarly support and feedback at various stages of this book's production. Prof. Ilia Delio, OSF, and Prof. Edward McCormack were the first to offer direction, support, and constructive feedback during the earliest stages of this project's development several years ago when the foundations for this book were first laid as I worked on my first master's degree. Prof. Terrance Tilley generously read early versions of some chapters and provided encouragement, helpful feedback, and constructive criticism. My friends Julianne Wallace and Jessica Coblentz read large parts of this project at various stages and offered fruitful comments. Thanks also goes to Jessica for her skillful assistance with the indexing of this book. This book has also been enriched by discussions at the American Academy of Religion regional conference at Syracuse University in 2011, where I presented a portion of the research from chapter 3, as well as in a systematics-area colloquium in the Department of Theology at Boston College in the 2012 fall semester, at which time Prof. Stephen Brown facilitated a discussion about themes related to this book. I am grateful to Prof. Thomas Williams for making some insightful yet unpublished conference papers available to me, and to Prof. Scott Williams for directing me to some other helpful resources. Additional conversations with others over the years about the subject matter explored here have no doubt positively shaped this book. Thanks go to Prof. Susan Abraham, Prof. Joshua Benson, Prof. Brian Robinette, Prof. Richard Gaillardetz, Rev. Benson Shelton, and David Golemboski, to name just a few. While so many people have been helpful to me in various ways, I must offer the requisite disclaimer that all errors are my own.

I am grateful for the opportunity to study at several institutions of higher education and learn as a member of these scholarly communities; key among these are St. Bonaventure University, The Franciscan Institute, The Washington Theological Union, and Boston College. Aspects of this project are indebted to each of these schools in different ways.

Finally, I must express thanks to my editors Michael Gibson and Lisa Gruenisen and to Fortress Press for the immediate enthusiasm and support shown to me from the very beginning. I am especially indebted to Mike's kind patience with me as I finished this book, more or less on schedule.

Introduction: The Return to the Narrative

Since the early 1990s, a new theological movement has captured the attention of scholars and students. This new school of theology was founded—at least incipiently—by John Milbank, and its motto is contained in the claim, "Once there was no 'secular,'" which graces the earliest pages of his now-classic book *Theology and Social Theory*.[1] In some sense, *Theology and Social Theory* serves as a manifesto of the nascent movement that first found its momentum at the Divinity School of the University of Cambridge. Soon Milbank was joined by former graduate students and colleagues who would bolster his early vision of a restoration of theology to a place of primacy that, he argued, was usurped by the elevation of social science over theological and philosophical inquiry. Rooted in a particularly idiosyncratic form of Thomism, Radical Orthodoxy, as the movement has come to be known, is largely concerned with the reinstallation of theology as the "queen of sciences."[2]

Milbank identifies the source of the decline of theological primacy with the advent of modernity and the emergence of "the secular." This new worldview, perhaps characterized best by the work of the

---

1. John Milbank, *Theology and Social Theory: Beyond Secular Reason*, 2nd ed. (Oxford: Blackwell, 2006), 9.
2. For the most comprehensive study of Radical Orthodoxy's use of Thomas Aquinas, see Paul DeHart, *Aquinas and Radical Orthodoxy: A Critical Inquiry* (London: Routledge, 2012).

modern philosophers of the seventeenth and eighteenth centuries, appears to have separated philosophical investigation from theology. The subsequent advancements in science and technology only contributed to the further subordination of theology. One of the fundamental claims advanced by Radical Orthodoxy thinkers is that a major source of the manifold problems present in today's society, culture, and academy can be traced to this place called the secular that "stands apart," as it were, from God. Radical Orthodox theologians believe that this space called the secular was not discovered so much as invented. This worldview relies on the reestablishment of the credibility of a metanarrative that situates theology at the heart of intellectual inquiry and reflection, no small task in the face of modern autonomy and the centrality of the subject, or the subsequent postmodern suspicion of master stories. It is in this light that Radical Orthodoxy sees itself as truly *post*-modern, or as a viable alternative to the problems of modernity. Those who generally identity with or are sympathetic to the Radical Orthodoxy movement seek a restorative vision that verges on the reactionary: the answer to the problems of our time, socially and academically, can be found in a return to the past and the selective *ressourcement* of a philosophical insight that is deeply theological. In other words, the Radical Orthodoxy movement's response to the perceived challenges of modernity and secularity has been to reconsider theology as the foundation for all intellectual inquiry. However, it is not just *any* type of theology that can serve as the requisite response to the problems Radical Orthodoxy has uncovered. As Paul DeHart explains, "To counter the dereliction in face of these threats that has plagued most theologies since the modern epoch, Radical Orthodoxy promotes the critical recovery of the unsullied ontological vision that predates the rise of modern ideas."[3]

The form of this process has been largely narrative in its foundation, taking a variety of subfields (ecclesiology, politics, aesthetics, epistemology, music and others) as dialogue partners, yet built upon an a priori theological system. The Radical Orthodoxy method is dependent on the rejection of modernity and its apparent implications. As Wayne Hankey has succinctly noted, "The retrieval of the pre-modern against modernity makes historical narrative essential to Radical Orthodoxy—indeed, as we shall see, re-narrating history is the only way it can establish the authority of its orthodoxy."[4] This has led Milbank and others to trace the development of modernity back to its origins, in order to more effectively diagnose intellectual and social ills. Whereas most scholars hold the work of Kant and other modern thinkers as the harbinger of what is popularly understood as modernity, Milbank and the Radical Orthodoxy theologians believe the trajectory that leads to the modern age actually begins much earlier, with the work of John Duns Scotus, the late-thirteenth-century Franciscan theologian and philosopher. This hypothesis is not entirely original to Milbank or those who follow his theological lead; however, it is because of Milbank's seminal work and its appropriation in the work of the other Radical Orthodoxy theologians that this particular narrative—Scotus as protomodernist—has become ubiquitous in a great deal of contemporary theological discourse. The Radical Orthodoxy movement has established their anti-Scotus narrative—what I will call the "Scotus Story"—as the reason par excellence for the problems of theology over the course of recent centuries. While Milbank

---

3. Ibid., 3.

4. Wayne Hankey, "Radical Orthodoxy's *Poiēsis*: Ideological Historiography and Anti-Modern Polemic," *American Catholic Philosophical Quarterly* 80 (2006): 7. For more on the idiosyncratic historiographical construction of John Milbank particularly and Radical Orthodoxy generally, see Paul Janz, "Radical Orthodoxy and the New Culture of Obscurantism," *Modern Theology* 20 (2004): 363–405.

admits that Scotus is not solely responsible for the problems associated with modernity and secularity, the subtle doctor nevertheless remains the primary object of scrutiny and blame, unsurpassed in criticism by Radical Orthodoxy adherents. For Milbank, Scotus represents decisively "the turning point in the destiny of the West."[5] As we will see in chapter 1, Milbank and his likeminded theological colleagues understand Scotus's original and innovative approach to the concept of being as the cardinal point of theology's downfall and the inauguration of what will become modernity. The Radical Orthodoxy Scotus Story portrays Scotus as proposing a problematic metaphysical claim, suggesting that *being* is something akin to a genus under which both God and creatures fall like two species. If this were in fact true, there might be something to their concern. However, as we will see in the second half of the book, this is not what Scotus argues.

Despite the lack of grounding in Scotus's actual writings that would support Radical Orthodoxy's interpretations and use of his thought, this Scotus Story has become well known. The proliferation of this perspective on the origins of modernity and the problems with Scotus's philosophical and theological outlook has gone largely unquestioned over the course of the last two decades, outside the occasional treatment offered by a handful of historical philosophers and Scotus specialists. As we will see in chapter 2, that this narrative has gained traction beyond the confines of the Radical Orthodoxy circle has been as fascinating as it is perplexing. There are at least a couple of reasons why this vilification of Scotus and his work might have flourished as it has. First, Scotus is a notoriously complex thinker, which can contribute to easy misinterpretation even by

---

5. John Milbank, *The Word Made Strange* (Oxford: Blackwell, 1997), 44. This sort of claim is repeated in numerous places throughout Milbank's writings and the broader Radical Orthodoxy corpus.

those who seek to understand the subtle doctor according to his own terms. In addition to the nuanced and painstakingly logical approach Scotus takes to philosophical and theological questions, the subtle doctor's early death and lack of any complete systematic work adds to the difficult scholarly terrain one must traverse in order to engage Scotus's thought as such. Richard Cross, a medieval specialist, explains that too many people approach Scotus as one might approach Thomas Aquinas (certainly a method well known to Radical Orthodoxy theologians). This is unhelpful because

> parts are very much work in progress, and in these areas it is hard to form one coherent systematically developed theory—most notably, [Scotus's] philosophy of mind and theory of cognition, but also (probably) his ethics. But his thought moves in such powerfully anti-Aristotelian directions, highly original, that it is tempting to suppose that he could not have achieved his goals without rejecting far more of Aristotle than he actually did.[6]

Unlike Aquinas, who lived nearly twice as long as Scotus, who was much more systematic in his thought, and who followed Aristotle more closely than Scotus, the subtle doctor is not as easily categorized and caricatured. The difficulty of the texts themselves, compounded by the distinct historical and intellectual context in which Scotus worked, makes him an easy target for misrepresentation, whether intentional or not. Even those who dedicate the requisite time and energy to studying Scotus's work are not able to escape the significant possibility that they will still not arrive at a clear understanding of his thought.

Second, most theologians never bother in any way to grapple with Scotus's complex thought in order to appreciate his extraordinarily nuanced, if at times still incomplete, arguments. Because of this,

6. Richard Cross, *The Medieval Christian Philosophers: An Introduction* (New York: I. B. Tauris, 2013), 164.

the majority of nonspecialists that refer to Scotus do so according to caricatures and overly simplistic interpretations that are merely repeated again and again. In his now-classic 1942 text on Scotus's philosophy and the univocity of the concept of being, Cyril Shircel wrote in a strikingly prescient way that

> the doctrine of the univocity of the notion of being and the univocal predication of being has become identified with Duns Scotus. Unfortunately, however, it has become identified with him in a very unfavorable and unjustifiable interpretation. Perhaps no other doctrine of the subtle doctor has been more misunderstood and misinterpreted for lack of scientific research.[7]

Long before Milbank, Scotist scholars recognized the propensity of nonspecialists to make sweeping and inaccurate generalizations about Scotus's thought. Perhaps because of the reasons named above, there exists a longstanding precedent for the passing on of (over-) simplified narratives. Because Scotus is rarely given the attention afforded to other medieval figures such as Anselm, Aquinas, or Bonaventure, the onus falls to individual scholars to return to the primary source material to evaluate received interpretations of his thought. The sad truth is, as Shircel noted decades ago, very few have bothered to read closely Scotus's own writings, and the result has been perennial reinscription of errant readings and presentations.

These and other complicating factors have paved the way for the easy dissemination and subsequent appropriation of Radical Orthodoxy's Scotus Story. This book is my modest contribution to offer a corrective response to this increasing trend.

---

7. Cyril Shircel, *The Univocity of the Concept of Being in the Philosophy of John Duns Scotus* (Washington: Catholic University of America Press, 1942), 7.

What This Book Is and Is Not

There already exist a number of fine overviews of Radical Orthodoxy.[8] Therefore, this book will not attempt to provide a general introduction to or survey of the development of the broad movement. Instead, the scope of this project is decidedly narrow. This book is my attempt, imperfect as it surely is, to respond to the Scotus Story in a critical and corrective manner in three ways. First, I highlight the ways in which key figures of the Radical Orthodoxy movement have initially constructed and subsequently developed their Scotus Story, which has since been appropriated by theologians, philosophers, and historians in various ways. Second, I survey the work of those who have previously responded to some of the claims Radical Orthodoxy has advanced regarding Scotus. Here, I am indebted to the excellent work that several historical philosophers and Scotus specialists have offered in disparate articles, conference papers, and symposia contributions. While much of these materials are more or less accessible in various scholarly journals, there exists no single study that surveys and evaluates the scholarship heretofore presented on the theme of Radical Orthodoxy's interpretation and use of Scotus. Third, I offer an alternative reading of Scotus's approach to the univocal concept of being in an effort to correct the egregious Scotus Story. I do not claim to be an expert on John Duns Scotus in the manner of a medievalist or a historical philosopher. As I noted above, I rely heavily on the excellent and careful work of many such scholars and it is upon their shoulders I stand to present this

---

8. For example, see D. Stephen Long, "Radical Orthodoxy," in *The Cambridge Companion to Postmodern Theology*, ed. Kevin Vanhoozer (New York: Cambridge University Press, 2003), 126–45; James K. A. Smith, *Introducing Radical Orthodoxy: Mapping a Post-Secular Theology* (Grand Rapids: Baker Academic, 2004); Steven Shakespeare, *Radical Orthodoxy: A Critical Introduction* (London: SPCK, 2007); and Simon Oliver, "Introducing Radical Orthodoxy: From Participation to Late Modernity," in *The Radical Orthodoxy Reader*, ed. John Milbank and Simon Oliver (London: Routledge, 2009), 3–27.

monograph. My efforts here aim at providing an alternative reading of Scotus that allows for a restoration of the subtle doctor's name in an age when his thought, innovative and original as it is, might aid theologians and philosophers rather than hinder their work.

In many ways I see this book as something of a companion volume to Paul DeHart's excellent 2012 monograph, *Aquinas and Radical Orthodoxy: A Critical Inquiry*. In his text, DeHart carefully examines many of Radical Orthodoxy's claims about Thomas Aquinas, concluding at times that their original approach departs significantly from what the angelic doctor wrote or intended. Whereas DeHart studies Radical Orthodoxy's use of Aquinas, who serves as the protagonist of Radical Orthodoxy's metanarrative, this book offers a comparable study of the movement's chosen antagonist, Scotus. Also like DeHart with Aquinas, I do not claim to offer an exhaustive treatment of the movement's use of Scotus, nor do I portend to provide the definitive account of the subtle doctor's work on univocity. Instead, I feel compelled to proceed with this study out of a sense of necessity, recognizing the need for a wider engagement with both Radical Orthodoxy and the thought of Scotus as such. To date, there exists no other monograph that deals in depth with this subject. Finally, as DeHart disclaims in his project, I do not intend to proffer an "attack" on Milbank and other Radical Orthodoxy thinkers or on the movement itself. There are many formidable aspects to the project that has grown under the aegis of Radical Orthodoxy, most notably a perceptible shift in the scholarly discourse surrounding the place of theology in the academy and its potential to shape and be shaped by other intellectual disciplines. My interest is in addressing erroneous readings of Scotus's work and the perpetuation of misrepresentative claims about his thought.

Before proceeding with this project, there is an important methodological consideration I must address. As I state above, my concern follows that of Richard Cross, Thomas Williams, and others who have likewise recognized the misrepresentation of Scotus and his thought throughout the Radical Orthodoxy corpus. Milbank and his fellow Radical Orthodoxy theologians present Scotus as a scapegoat, and his thought as the intellectual locus that irrevocably shifts the course of theology and philosophy. While I have serious concerns about the post-Scotus genealogical narrative Radical Orthodoxy posits, my focus here is not to contest the possibility that how Scotus's thought was subsequently received, interpreted, and used might have led to the conclusions Milbank and others suggest. How the subtle doctor's thought was or was not interpreted and used after the fact is not something for which the medieval Franciscan himself can be held accountable. Nor should the real or imagined interpretations and subsequent usages be read into the subtle doctor's work per se.

Another way to talk about this distinction is to follow the insightful demarcation that Christine Helmer makes in her review of Milbank and Pickstock's coauthored book *Truth in Aquinas*. Helmer notes,

> In historical theology and philosophy, there are two major ways in which a canonical figure can be appropriated for the contemporary discussion of a topic. Firstly, a historical figure can be studied in order to pursue a topic in detail that, although perennial, is given a distinctive shaping by the author in question. To borrow from Schleiermacher's famous definition of hermeneutics, this path requires mustering an apparatus of interpretative tools (i.e., philological, hermeneutical, histocial-critical) in order to understand a text (and its author) as correctly as possible. In view of this option, the reader will find errors in the interpretation of Aquinas. . . . Secondly, a historical figure can be used as a springboard for launching contemporary concerns. With this option, correct interpretation is clearly not as important as making use of that figure to inspire a vision addressed to a present-tense audience.[9]

9. Christine Helmer, review of *Truth in Aquinas*, *International Journal of Systematic Theology* 5 (2003): 93–94.

Helmer goes on to suggest that a reader evaluating the work of Milbank and Pickstock, at least in their *Truth in Aquinas* (and I would argue in nearly all of their texts), will find their understanding and presentation erroneous according to the first hermeneutical approach (that of *interpretation*). Yet, if a reader were to look at their project through the lens of the second hermeneutical approach (that of *use*) there might be merit to their project. While I see the value of reading all texts with a hermeneutic of generosity, the claims Radical Orthodoxy makes are ultimately presented according to Helmer's hermeneutic of *interpretation*, despite the fact that the Scotus Story could only result from the latter method, Helmer's hermeneutic of *use*. I am not interested in evaluating the doxagraphical quality of Radical Orthodoxy's use of Scotus.[10] Rather, I am deeply concerned about the reduction of a formidable thinker's work to nothing more than a straw argument against which to establish a self-serving genealogy and metanarrative. Because Milbank and the Radical Orthodoxy thinkers that follow him ascribe certain claims to Scotus, rooted in their *interpretations* of Scotus's work, there is need for redress. That is the point of this book.

I intentionally limit this study to what Radical Orthodoxy theologians say about Scotus and his thought, as well as how they ultimately deploy those interpretations. I do so in an effort to restore the good name of the medieval thinker. Whether or not Radical Orthodoxy's subsequent metanarrative of the emergence of modernity continues to hold after a corrective reading of Scotus's *actual* view on the univocal concept of being is presented remains

10. By "doxographical quality" of the argument posited by the Radical Orthodoxy movement, I am referring to the practice of transmitting a previously held opinion, belief, or view that does not take into account the original source material of a given thinker. This will be taken up in greater detail in chapter 3. For more, see Simon Blackburn, "Doxography," in *Oxford Dictionary of Philosophy* (New York: Oxford University Press, 2005), 105: "The practice of recording the opinions of other philosophers, practiced by classical philosophers and historians."

for others to determine. One might alternatively read this book as a theological amicus brief written to offer evidence on behalf of Scotus's historical exoneration, an attempt to let Scotus speak for himself and permit contemporary theologians to engage the medieval thinker's work on its own terms. For, as Shircel wrote, "Whether one agrees with the subtle doctor, Duns Scotus, or not, we are convinced that his critique of the concept of analogy and his subsequent adoption of univocity of being bring out the problem of our naturally acquired knowledge of God to greater precision."[11] The reader might not ultimately side with Scotus, but agreement is not the point. A rejection of Scotus's approach is only conceivable after an accurate reading of his argument, something that Radical Orthodoxy has not demonstrated.[12]

The Structure of this Book

The first chapter is an examination of Radical Orthodoxy's use of John Duns Scotus and the formation of the subsequent Scotus Story that posits the subtle doctor as the primary progenitor in the genealogy of modernity. Beginning with the foundational work of John Milbank and his establishment of the nascent Scotus Story, this chapter also includes a detailed consideration of the work of Catherine Pickstock. Pickstock has been the most vocal critic of Scotus, and the most persistent proponent of the Radical Orthodoxy Scotus Story after her *doktorvater*'s initial drafting of the narrative.

11. Shircel, *The Univocity of the Concept of Being*, 2.
12. In addition to DeHart's *Aquinas and Radical Orthodoxy*, for more on Milbank's (and Radical Orthodoxy's) approach to history, historiography, and theology, see John Bowlin, "Parts, Wholes, and Opposites: John Milbank as *Geisteshistoriker*," *Journal of Religious Ethics* 32 (2004): 257–69; and Scott MacDougall, "Scapegoating the Secular: The Irony of Mimetic Violence in the Social Theology of John Milbank," in *Violence, Transformation, and the Sacred: "They Shall Be Called Children of God,"* ed. Margaret Pfeil and Tobias Winright (Maryknoll: Orbis, 2012), 85–98.

The chapter closes with a short overview of how Radical Orthodoxy theologians Conor Cunningham, Graham Ward, and Gavin Hyman appropriate and advance the Scotus Story.

The second chapter offers a brief survey of the way Radical Orthodoxy's Scotus Story has been subsequently appropriated in wide-ranging ways from theology to history. From among the diverse areas of influence, this chapter examines several contemporary examples of how the Scotus Story has been appropriated in the work of both academic and popular writers including Adrian Pabst, Stanley Hauerwas, Karen Armstrong, Francis Cardinal George, Robert Barron, and Brad Gregory.

The third chapter offers a detailed assessment of the Radical Orthodoxy movement's use of John Duns Scotus as outlined in chapter 1. Subdivided into three sections, the first two sections are concerned with presenting the critical insights of two major Scotist scholars in response to the Radical Orthodoxy narrative. The first, Richard Cross, offers some keen elucidatory insights that help clarify some of the most problematic characteristics of the Radical Orthodoxy interpretation of Scotus. The second, Thomas Williams, argues for the validity of Scotus's doctrine of the univocity of being as both true and salutary. The third section focuses on additional dimensions of the Scotus Story in need of further explication and analysis.

The fourth chapter is dedicated to presenting Scotus's univocity of being in an accurate format so as to offer a corrective to the Radical Orthodoxy Scotus Story. Organized in two parts, this chapter provides both a contextual and an expository presentation. The first part focuses on the often-overlooked and important role of Henry of Ghent in the formation of Scotus's position. The second part, the larger of the two, is a corrective reading of Scotus's univocity of being, rooted in primary sources and supported by sound Scotist scholarship.

This book is a return to the narrative, the Scotus narrative.

Modeled after Radical Orthodoxy's contention that ideas have a history, I believe that Scotus's work is not really the problem-inducing source of protomodernity that Milbank and others believe. While I acknowledge Scotus's thought—like that of any thinker—can be used for ill purposes or misconstrued to suit particular agendas not original to the author, I believe that Scotus can actually be a resource for contemporary theological inquiry in a postmodern age. A return to the Scotus narrative requires critical analysis that follows to uncover a more accurate reading of the theological and philosophical positions the subtle doctor developed. In the process, the shifts and errors that mark the history of Radical Orthodoxy's Scotus Story in contradistinction to Scotus's thought as such will emerge. In the end, while no thinker is ever completely protected from the critique that is constitutive of academic study, it is my hope that Scotus might be freed from much of the malevolent reputation and historical misreading to which he has been subjected over the years. Only then might an accurate Scotus Story, one for our time, be written.

1

———

Radical Orthodoxy's Use of John Duns Scotus

The establishment of an explicit genealogy that traces modernity, and, subsequently, the concept of nihilism as substantial *res*, back to John Duns Scotus (d. 1308) occurred through an evolutionary process. In recent history, this genealogy finds its advent in the seminal work of John Milbank, and it is upon the foundation of his work that others have constructed edifices built on the narrative of Scotus as *the* protomodern antagonist. Displacing the early modern Enlightenment thinkers, Scotus serves as the inaugurator of all that is ill with modernity. While Milbank is correct in pointing to the existence of scholarly opinions prior to his own that suggest Scotus's work anticipated the dawn of modernity, thereby paving the way for post-Enlightenment creation of the "secular,"[1] it is Milbank's

---

1. Here Milbank names several prominent philosophers and theologians to support his case, but the position he maintains follows most closely that of Étienne Gilson. While the matter of Milbank and others' reading of Gilson will be addressed below, the legitimacy of Milbank's study of these and other authors cited to support this reading of Scotus is questionable, given the

adoption and integration of this narrative into his theological project that launched the ensuing onslaught of contemporary anti-Scotist polemics. Most notable among those voices contributing to this discourse is the Milbank protégé and Radical Orthodoxy contributor Catherine Pickstock. Pickstock, following Milbank's lead, focuses her attention on the subtle doctor in an effort to advance her conviction that Thomas Aquinas's understanding of *analogia entis* is the most correct way to consider God and being (*esse*). Pickstock has engaged in public scholarly debates, always maintaining that her reading of Scotus is accurate, while attempting to fend off critiques from scholars who specialize in Scotus's philosophy and theology who argue that her claims represent a misreading and misinterpretation of the medieval Franciscan's thought.

The Creation of the Scotus Story

Beyond his initial engagement with and interpretation of Scotus's concept of the univocity of being as the impetus for nominalism[2] and the subsequent emergence of the "secular," Milbank has not

subsequent reevaluation by Scotus scholars of Gilson's presentation as an unfairly oversimplified view of Scotus. Milbank's primary resources in this apparently antecedent line of thinkers who attributed the seeds of modernity to Scotus are Étienne Gilson, *Jean Duns Scot* (Paris: Vrin, 1952); and Gilson, *Études sur le role de la pensée médiévale dans la formation du système Cartésien* (Paris: Vrin, 1930). Milbank also directs the reader to Ludger Honnefelder, *Scientia Transcendens: Die Formale Bestimmung der Seiendheit et Realität in der Metaphysik der Mittelalters und der Neuzeit*, Paradeigmata 9 (Hamburg: Fleix Meiner, 1990). See John Milbank, *Theology and Social Theory: Beyond Secular Reason*, 2nd ed. (Oxford: Blackwell, 2006), xxv n41.

2. While this point of contention will be addressed in greater detail below, it is important to note from the onset that Scotists do not support the claim advanced by Milbank et al. that Scotus was ever a "nominalist" in the strict sense. There is no apparent scholarly evidence to suggest that Scotus was a "protonominalist" akin to the accusations leveled against William of Ockham (a position that is also debated). For more, see Thomas Williams, "The Doctrine of Univocity is True and Salutary," *Modern Theology* 21 (October 2005): 575–85; and Williams, "Radical Orthodoxy, Univocity and the New Apophaticism," unpublished paper delivered at the International Congress for Medieval Studies (Kalamazoo, MI, 2006).

In his more recent work, *Beyond Secular Order: The Representation of Being and the Representation of the People* (Oxford: Wiley-Blackwell, 2014), Milbank seems to more returned to the subtle doctor to further develop his initial claims.[3] As a result, this has left Pickstock to represent both her own and, vicariously, his voice on the matter in the subsequent theological conversation. Pickstock has clearly become the champion of the anti-Scotist cause, remaining the loudest of the critics positioned in the Radical Orthodoxy camp.[4]

Following the foundational work of Milbank and Pickstock, nearly every contributor to the theological conversation within Radical Orthodoxy has either plainly adopted this "Scotus-as-villain" narrative as axiomatic or, through some variation on the theme, retraced a similar sequence found in the first monographs of the

adequately acknowledge a distinction between Scotus and the later nominalist school, as when he writes, "I am thinking of Scotus and then of the nominalists" (23).

3. Shortly before the completion of this book, Milbank had not developed further his arguments about Scotus beyond what was presented early in his work, although he had frequently returned to those claims in subsequent essays and lectures, reiterating his earlier narrative. However, as this current book was in the final editorial stages of production, and as luck would have it, Milbank released *Beyond Secular Order*, which he presents as a "successor volume to *Theology and Social Theory*, [that] seeks to deepen its analyses" (1). The untimely coincidence of these two publications' overlap has prohibited me from substantively studying and incorporating this new Milbank text into *Postmodernity and Univocity*. Where I have been able, I include relevant references to *Beyond Secular Order*, but I do not claim to have given this latest book a thorough examination. This will have to be reserved for another time. Suffice it to say, as I note in the conclusion, that while Milbank devotes nearly half of this new book to expanding and reinforcing his earlier Scotus Story, little is added by way of correction or satisfactory response to critiques of his original and subsequently repeated interpretation of the subtle doctor and his work. Instead, the bulk of additional references in *Beyond Secular Order* tend to come from those figures discussed later in chapter 1 and in chapter 2 that inherit and represent the Radical Orthodoxy Scotus Story—these figures include Catherine Pickstock, Conor Cunningham, Adiran Pabst, and Charles Taylor, among others. The story has not changed, but instead it has been bolstered by those who have already confirmed Milbank's theses concerning Scotus.

On a related note, Milbank has another monograph in press, which also returns to the general themes of *Theology and Social Theory*. See his forthcoming *Philosophy: A Theological Critique* (Oxford: Blackwell, 2014).

4. See especially Catherine Pickstock, "Duns Scotus: His Historical and Contemporary Significance," *Modern Theology* 21 (October 2005): 543–74; Pickstock, "The Univocalist Mode of Production," in *Theology and the Political*, ed. John Milbank, Slavoj Zizek, and Creston Davis (Durham, NC: Duke University Press, 2005), 281–325; Pickstock, "Modernity and Scholasticism: A Critique of Recent Invocations of Univocity," *Antonianum* 78 (2003): 3–47; and Pickstock, *After Writing: On the Liturgical Consummation of Philosophy* (Oxford: Blackwell, 1998).

movement. After Pickstock, the most detailed treatment of the Radical Orthodoxy position on Scotus comes in the form of Conor Cunningham's *Genealogy of Nihilism*.[5] Cunningham focuses his attention in the entire first half of this text on the development of, and the logic behind, nihilism. In doing so, he focuses on John Duns Scotus with particularly severe scrutiny, identifying his philosophical system as significantly informing the would-be nominalist project of the subtle doctor's philosophical and theological successor William of Ockham (d. 1347). Cunningham, perhaps more so than his Radical Orthodoxy predecessors, is willing to associate Scotus with Ockham in an accomplice-like manner. This is highly problematic for reasons to be addressed later in this book.

Alongside Cunningham stands the coeditor of the *Radical Orthodoxy* volume, Graham Ward. Ward has appeared less concerned with contributing to the Scotus Story posited by Milbank than Pickstock and Cunningham have been, and more interested in building upon the narrative already constructed.[6] Ward's acceptance of the Scotus Story is important, in that his work is given gracious latitude of deference and has been influential within the Radical Orthodoxy movement. Ward's reception of the Scotus Story contributes to the validation of a narrative that accepts Scotus as villain antecedently to modernity and the "secular." The participation of Ward in postmodern theological discourse, a position within which he holds a place of prominence, coincides with the ongoing creation of a grammar based on presuppositions of Scotus's culpability.

---

5. Conor Cunningham, *Genealogy of Nihilism: Philosophies of Nothing and the Difference of Theology* (London: Routledge, 2002). This treatment will be explored in more detail at the end of this chapter.
6. See Graham Ward, *Cities of God* (London: Routledge, 2000), esp. 155–60, 190, and 252–56.

Like Ward, there are numerous contributors to and sympathizers with Radical Orthodoxy that adhere to the Scotus Story and adopt the modern/secular/nihilistic genealogy that begins with the subtle doctor. Some of these thinkers include Tracey Roland, Gavin Hyman, Philip Blond, Stephen Long, Simon Oliver, and Daniel Bell, among others. [7] Additionally, James K. A. Smith, a voice from the Reformed Christian tradition who has written sympathetically to Radical Orthodoxy, accepts the Scotus Story, though he is not very concerned as such about pre-Cartesian influences on the subsequent emergence of modernity.[8]

In this chapter, I present the position on John Duns Scotus held by the founding scholars of Radical Orthodoxy, with a particular focus on their interpretation and use of his work in the construction of a narrative that continues to serve as the foundation for subsequent theological inquiry and the historical critique of modernity under the aegis of the Radical Orthodoxy movement. The presentation will take both an author-based and a quasi-chronological outline. While these two forms of qualified analysis often follow a parallel trajectory over the course of Radical Orthodoxy's short history, I have selected to forego a strict chronological-historical approach in favor of an organization based on individual thinkers (or group of thinkers). This method, I believe, will allow the reader to acquire an appreciation for the development of what I am calling the Scotus Story over the course of its scripting. We will trace the Scotus Story from its nascent

7. See Tracey Roland, *Culture and the Thomist Tradition: After Vatican II* (London: Routledge, 2003), esp. 189n30 and 197n69.; Gavin Hyman, *The Predicament of Postmodern Theology: Radical Orthodoxy or Nihilist Textualism?* (Louisville: Westminster John Knox, 2001); Philip Blond, *Post-Secular Philosophy* (London: Routledge, 1998); D. Stephen Long, *Divine Economy: Theology and the Market* (London: Routledge, 2000); Simon Oliver, *Philosophy, God and Motion* (London: Routledge, 2005); and Daniel Bell, *Liberation Theology After the End of History: The Refusal to Cease Suffering* (London: Routledge, 2001).

8. See James K. A. Smith, *Speech and Theology: Language and the Logic of Incarnation* (London: Routledge, 2002) and Smith, *Introducing Radical Orthodoxy: Mapping a Post-Secular Theology* (Grand Rapids: Baker Academic, 2004), esp. 87–122 and 185–229.

composition in the seminal work of John Milbank through the more polemical scholarship of Catherine Pickstock to its present state as it is received and repeated.

The first section of this chapter focuses on Milbank and his *Theology and Social Theory*. Here we see the Scotus Story in its most primitive stage. Following a reading of this text, we will explore Milbank's later work, in which he contributes to continuing conversation about univocity and the role of Scotus in the establishment of modernity and the secular. After Milbank, our attention will turn to Pickstock and her significant contribution to this narrative. This section will focus on her work in *After Writing*, her contribution to *Truth in Aquinas* and her many articles on the subject.[9] This chapter will conclude with a short summation, before moving on to the next chapter, in which we will survey how the Scotus Story has been subsequently received and appropriated in theological, philosophical, and historical circles.

John Milbank, *Theology and Social Theory*, and the Birth of a Story

Central to John Milbank's conception of modernity is the understanding that ideas have a history. This includes the notion of the secular, an idea that Milbank believes has a particular and accessible chronology, and for which he attempts to sketch out a narrative map. In a classic manner, Milbank begins his story with the now-famous line, "Once, there was no 'secular.'"[10] From here, he develops a complex schema that accounts for the presecular condition of divine participation and suspension. In other words, prior to the dawn of this "idea" of the secular, which is ultimately a construct of

9. John Milbank and Catherine Pickstock, *Truth in Aquinas* (London: Routledge, 2001).
10. Milbank, *Theology and Social Theory*, 9.

modernity, everything was understood in relationship to the divine. Milbank (with Graham Ward and Catherine Pickstock) explains that what is meant by this participatory relationship to, or suspension from, the divine is more precisely that understanding "as developed by Plato and reworked by Christianity, because any alternative configuration perforce reserves a territory independent of God."[11] Herein lies the problem. The secular, this conceptual modern construction, reserves a space outside of the divine. D. Stephen Long offers a summary of this fabricated location:

> Modernity is the construction of a space and time where the conditions for the possibility of knowing (the transcendental) are given not in "things" but in our ability to transcend such objects by way of a critical reflective standpoint that assumes a "secure" subjective presence. Through this transcendental standpoint, objects of knowledge are given meaning.[12]

Milbank explains that the only solution to this problem is to ground all human inquiry and each academic discipline in theology. Without this foundational theological perspective, Milbank asserts, these disciplines will define a space outside of God.[13] As such, this space is therefore grounded in "nothing," a path that is, by definition, nihilistic.

The story continues with the claim that before the arrival of the secular, there was no "objective, autonomous, or neutral reason, no state, no public or private sphere, and no space that was not always already understood to be liturgical and doxological—oriented toward praise of the divine."[14] It is again important to note the active sense of

---

11. John Milbank, Graham Ward and Catherine Pickstock, "Introduction: Suspending the Material: The Turn of Radical Orthodoxy," in *Radical Orthodoxy: A New Theology*, ed. John Milbank, Graham Ward, and Catherine Pickstock (London: Routledge, 1999), 3.
12. D. Stephen Long, "Radical Orthodoxy," in *The Cambridge Companion to Postmodern Theology*, ed. Kevin Vanhoozer (New York: Cambridge University Press, 2003), 127.
13. Milbank et al., "Introduction," 3. Also, see Smith, *Introducing Radical Orthodoxy*, 88.

the word *arrival* in observing the presence of the idea of the secular.[15] For Milbank, modernity and secularity are always understood in terms of process and development. These concepts are neither a priori nor atemporal, but have a determinable origin.

The quest to identify the origin of modernity, and therefore the secular, is not new. Many popular accounts isolate the origin of modernity within what has been termed the "early modern" period of philosophy, associated with names like Descartes, Kant, Locke, Hobbes, and Smith. The seventeenth and eighteenth centuries have therefore been considered the historical locus of emergent modernity. Milbank offers an alternative genesis. His suggestion is that we look past the Enlightenment to focus instead on the late Middle Ages.

Milbank's turn toward the late Middle Ages begins with his analysis of political theology and his critique of sociology. Like the notion of the secular, the idea of the political (which Milbank defines as "a field of pure power"[16]) is the product of the new scientific conceptualization of society that understands society as an autonomous object. A hallmark of this new object is the novel definition of practical reason that is contrary to the Aristotelian (or Thomistic) telos of the good, and is understood instead as a series of theoretical reflections on the need for individual self-preservation.[17] This understanding is present in the work of Grotius, Hobbes, and Spinoza (to name a few) in its earliest manifestations, but continues to be present today in the work of not just social scientists, but theologians as well. Harvey Cox, to highlight one example, suggests

---

14. Smith, *Introducing Radical Orthodoxy*, 88. This is Smith's summary of some of the points made by Radical Orthodoxy contributors following Milbank.

15. For another perspective, see Charles Taylor, *A Secular Age* (Cambridge: Belknap, 2007), esp. 423–538. For a theological response to this perspective, see Daniel Horan, "A Rahnerian Theological Response to Charles Taylor's *A Secular Age*," *New Blackfriars* 95 (January 2014): 21–42.

16. Milbank, *Theology and Social Theory*, 10.

17. Ibid.

that the biblical "dominion" granted to Adam in Eden is indeed the "area of the free play of human constructive choice" that we might today name the secular.[18] For Milbank, this way of thinking is highly problematic, for it begins to suggest that there is something beyond the divine; namely, secular space as "pure power," that is the foundation for all human experience, inquiry, and reason.[19] This secular space of pure power is the location from which everything is predicated. From this vantage point, one begins to see the *dominium* of Adam no longer as a participation in the divine life, but now redefined as "power, property, active right, and absolute sovereignty" all directed toward the autonomy, self-mastery, and individuality of each person.[20]

This concurrently theological and sociological/political shift occurred most notably in the early and late period of modern philosophy. The lasting imprint of thinkers such as Hobbes, Locke, and Smith clearly attest to such a claim. So why does Milbank see a need to move beyond these figures to an earlier period? The answer rests in his conviction that all ideas have a history.

Theology as the Vehicle of Modernity

While the clearest example of the shift remains the epistemological (and, therefore, nonontological) innovations of modern philosophy, Milbank insists that this period represents only a single installment in the broader history of modernity and the emergence of the secular. In fact, this relatively recent contribution to the genealogy of the secular can be seen as both in continuity with and as a capstone to what Milbank terms the "nominalism-voluntarism" trend.[21] Milbank

---

18. Harvey Cox, *The Secular City* (London: SCM, 1967), 21–24.
19. Milbank, *Theology and Social Theory*, 13.
20. Ibid.

argues that this philosophical trend resulted in a problematic and atheological view of humanity. This anthropology, which is oriented toward the autonomy, self-mastery, and individuality of each person, is legitimized and ushered in by means of theological reflection.[22] This view of the human person did not arise spontaneously in the seventeenth and eighteenth centuries, as if generated ex nihilo. Rather, according to Milbank, it is the natural progression along the so-called nominalist-voluntarist trajectory that began centuries earlier. Following his reading of Étienne Gilson's *Jean Duns Scot*, Milbank summarizes the connection between the modern philosophical-anthropological worldview and the nascent nominalism-voluntarism of the late Middle Ages.

> In the thought of the nominalists, following Duns Scotus, the Trinity loses its significance as a prime location for discussing will and understanding in God and the relationship of God to the world. No longer is the world participatorily enfolded within the divine expressive *Logos*, but instead a bare divine unity starkly confronts the other distinct unities which he has ordained.[23]

We see made here the earliest explicit connection between the condition of the modern conception of subjectivity and the medieval harbinger of such a shift from the default analogical/participatory metaphysic of the time. What we understand as the secular is that which replaced the participatory or suspended dependence on the divine and now is seen as a space of human autonomy. Milbank sees this move not as a reaction to theology as a means to "liberate" science or reason, but rather the creation of the secular is something

21. Ibid., 14.
22. Milbank is not the only voice advancing the claim that modernity was promoted through shifting theological views. While not in complete accord with Milbank's explanatory narrative, Michael Gillespie has also recently drawn attention to the infrequently considered place of theology in the history of modernity. See Michael Allen Gillespie, *The Theological Origins of Modernity* (Chicago: Chicago University Press, 2008), and Taylor, *A Secular Age*.
23. Milbank, *Theology and Social Theory*, 15.

of a countertheology, or the product of a particular theological anthropology.

Milbank explains how he sees modernity and the creation of the secular as a product of a theology:

> I am suggesting that *only* the theological model permits one to construct the *mythos* of the sovereign power, or sovereign person, so that it is not a case of "essentially" secular and pragmatic realities being temporarily described in antique theological guise. In the midst of the crisis posed by religious conflict, Bodin and Hobbes contrived solutions at once sacred and pragmatic, founded upon a new metaphysics of political power. Only *within* the terms of their new theology is divine sanction pushed into the remote background, and this sanction is nonetheless still required to legitimate the human power which authenticates itself in the foreground, as the purely arbitrary.[24]

Milbank, tracing beyond the "modern" work of philosophers such as Hobbes, sees the movement toward human subjectivity and the creation of the space of the secular as coinciding with a "somewhat contrariwise theological insertion."[25] In other words, God is not the ultimate *arbitrary* authority that grounds and powers human *arbitrary* power. Instead, God is simply *present* to human society, securing its existence in a manner akin to Isaac Newton's conceptualization of a God who keeps planetary bodies in space.[26] This theological worldview confirms and protects the concept of the secular, offering an implicit narrative that suggests secular space was preordained and is discoverable, as opposed to something fabricated by humanity.

According to Milbank, the shift occurring *within* theology that ultimately results in the creation of the secular finds its origin in Scotus's doctrine of univocity. It is Scotus's work in contradistinction to Thomas's analogical predication of being that, for Milbank, marks

---

24. Ibid., 27. Italics are from the original.
25. Ibid., 28.
26. Ibid.

the commencement of the genealogy of the secular. Milbank, drawing on the work of Amos Funkenstein, describes this theological shift as an orientation toward "secular theology," understood as a "discourse which collapses together empirical discussion of finite realities and invocation of the transcendent."[27] In other words, it is a theology that embraces the predication of terms (e.g., *cause, power*, etc.) univocally of both human and divine agents. Funkenstein and Milbank hold that this "secular theology" that sanctifies secular space is the heir to Scotus's univocity of being. Therefore, the foundation for the history of modernity is laid with the establishment of the Scotus Story.[28]

Tracing the Origins of Modernity Back to Scotus

The Scotus Story, as sketched out by Milbank in *Theology and Social Theory*, commences with the assertion that a nihilistic genealogy (or the history of modernity and the ultimate fabrication of the secular) necessarily requires an ontology of violence.[29] Milbank is clear in his critique of those thinkers that claim genealogy is per se objective or neutral. The crosshairs of critique are first aimed at Nietzsche, as one might expect.[30] Nietzsche held that historical reflection yields a genealogy that presents a universal human condition; namely, that

27. Ibid., 55. Also, see Amos Funkenstein, *Theology and the Scientific Imagination* (Princeton: Princeton University Press, 1986), 25–31 and 54–59.

28. Milbank is not shy about expressing this belief in explicit terms. Take, for example, this statement originally published in an explanatory response essay collected in an issue of the journal *Arachne* 2, no. 1 (1995), which was partly devoted to Milbank's *Theology and Social Theory*: "Thereby, at a stroke, Scotus anticipated transcendental philosophy, idolized God, obscured the ontological difference, and implied (unlike Augustine or Aquinas) that any being can be fully 'present.' In this fashion the Oxford theologian set us on the intellectual course to modernity." See Milbank, "On Theological Transgression," in *The Future of Love: Essays in Political Theology* (Eugene, OR: Wipf and Stock Publishers, 2009), 159.

29. Milbank, *Theology and Social Theory*, 279.

30. See Friedrich Nietzsche, *On The Genealogy of Morals: A Polemic*, trans. Douglas Smith (New York: Oxford University Press, 2009).

society celebrates playful competitive struggle. This is further expressed in the history of violence that can, according to a particularly nihilistic narrative, be observed in the ostensible political and social propensity toward war and injustice. Milbank objects to the Nietzschean declaration of a universal genealogy of this kind. He responds to Nietzsche with the case of Christianity, positing, in accord with Nietzsche's own handling of Christianity, that Christianity is the "precise opposite of nihilism."[31] As such, it is the exception that disproves the rule. Therefore, because Christianity cannot be positioned in a genealogy of violence that claims every event as an event of warfare, the possibility of a so-called counterhistory to the Nietzschean genealogy remains tenable, particularly with an eye toward Augustine's work.[32] Milbank's focus on this theme of ontological violence is important to see why he pinpoints the genesis of modernity with the work of Scotus. Milbank sees in Scotus's univocal predication of being a foretaste of Nietzsche's genealogy of violence. To further flesh out this connection, Milbank offers a reflection on Heidegger's *Being and Time*, stating that it is this work that marks a real shift in contemporary philosophy vis-à-vis metaphysics.[33] Whereas Kant needed an a priori element in his system (i.e., the prethematic categorical schematization of a posteriori empirical intuitions), Heidegger holds nothing positive in this respect. Rather, he sees finitude as the need for *Dasein* to struggle with complete

---

31. Milbank, *Theology and Social Theory*, 295.

32. Ibid.

33. See Martin Heidegger, *Being and Time*, trans. John Macquarrie and Edward Robinson (San Francisco: HarperCollins, 2008). It is well known that Heidegger studied both Scotus's legitimate and spurious texts extensively and wrote his *Habilitation* thesis on the subtle doctor. See Martin Heidegger, *Die Kategorien–und Bedeutungslehre des Duns Scotus* (Tübingen: Mohr-Siebeck, 1916); and Sean McGrath, *The Early Heidegger and Medieval Philosophy: Phenomenology for the Godforsaken* (Washington, DC: Catholic University of America Press, 2006), esp. 88–119.

contingency, illustrated by his now-famous concept of the inescapable ontological "fall." Milbank elaborates,

> There is therefore a kind of primordial violence at work here, which can only be countered by a mode of interpretation which is itself a "doing violence" (*gewaltsamkeit*), and which follows the opposite course from the "falling tendency" of being and of customary understanding. In *Being and Time* there is an emphasis on the negating of forgetfulness, of recovering a primordial experience of being itself; this stress never quite disappears in the later works, but is more and more insisted that Being only *is* in the event of its own self-occlusion and the arbitrary series of differential breaks which constitute the battles of history, the replacement of one cultural regime by another.[34]

Heidegger, in an effort to remain in the realm of the philosophical without invocation of theological categories, maintains a primordial and fundamental "fall" and (nonmoral) "guilt" that is antecedent to sin. Heidegger's concern with the theological assertion of fall and guilt is that there would be something lacking in the human being (*Dasein*); the consequence, therefore, would be something missing in *Dasein*, something for which Heidegger has no place, given his position that *Dasein* fully "is."[35] This stands in stark contrast with Augustine (and perhaps Aquinas) who sees in sin ("fallenness" and "guilt") a privation, a lack. Heidegger, Milbank asserts, has "flattened everything out, and still (like any positivist or neo-Kantian) turns historical differences into so many value-neutral facts . . . he sees the ontological 'not,' the reverse copula, as indicating transcendental violence, a fundamental rift sundering ourselves from ourselves and ourselves from others."[36] Having worked to avoid associating any privation with *Dasein*, Heidegger has necessarily transferred the concept of a "(pre)historical fall" to an ontological one, thereby

34. Milbank, *Theology and Social Theory*, 302.
35. Ibid., 303.
36. Ibid., 304.

28

necessitating an ontology of violence.[37] The struggle of *Dasein* to grasp at being and reconcile one's "thrownness" (*Geworfenheit*) ultimately supports the notion of an autonomous realm of human self-mastery.[38] In other words, this ontological struggle—not adherence to doctrine, moral codes, or participation in the Divine—is what is actually the condition of the possibility for authenticity or inauthenticity.

Milbank reads Jacques Derrida as suggesting that this Heideggerian notion of ontological struggle and violence originates not with Heidegger, but is the natural continuation and further development of the genealogy of violence best characterized by Nietzsche and first initiated by Scotus.[39] Scotus is implicated as co-conspirator with all of these modern thinkers because, in Milbank's narrative, it is the subtle doctor who first speaks of being outside the confines of participatory ontology or analogous language. Simply put, Scotus seemingly separates metaphysics from theology in order to predicate being univocally.

37. Ibid. This concept is drawn out in greater detail vis-à-vis Scotus in contradistinction to Aquinas in Milbank and Pickstock, *Truth in Aquinas*, 62.

38. In a later work, Milbank returns to this theme, expounding, "*Dasein remains* in a fashion both a Cartesian *cogito* and a Husserlian transcendental ego. For if Being is only apparent in *Dasein*, and even only *is* in *Dasein* (since otherwise it 'nihilates' itself in beings) then it requires *Dasein*'s thinking of itself as a site of exposure, reflection and decision." Milbank, *The Word Made Strange: Theology, Language, Culture* (Oxford: Blackwell, 1997), 37.

39. Jacques Derrida, *Writing and Difference*, trans. Alan Bass (Chicago: University of Chicago Press, 1980), 79–153 and esp. 319n84: "Theology, the thinking of the existent-God, of the essence and existence of God, thus would suppose the thinking of Being. Here we need not refer to Heidegger in order to understand this movement, but first to Duns Scotus, to whom Heidegger had devoted one of his first writings, as is well known. For Duns Scotus, the thought of common and uniform Being is necessarily prior to the thought of the determined existent." Derrida goes on to qualify what he understands Scotus to mean and *not to mean* by this, something not present in Milbank's usage. Derrida, however, relies heavily on Gilson for his interpretation of the subtle doctor.

Also, see Gillian Rose, *Dialectic of Nihilism: Post-Structuralism and Law* (Oxford: Blackwell Publishing, 1984), 104–8. Milbank highlights this connection more strongly in his coining of the phrase "pre-theological, Scotist-Heideggerian apprehension" in reference to human thought and the conception of *esse*. See Milbank, *The Word Made Strange*, 175.

The Problem With Scotus's Philosophical Vision

Milbank's concern with Scotus's philosophy must always be placed within the context of Milbank's simultaneous reading of Aquinas's approach. Milbank holds that there is no metaphysics apart from revelation. Metaphysics serves to provide an account of being; as such, it cannot be separated from theology. The reason, Milbank argues, is that the subject matter of metaphysics (being) refers completely to a "first principle" (God), which is the subject matter of an even higher science that is accessible to us only by way of revelation.[40] Therefore, it necessarily follows that metaphysics is completely subsumed by theology.[41] Any attempt to separate metaphysics from theology is de facto problematic and ultimately nihilistic. Yet, as Milbank asserts, Scotus is the first to attempt just such a move.

As Milbank's narrative goes, Aquinas—contrary to the sweeping claim of Heidegger concerning the whole history of Christian philosophical appropriation resulting in ontotheology—does not develop a "conceptual idol" with his understanding of *esse*. Instead, Aquinas "speaks of God creating being as such and not just beings, and conceives the divine *esse* as incomprehensibly other to the *ens commune* of creatures, because it uniquely coincides with his essence, or his infinite 'whatever he is.'"[42] In some sense, Milbank is acquitting the angelic doctor of the Heideggerian charges of problematic metaphysical inquiry (or engagement in "ontotheology"), seeking instead to uphold Thomas as a mystic prone to apophatic God talk. This approach fits well with Milbank's theological narrative because it frees Aquinas to discuss being only in terms of negation or analogy.[43] As such, Aquinas remains entirely within the purview of theology,

40. Milbank, *The Word Made Strange*, 44.
41. Ibid.
42. Ibid., 41.

always necessarily drawing on theological terms, because for Aquinas the proper subject of metaphysics is simply God.

In stark contrast to Aquinas, Scotus distinguishes between philosophy, understood as the science of being, and theology, which is the science of God. Milbank uses a variety of terms to demarcate these two approaches. There are references to Aquinas's method as "participatory metaphysics"[44] or "theological metaphysics,"[45] while Scotus's approach is described as "autonomous metaphysics"[46] or "proto-transcendentalist metaphysics."[47] Milbank believes that a problem arises as a result of such a methodological innovation on the part of Scotus. The first issue to surface centers on the understanding of being that emerges in Scotus's philosophy when he removes metaphysics from the "purely theological." Whereas Thomas's understanding of being was entirely dependent on the theological nature of metaphysical inquiry (since the object of metaphysics was the first principle), Scotus introduces an approach that considers the nature of being apart from God. As such, "to be" can in effect be predicated, not just of created be-*ings*, but also of God. Milbank summarizes this shift in the following way:

> Being, [Scotus] argued, could be either finite or infinite, and possessed the same simple meaning of existence when applied to either. "Exists," in the sentence God "exists," has therefore the same fundamental meaning (at a logical and ultimately metaphysical level) as in the sentence, "this woman exists." The same thing applies to the usage of transcendental terms convertible with Being; for example, "God is good" means that he

---

43. This theme is recurring, found most developed in Milbank and Pickstock, *Truth In Aquinas*, esp. 6–11 and 24–59. Also, see Milbank, *Theology and Social Theory*, 304–9; Milbank, "On Theological Transgression," 156–65; and Milbank, *The Word Made Strange*, esp. 7–32, 36–50 and passim.

44. Smith, *Introducing Radical Orthodoxy*, 97.

45. Milbank and Pickstock, *Truth in Aquinas*, 35.

46. Smith, *Introducing Radical Orthodoxy*, 97.

47. Milbank, *The Word Made Strange*, 9.

is good in the same *sense* that we are said to be good, however much more of the quality of goodness he may be thought to possess.[48]

Milbank succinctly abstracts this philosophical shift with the description of the move as Scotus's desire to establish a "pure ontology independent of theology."[49] Herein lies the ultimate source and primary impetus for modernity. Milbank insists that it is with Scotus's univocal predication of being—rooted in the separation of metaphysics from theology—that a space begins to be created that stands apart from God.[50] "Scotus, therefore, invented a separation between ontology and theology, which depends upon our having a fixed and stable—almost, one is tempted to say, an a priori—sense of the meaning of 'Being,' 'Goodness,' and so forth."[51] We can begin to see how Milbank traces through Derrida, Heidegger, Nietzsche, and so on back to Scotus.[52] There is a contiguous relationship between the modern philosophers' ontological conceptions and the a priori ontology of univocally predicated being found in Scotus's philosophy. Likewise, one could see a connection between the Scotist conception of being apart from theology and the Cartesian *cogito ergo sum*. For Descartes, there is an apparent a priori recognition of being apart from and independent of God. For Aquinas, such a formulation would have been absurd. For the angelic doctor, things only "are" inasmuch as they "are" in a derived, approximate, and analogical sense vis-à-vis God.[53]

---

48. Milbank, *Theology and Social Theory*, 305.
49. Milbank and Pickstock, *Truth in Aquinas*, 33. In his earlier work, Milbank describes this move as one toward a "fundamental ontology." See Milbank, *Theology and Social Theory*, 305.
50. This is later reiterated by Simon Oliver in his essay "Introducing Radical Orthodoxy: From Participation to Late Modernity," in *The Radical Orthodoxy Reader*, ed. John Milbank and Simon Oliver (London: Routledge, 2009), 21–24.
51. Milbank, *Theology and Social Theory*, 306.
52. Heidegger, according to Milbank, is a clear heir to Scotus's position that there can be a "non-theological, non-mystical, discourse about Being" thereby reacting against the so-called ontotheology of metaphysics. See Milbank, "On Theological Transgression," 159–60.
53. Milbank and Pickstock, *Truth in Aquinas*, 33.

Milbank sees Scotus as having elevated being (*ens*) to a place above and apart from God. The result is a different (i.e., "new") conceptualization of God that Milbank deems the advent of "ontotheological idolatry."[54] In addition to making being out to be something that is "anterior to God's self-revelation,"[55] this idolatry changes the previously conceived notion of creatures. In a Thomist metaphysical world of participation, creatures have their existence and meaning in God. In this Scotist metaphysical world (independent of theology), creatures have their own subsistence and autonomy because they "are" as much as the infinite; the only qualification that remains is their finitude.[56] No longer are creatures finite beings dependent on God or granted being by anything beyond themselves. In effect, we are left with a reduction of God and an exaltation of creatures, something Milbank terms "the double idolatry" of univocity.[57]

Milbank's Conclusive Position

This is as far as Milbank goes in his assessment of the subtle doctor's role in the establishment of the secular and the genealogy of nihilism that coincides with the modern era. Milbank has effectively traced the genealogy from the "usual suspects" of modernity and the Enlightenment (and some poststructuralist, transcendentalist, and other generally "postmodern" thinkers) back to Scotus. The place Scotus holds in Milbank's narrative is an important, if not a controversial, one. In his *Theology and Social Theory*, Milbank inaugurates the Scotus Story by broadly sketching a chronology that

54. Milbank, *The Word Made Strange*, 44.
55. Smith, *Introducing Radical Orthodoxy*, 98.
56. Milbank and Pickstock, *Truth in Aquinas*, 33–34.
57. Milbank, *The Word Made Strange*, 47 and passim.

places the subtle doctor at ground zero. Milbank argues that the thought processes of thinkers such as Nietzsche and Heidegger are in some way aligned with, if not indebted to, the philosophical insights and innovations of John Duns Scotus. After his work *The Word Made Strange*, Milbank no longer engaged Scotus in a new way. Instead, his later work refers back to the initial genealogical sketch first published in *Theology and Social Theory* and later expanded in *The Word Made Strange*, or he cites his protégé Catherine Pickstock's later and more explicit engagement with Scotus.[58] In effect, Milbank has drawn his conclusion about Scotus's place in the history of modernity. His position remains that Scotus, although not quite *solely* culpable,[59] is the initiator par excellence of the intellectual course to modernity and planter of the ontological seeds of what will later grow into "the secular."

Catherine Pickstock and the Advancement of the Scotus Story

As with John Milbank, Catherine Pickstock blames John Duns Scotus for distorting the "authentically Christian understanding of God and truth."[60] A former student of Milbank, Pickstock has been associated with the Radical Orthodoxy movement from its earliest stages. Whereas Milbank has largely remained silent in his subsequent theological writing on matters directly related to Scotus, Pickstock has in a way continued where her former mentor left off. Milbank seems to have found it sufficient to name Scotus as the key figure responsible for the breakdown of the participatory ontology and the

58. See the next section of this chapter below.
59. For a detailed response to initial criticisms concerning the invocation of Scotus in *Theology and Social Theory*, see Milbank, "Preface to the Second Edition," in *Theology and Social Theory*, esp. xxv n41.
60. Steven Shakespeare, *Radical Orthodoxy: A Critical Introduction* (London: SPCK, 2007), 11.

analogical worldview Milbank has so closely associated with Aquinas. Satisfied with this isolation of the protomodernist par excellence, Milbank appears disinterested in returning to the subtle doctor to either defend his claim or further explore the implications of such a position.[61] Reference to Scotus in Milbank's later work takes the form of citing either his previously published explication[62] or, interestingly, subsequent publications by his theological protégé, Pickstock. For this reason, Pickstock can clearly be seen as the recipient, deliberately or otherwise, of the role of master narrator in the effort to continue the Scotus Story.

Milbank's Foundationalism

Pickstock's starting point is the foundation formed in the nascent construction of the Scotus Story according to Milbank. I suggest that what Milbank has created, and Pickstock the first to adopt, is a form of Scotus Story–based genealogical foundationalism upon which Radical Orthodoxy's entire system and subsequent subfield projects are built. In other words, after Milbank's Scotus Story sketch, first outlined in *Theology and Social Theory* and later minimally fleshed out in *The Word Made Strange*, his position on the origin of modernity becomes axiomatic for all those associated with the Radical Orthodoxy movement. Milbank's foundationalism[63] becomes

---

61. Milbank returns to Scotus, without adding substantial changes to his Scotus Story, in his recent *Beyond Secular Order* (2014).
62. Namely, *Theology and Social Theory* and *The Word Made Strange*.
63. This is my term, roughly analogous to the philosophical concept of *foundationalism* generally associated with the subdiscipline of epistemology. Whereas epistemological foundationalism is concerned with grounding knowledge in secure and certain foundations, I suggest that Milbank's *modus* with regard to his construction of the Scotus Story rests in his intention to create a foundation upon which to build the historical-narrative genealogy of modernity. Those who subscribe to Milbank's foundationalism (e.g., Pickstock, et al.) ground their subsequent theological work in his narrative.

the normative attitude that sets the tone for much that follows in this vein.

Not only does Pickstock inherit this foundationalism, she is also the most prominent voice from the Radical Orthodoxy movement that engaged in the defense of it after Milbank. She has, in recent years, published several major works that prominently feature Scotus. Perhaps the most notable is her monograph *After Writing: On the Liturgical Consummation of Philosophy*. Additionally, she contributed in large part to the text *Truth in Aquinas*, which she coauthored with Milbank. While these books have certainly shaped the discourse surrounding and related to the Scotus Story, her most concentrated efforts to defend and develop the narrative passed on from Milbank are found in two articles published in the early part of the last decade. The first, "Modernity and Scholasticism: A Critique of Recent Invocations of Univocity," appeared in the European Franciscan journal *Antonianum* in 2003.[64] The second article appeared in a special issue of the journal *Modern Theology* in 2005 dedicated solely to the role of Scotus in contemporary theological discourse. Pickstock's article was the centerpiece to which several other articles were published in response. The title of this second article is "Duns Scotus: His Historical and Contemporary Significance."[65]

---

64. *Antonianum* 78 (2003): 3–47. It was published in response to several pro-univocity articles by a number of European Scotist scholars, including Richard Cross, whose work had appeared in the same journal two years prior. It is safe to say that it went largely unnoticed in the United States. Few, if any, scholars have taken note of that article, including those sympathetic to Pickstock's position. It was reprinted in a collection of essays in 2005, which has made the article much more accessible. (For one illustration of how the scholarly community has overlooked the previous *Antonianum* article, see Alexander Hall, *Thomas Aquinas and John Duns Scotus: Natural Theology in the High Middle Ages* [London: Continuum, 2007]. Hall cites only Pickstock's *After Writing* and her later [2005] *Modern Theology* article). The *Antonianum* article was later reprinted as "The Univocalist Mode of Production." All subsequent references to this article will be cited as it appears in the Duke University Press *Theology and the Political* volume, due to the greater accessibility of that text.

65. This article received much more attention than her previous article on the subject.

Before examining the ways Pickstock has advanced the Scotus Story through her continued focus on the subtle doctor's role in the initiation of the process ending in the establishment of modernity, it is worthwhile to highlight those aspects of Milbank's foundationalism she adopts to form a contiguous relationship between his work and her own.

The first aspect of the Scotus Story that Pickstock inherits are the sources of secondary literature that Milbank draws upon to support his antiunivocalist narrative. The major authors include Étienne Gilson, J. F. Courtine, Olivier Boulnois, and others.[66]

The second feature of Milbank's initial sketch of the Scotus Story that Pickstock adopts is the concept of the loss of participation or, more specifically, the rejection of the Platonic notion of μέθεξις (*methexis*). Like Milbank, Pickstock sees Scotus's univocal ontology as rupturing the bond of suspension that connects creation to the Divine. Both Milbank and Pickstock refer to this as a "flattening out" of the world into a single plane on which is found God and creation

---

66. In her *Antonianium* response to pro-univocity critics of her (and her colleague's) work within the Radical Orthodoxy movement, Pickstock lists an extensive collection of secondary sources she claims to have drawn on to support her interpretation. That list, because of the controversial nature of the Radical Orthodoxy movement's interpretation of Scotus, is worth replicating here in large part. For the entire list with her commentary, see Pickstock, "The Univocalist Mode of Production," 318n2. Étienne Gilson, *Jean Duns Scot: Introduction á ses positions fondmentales* (Paris: Vrin, 1952); Olivier Boulnois, "Quand commence l'ontothéologie? Aristote, Thomas d'Aquin et Duns Scot," *Revue Thomiste* 95 (1995): 84–108; Olivier Boulnois, *Etre et representation* (Paris: P.U.F., 1999); Olivier Boulnois, *Duns Scot: Sur la connaissance de Dieu et l'univocité de l'étant* (Paris: P.U.F., 1990); J. F. Courtine, *Suarez et le systéme de la métaphysique* (Paris: P.U.F., 1990); Éric Alliez, *Capital Times: Tales from the Conquest of Time,* trans. Georges Van Den Abbeele (Minneapolis: University of Minnesota Press, 1996), 197–239; Bruno Puntel, *Analogie und Geschichtlichkeit* (Fribourg: Herder, 1969); C. Exposito, *Introduzione a Suarez: Meditazioni metafische* (Milan: Rusioni, 1996); David Burrell, *Knowing the Unknowable God: Ibn-Sina, Maimonides, Aquinas* (Notre Dame: University of Notre Dame Press, 1986); John Inglis, "Philosophical Autonomy and the Historiography of Medieval Philosophy," *Journal of the History of Philosophy* 5 (1997): 21–53; Inglis, *Spheres of Philosophical Inquiry and the Historiography of Mediaeval Philosophy* (Leiden: Brill, 1998); and H. Möhle, *Ethik als Scientia Practica nach Johannes Duns Scotus: Eine Philosophische Grundlegung* (Münster: Aschendorff, 1999).

"existing."[67] Pickstock also uses the word *unhinged* in her discussion of Scotus's ontology.[68] The concept is essentially the same in both thinkers. Scotus's approach, Milbank and Pickstock argue, is always in contradistinction to that of Aquinas. As such, any occasion that provides opportunity to highlight substantial difference is taken by Pickstock as a means for associating Scotus with the origins of a new metaphysical and subsequently "nihilistic" method.

The third area of continuity is found in Pickstock's adoption of Milbank's concern with Scotus's distinction between philosophy and theology. Both thinkers, following their reading of Aquinas, see theology as the proper context for metaphysical inquiry. The separation of metaphysics from theology in Scotus's method is highly problematic, not because of its initial failure, but because of the trajectory (toward an isolated and freestanding realm or space apart from the Divine) that follows such a philosophical move.[69] The end result is a form of fundamental ontology that is divorced from God talk.

While these three points summarize the foundationalism Pickstock inherits, one significant point of departure should be noted before continuing with an examination of Pickstock's efforts to advance Milbank's foundationalism to further the Scotus Story. The most noticeable point of departure from Milbank is found in Pickstock's treatment of the terms *voluntarist* and *nominalist*. Her adjudicative prowess surpasses Milbank's in her careful invocation of both terms throughout her work. Unlike Milbank, Pickstock is hesitant to conflate voluntarism and nominalism. She is also attentive to the ways in which Scotus is removed from both schools of thought.

67. For example, see Milbank, *Theology and Social Theory*, 304; Pickstock, "Duns Scotus: His Historical and Contemporary Significance," 545 and 568; Pickstock, "The Univocalist Mode of Production," 282; and passim.
68. Pickstock, *After Writing*, 127 and passim.
69. See Milbank and Pickstock, *Truth in Aquinas*, 24–36.

The temptation to caricature the work of Scotus (and his successor William of Ockham) as *simply* voluntarist or nominalist is one often indulged by many nonspecialists. Pickstock departs from Milbank's term *nominalism-voluntarism trend*[70] in such a way as to suggest her more careful reading of the secondary literature.[71]

Having provided a survey of the overlap between the work of Milbank and Pickstock, we can move on to look at the way in which Pickstock makes her own contributions to forwarding the Scotus Story.

Univocity, Formal Distinction, and the Distant Divine

The univocal predication of being in the philosophy of John Duns Scotus maintains a place of prominence in the thinking of Catherine Pickstock. In her book, *After Writing*, Pickstock offers a reflection on what she sees as problematic with univocity. Her approach, less concerned with positing the origins of modernity and more concerned with confirming the earlier Scotus Story, is one focused on liturgy. Pickstock suggests that before she is able to delve into the business of restoring the primacy of liturgy in place of what she views as the "sophistic, modern and postmodern refusal of liturgical life," we must "grasp how the modern secular order mimics the liturgical, and also rid ourselves of the theological legacy of this corruption which prevents us from envisioning the liturgical in its genuine character."[72] Her agenda, therefore, is focused on the goal of restorative liturgics, an effort that is both a reclamation (her desire to *return* to a period of liturgical hegemony that she believes rests in the "genuine liturgy

---

70. See Milbank, *Theology and Social Theory*, 14; and my "Theology as the Vehicle of Modernity" section above.

71. For example, see Pickstock, *After Writing*, 122–166.

72. Ibid., 121.

of the medieval Roman Rite"[73]) and something oriented toward a telos consisting of a "beyond modern" response to the problems of secularity and modernity.[74] She appears to understand her role in the narrating of the Scotus Story as clarifier and expositor. This exposition begins with the univocity of being. Pickstock's starting point is clear:

> Duns Scotus asserted the metaphysical priority of Being over both the infinite and the finite alike. Thus God is deemed "to be" in the same univocal manner as creatures, and although God is distinguished by an "intensity of being," He nonetheless remains within, or subordinate to the category of Being (which now becomes the sole object of metaphysics).[75]

Pickstock introduces Scotus's univocity by contrasting it to "the Thomistic framework of *analogia entis*."[76] This, the operative expression of ontological predication for Radical Orthodoxy, is seen as radically threatened by Scotus's new metaphysics. Pickstock terms the result of Scotus's univocal approach as "indifferent Being." By this she means that *being* is nondiscriminative, equally able to be predicated of both finite and infinite *beings*. Or, to put it another way, "finite creatures, like the infinite creator, nakedly 'are,' as opposed to 'not being' in a punctiliar fashion—they are 'the same' *in quid* as regards existing that belongs to them as an essential property, just as substance and accident, genus, species, and individuality all exist in the same fashion."[77] Whereas being was previously—in the Thomistic analogical sense—understood as rightly associated with the divine and by way of participation analogously related to creatures, Pickstock

---

73. Ibid., 170.
74. *Beyond modern* is my term, offered in deference to the Radical Orthodoxy preference not to be associated with postmodernity in its manifold expressions.
75. Pickstock, *After Writing*, 122.
76. Ibid.
77. Pickstock, "The Univocalist Mode of Production," 283.

sees Scotus making a move that ascribes being as an attribute common to *everything* that *is*.

How then does one understand the difference between creatures and the Creator in the context of univocal predication? Pickstock explains that it is a matter of degree, and Scotus's formal distinction provides the key to conceptualizing difference in an univocalist mode. The difference in degree is expressed in the qualification of finite versus infinite beings. Another way to conceptualize the distinction present in various degrees of being is by intensity. Pickstock is critical of this manner of differentiation because, as she writes, "The difference of intensity is continuous with an individuating modality which radically distinguishes the finite from the infinite, but without in any way modifying the common essence of Being."[78] One can follow the path of her concern from a seemingly elusive conceptualization of "more or less being" to her interpretation of such qualification. Rather than drawing creatures closer to the Creator, Pickstock sees univocal predication of being as creating a distance concomitant with differentiation by degree. She continues,

> Thus, the univocity of Being between God and creature paradoxically gives rise to a kind of equivocity, for the difference of degree or amount of Being disallows any specific resemblance between them, and excludes the possibility of figural or analogical determinations of God that give us any degree of substantive knowledge of His character. By withdrawing the means through which creatures might distinguish themselves ontologically from God through figuring or analogically drawing near to Him, the distance between the infinite and the finite becomes an undifferentiated and *quantified* (although unquantifiable) abyss. Thus, the "same" becomes the radically disparate and unknowable.[79]

Whereas Milbank was largely disturbed by the apparent establishment of a secular realm *from which* one could predicate being

---

78. Pickstock, *After Writing*, 123.
79. Ibid.

univocally of both creatures and God, Pickstock is concerned with the *actual predication* of being as such. Aside from the secular space devoid of the divine, the process of conceptualizing being in the Scotist mode seems to distance God from creatures. This, for Pickstock, is the greatest problem with univocity.

This distance presents the challenge of knowing anything of God. Whereas Scotus makes his argument for univocity from the understanding of our a priori capacity to know the divine, Pickstock believes in fact that this move unavoidably and irreparably prohibits us from knowing God. She explains, "Univocity appears to encourage dualities without mediation: God is unknowably and equivocally remote as regards His being *in quale*; this gap can be bridged only by positive revealed disclosures—yet this means that the space of revelation is philosophically predetermined as a space of facts or empirical propositions."[80] Pickstock views this distance as the emergence of equivocity from univocity. Ironically, it is precisely the argument Scotus makes against Henry of Ghent and Thomas Aquinas in reverse; namely, analogical language, Scotus argues, ultimately yields equivocity because there is in fact no such thing as a semantic middle way. Pickstock argues that if being is the same for Creator and creatures, then the difference between the two *necessarily* results in an impassible infinite gap.

Additionally, Pickstock takes issue with Scotus's establishment of what he calls "the formal distinction." Moving from the infinite distance created between Creator and creature resulting from the univocal mode of predication, Pickstock asserts that Scotus's philosophy additionally distances "creatures from each other, and each creature from itself."[81] This is the means of differentiation that relates being *in se*, which is "neutral and indifferent," to difference.[82]

---

80. Pickstock, "The Univocalist Mode of Production," 291.
81. Pickstock, *After Writing*, 123.

Pickstock spends relatively little time on the formal distinction and understandably so, since it is generally held to be the most difficult concept in Scotus's work. Simply put (if such an explanation is possible), Scotus holds those things to be formally distinct that are existentially inseparable yet maintain the potential to be known distinctively. In other words, Scotus is talking about one *thing* that is knowable in a *formally* (not *essentially*) distinct way. By definition, each formally distinct thing exhibits different properties, but cannot be conceived of independently of the object considered.[83] Mary Beth Ingham describes this as "a midpoint between conceptual distinction and a real distinction."[84] Pickstock's reading of the formal distinction is different. She reads Scotus's formal distinction as a compromise between the Thomist categories of "real distinction" and "intellectual distinction."[85] Pickstock considers the formal distinction to exist in a somewhat contradictory manner, as something that is at once both "real and logical, and neither real nor logical."[86] Pickstock believes the object of Scotus's metaphysics to be "univocal being" as such, which she understands as not capable of being satisfied by real or intellectual distinctions. She describes this new object of metaphysics as an "in-between being" that is "neither being nor being, neither particular nor universal, neither wholly real nor wholly thought; it is a *formality*."[87] Pickstock posits that this results in an abstraction of being that arises from univocal predication within a context of formal distinction. In other words, being is made a "virtual reality,"

82. Ibid.
83. For more, see Peter King, "Scotus on Metaphysics," in *The Cambridge Companion to Duns Scotus*, ed. Thomas Williams (New York: Cambridge University Press, 2003), 22–26.
84. Mary Beth Ingham, *Scotus for Dunces: An Introduction to the Subtle Doctor* (St. Bonaventure, NY: Franciscan Institute, 2003), 227.
85. Pickstock, *After Writing*, 123–24.
86. Ibid.,124.
87. Ibid.

or something that is neither an empirical quality that is commonly found between things, nor a logical necessity.[88]

This distancing of God from creation is seen as additionally problematic for Pickstock, because it has a direct impact on our understanding of divine revelation. She holds that the infinite gap that is created between Creator and creatures can only be bridged by "positive revealed disclosures."[89] Pickstock insists that this necessitates a philosophically predetermined space of revelation. This is viewed as an a priori space within which facts or empirical propositions are communicated. The reason this is problematic is that it threatens the mystery of God's divine revelation. Pickstock reads Scotus's univocity in such a light as to diminish (if not eliminate) "the paradoxical presence of unlikeness within likeness in analogy," which ultimately results in the suppression of the mysterious.[90] Divine revelation is prescribed in Pickstock's understanding of univocity. "To put this another way, the space for the *Logos* to amend even our logic may be somewhat lacking on Scotist premises."[91] Finally, Pickstock sees the doctrine of creation affected by the optic of univocity vis-à-vis divine revelation. Creation, Pickstock argues, imposes certain "mysteries" to which the incomprehensible logic of analogy seems to be sensitive. The Scotist mode, however, appears to demystify such revelations, seemingly uncovering being and other concepts. Such is the case with beauty as mediated between goodness and truth. Pickstock believes that an aesthetic is "always secretly fundamental for Aquinas (as also for Bonaventure and other Franciscans)," but becomes something that is converted "at once into an empirical aggregate" and "to analyzable proportion" in Scotus.[92]

88. Ibid., 124–25.
89. Pickstock, "Duns Scotus: His Historical and Contemporary Significance," 554.
90. Ibid.
91. Ibid., 555.
92. Pickstock, "Univocalist Mode of Production," 295.

Prioritization of Possibility

While univocity of being and the formal distinction of Scotus play a major role in Pickstock's critique of the subtle doctor's philosophical vision, the apparent elevation of the possible over the actual takes center stage in Pickstock's assessment. Her analysis begins with the concepts of univocity and formal distinction inasmuch as they provide a "priority of essence over existence."[93] The argument goes as follows: being is distinguished formally between creatures and God in such a way that the differentiation does not, in any manner, modify the univocity of their essence insofar as this is *being*.[94] The formal distinction elevates this essence even beyond that of existence, so that it becomes possible to differentiate not only the Creator from creatures (vis-à-vis their univocal *being*), but it provides the means for making distinctions within God, between one creature and another[95] and between one creature and itself.[96] Pickstock holds that this emphasis on the formal distinction (within the context of being predicated univocally) produces a priority of essence over existence because essence *necessarily* mandates *existence* (although in varying "degrees" or "modes"). It logically follows, she argues, that such a move equalizes the actual and the possible, thereby leveling the Thomistic understanding of the priority of *act* over *potentiality*. Pickstock explains:

For the necessity of existence attached to any essence now applies as

---

93. Pickstock, *After Writing*, 126.

94. Ibid., 125.

95. Noticeably absent from Pickstock's present discussion is any treatment of Scotus's principle of individuation, commonly referred to as the doctrine of *haecceitas*. For more on this, see Daniel Horan, "Beyond Essentialism and Complementarity: Toward a Theological Anthropology Rooted in *Haecceitas*," *Theological Studies* 75 (March 2014): 1–24.

96. Pickstock, *After Writing*, 125.

much to *possible* essences (which continuously urge towards Being) as to *actual* essences, since, according to the Scotist priority of the essential over the existential, all essences, even actualized ones, were themselves at some stage only potential or possible essences. That is to say, by formally distinguishing essence and existence, despite the fact that this would seem to tie existence more firmly to essence than the Thomist real distinction of the two, Scotus opens the possibility for a thing to be radically transposed into another thing, thereby relativizing a thing in favour of all that it *could* be, rather than affirming the actuality of all that it *is*.[97]

Such a reading is problematic because it suggests, Pickstock contends, that because the purely possible (understood as distinct from the actual) is only realized in thought (or, she suggests, "in some prior or virtual realm"[98]), Scotus's philosophical outlook effectively inaugurates the priority of epistemology over ontology and the rational over the actual. In doing so, Scotus, Pickstock insists, opens the way for modern metaphysics, a philosophy divorced from being and divine participation.[99]

Pickstock sees this as problematic because, in addition to the establishment of a protomodern epistemological preference, it ultimately appears to elevate the role of contingency with regard to created things. She sees this as an internal division within actuality, "for actuality now *testifies* that its specific arrangement is one of an apparently endless arrangement of equally viable alternatives."[100] Necessity seems to be dead. Pickstock interprets this further to suggest that nothing "real" is considered necessary, while nothing "unreal" is regarded as unnecessary. "This gives rise to a tendency in Scotus to assume that the possible, if it can be thought at all, requires formalization."[101] Pickstock sees in this move the establishment of

97. Ibid., 126.
98. Ibid., 127.
99. Ibid.
100. Ibid., 128.

a new schema, attributed by her to Scotus, for epistemology and scientific inquiry. Through his formal distinction, Scotus appears to introduce a new mode of knowledge that arises from a priori analysis of "clear and distinct concepts" formed by understanding.[102] In this way, Scotus is seen as the clear precursor to Descartes and Kant. Although Milbank sketched out a rough draft for the way Scotus anticipates philosophers of the modern period, Pickstock goes to great lengths to fill in the lines and flesh out the initial intimations.

Pickstock and the (In)conclusion of the Scotus Story

Catherine Pickstock, deeply steeped in the foundationalism of Milbank, continued the crafting of the Scotus Story in a way that her mentor and colleague no longer could or cared to proceed. Her examination of the manner in which Scotus's univocal predication of being provides a reading of and method for a new metaphysics necessarily led her to explore the meaning of the formal distinction. In light of her analysis of univocity concomitant with the formal distinction, she posited an insurmountable divide or infinite gap between the Creator and creatures, the divine and all else. Pickstock believes that this separation radically ruptured the capacity for human knowledge of God and the possibility of divine communication in terms of revelation. Furthermore, Pickstock believes that Scotus's seeming prioritization of possibility over actuality necessarily created an opportunity for the subordination of ontology to epistemology, clearly anticipating the subsequent philosophy of the modern era. In outlining these points, she engaged the Scotus Story in a more concentrated and focused manner than her predecessor. Her advancement of the narrative that implicates Scotus as protomodern

101. Ibid., 129.
102. Ibid., 130.

antagonist is unsurpassed and remains the most carefully, if controversially, executed examination of the subtle doctor's work vis-à-vis the Radical Orthodoxy schema.

A Survey of Subsequent Radical Orthodoxy Commentators: Scotus as Patriarch of Nihilism

This last major section of this chapter is focused on providing a brief overview of those Radical Orthodoxy interlocutors that have most explicitly engaged the Scotus Story after Milbank and Pickstock. As we will see in the next chapter, the reach of this narrative extends far beyond the idiosyncratic theological world of those who have constructed this particular interpretation of Scotus's thought. Nevertheless, most scholars who align themselves with the Radical Orthodoxy movement, either explicitly through the publication of a book in the twelve-volume Radical Orthodoxy book series,[103] or implicitly by other means, have uncritically adopted the Scotus Story as narrated by Milbank and Pickstock. This is seen most clearly in the way that these scholars rely not on the critical texts of Scotus in presenting their particular iteration of the Scotus Story, but on the recent work of Milbank and Pickstock.[104] Here we will look at the work of Connor Cunningham, Graham Ward, and Gavin Hyman.

---

103. This series was published by Routledge and edited by John Milbank, Catherine Pickstock, and Graham Ward. While the Radical Orthodoxy series has concluded, its general ideological mission has been carried on in the Wiley-Blackwell monograph series Illuminations: Theory and Religion, also edited by Catherine Pickstock, John Milbank, and Graham Ward.

104. One notable exception to this rule is Conor Cunningham in his *Genealogy of Nihilism*. While he adopts a similar approach, ultimately assuming the same thesis and historical-philosophical trajectory as Milbank and Pickstock, he opts to trace his own path through the work of Scotus.

Conor Cunningham

Unlike Milbank and Pickstock in their earliest explications, Conor Cunningham begins his genealogy prior to when Scotus arrives on the scene. Tracing the Plotinian concept of the One (*hen*) through the work of Avicenna, Henry of Ghent, Scotus, Ockham, Suarez, Spinoza, Kant, and Hegel, Cunningham posits that because Plotinus developed a *meontological* philosophy (the prioritization of nonbeing as highest principle) and these subsequent thinkers have adopted this Plotinian philosophical view, they ultimately argue for the existence of *nothing* as a thing (*res*).[105] If this were not the case—that something exists from which the One can be distinguished—then there would not be a way to identify the One *in se*.

Cunningham notes that the two greatest influences on the thought of John Duns Scotus were Henry of Ghent and Avicenna.[106] He traces in Scotus a development of thought from the earliest commentary on the *Sentences* in the *Lectura* (where Scotus, following Henry and Avicenna, sees a two-step movement in divine foreknowledge) through the more reflective *Ordinatio* (where Scotus, writing more logically, posits a four-step subdivision) that ultimately results in the affirmation of an *esse diminutum*, which is asserted, according to Cunningham, as "nothing" understood in positive terms.[107]

Cunningham's agenda differs in part from those who were otherwise engaged in outlining the nascent Scotus Story. His concern is focused on presenting a historical-philosophical sequence of nihilism; he also sees Scotus as located in the center of the advent of modernity, the creation of the secular, and the instigator par excellence of nihilism, which is Cunningham's primary contribution

---

105. See Cunningham, *Genealogy of Nihilism*.
106. Ibid., 16–17.
107. Ibid., 17.

to the ongoing development of Radical Orthodoxy's Scotus Story. This is manifested in his attention to Scotus's formal distinction, stemming from univocity, and a prioritization of possibility over actuality that Cunningham believes (drawing on Alliez) supports a metaphysics that gives "objective reality" to all conceivable parts of anything.[108] Whereas for Pickstock, this apparent move suggests an infinite impasse between God and creatures, Cunningham sees this as leading to a loss of "ontological unity" wherein Being qua Being, the subject of Scotist metaphysics, becomes "ontologically drained." Cunningham explains,

> Because each reality is mediated by a logical sameness of being, knowledge of being starts to usurp the primacy of theology. And since univocity thereby operates already as the possibility for all knowing, the measure of knowing begins to be a clear and distinct grasp of logically distinguishable items. In this way the primacy of adequation involving a real relation between knower and known starts to fade. Cognition is no longer necessarily about actual objects, but by way of the *potentia absoluta* is possible in principle without one.[109]

As is evident from this passage, Cunningham echoes the concerns of Milbank (Scotus initiating the subordination of theology) and Pickstock (elevation of potency over act), and moves to identify Scotus as anticipating Descartes ("clear and distinct grasp"), an intimation made explicit when Cunningham later writes, "This is to some degree a precursor to the Cartesian reversal from '*ab esse ad nosse valet consequentia*' to '*a nosse ad esse valet cosequentia.*'"[110] He summarizes Scotus's work, borrowing a line from Gerard Manley Hopkins (himself deeply indebted to Scotus's thought), where

108. Ibid., 21. Also see Alliez, *Capital Times*, 201.

109. Cunningham, *Genealogy of Nihilism*, 21.

110. Ibid., 21–22. Later, in summarizing his reading of Scotus, he writes, "This points us in the direction of Descartes in terms of the practical representation of cognition, and Spinoza and Hegel in so far as God and Nature, infinite and finite, are seen as an aspectual dialectic of a monistic whole in the fashion of Jastrow's *duck-rabbit*" (32).

Hopkins apparently described Scotus as "the unraveller."[111] This curt summation is carried throughout the rest of Cunningham's presentation of Scotus.

So if Cunningham seems to follow Milbank and Pickstock, granted in his own way, what is his contribution to the Scotus Story? Beyond a reinterpretation of the Scotus Story as found in the earlier work of Milbank and Pickstock that results in an affirmation of Scotus's role in the establishment of an ontology that conceives of nihilism as substantial *res* (and this is no small contribution), Cunningham also seeks to dismantle the legitimacy of Scotus's doctrine of contingency. Adopting a methodology akin to Pickstock's, Cunningham reads Scotus's definition of contingency in a manner that reverses the subtle doctor's conclusions and intent. Cunningham insists that what Scotus really does by emphasizing contingency is establish a "contorted form of necessitarianism." He writes, "There is no longer any actual contingency but instead virtual necessity."[112] Furthermore, in this move, Cunningham sees Scotus as a forerunner to Ockham, noting that "[the priority of] the possible, in being potentially intelligible (*esse intelligible*), is independent of God and does not receive this potential from God. Instead the creature is possible in itself."[113] What Cunningham sees culminating in modernity's assertion of a space of human autonomy begins in Scotus's metaphysics and coincides with what is labeled as the onset of nihilism as *res*. Cunningham summarizes his conclusive view of Scotus's work:

> I am arguing that for Scotus *being is not* (since it is a partially determined essence), and that *there is but one being*, which in its unity is formally distinct from itself, such that univocity of being again for this reason "is not" being; already as one being it departs from pure existence. This is the *meontotheology* of nihilism's logic: nothing *as* something. It is this

111. Ibid., 22.
112. Ibid., 23.
113. Ibid.

which finite and infinite share. Certainly it was not Scotus's intention to develop a metaphysical system that permits such an interpretation, but this does not mean that such an interpretation is illegitimate.[114]

Cunningham's major contribution to the Scotus Story is his assertion of a reading of Scotus's work that yields an affirmation, not of Being qua Being in a univocal sense, but Being qua *no-thing*.

Graham Ward

Graham Ward begins his *Cities of God* with this assertion: "An analogical world-view is, necessarily, a theological world-view. For the analogical cannot pertain to values and meanings which are only immanent."[115] While Ward rarely addresses the contradistinct proposal of univocity in any explicit form, a fundamental theme that guides his project is a conviction that the lack of analogical ontology in the polis has ushered in the necessary reconsideration (or recreation) of a theological cosmology. He describes this cosmology as "founded upon dwelling in analogical relation, in complex communities which constitute cities of God."[116] The starting point is the contemporary city, which Ward retitles throughout his project. Suffice it to say that he is discussing the postmodern city, the capitalist city, the nonparticipatory city, and the city of disordered desire. For this reason, it could be said that Ward is not interested in recapitulating the Scotus Story, nor is he concerned with its modification. Rather, Ward adopts the Scotus Story as it has been

---

114. Ibid., 31. Emphasis is in the original. How Cunningham is able to defend such a claim remains unanswered. While seemingly conceding to the impossibility of such a reading of Scotus's work with certain concession to the subtle doctor's clear intent, Cunningham nevertheless asserts his right to "read" or "interpret" Scotus's metaphysics as he pleases.

115. Ward, *Cities of God*, ix. Also see Ward, *Cultural Transformation and Religious Practice* (Cambridge: Cambridge University Press, 2005); and Ward, *Politics of Discipleship: Becoming Postmodern Citizens* (Grand Rapids: Baker Academic, 2009).

116. Ward, *Cities of God*, ix and passim.

developed by Milbank, Pickstock and, to a certain degree, Conor Cunningham.[117] His use of the Scotus Story is manifest in an implicit thread of continuity that is sewn throughout his work. The one time in *Cities of God* that he explicitly names John Duns Scotus is in association with the deconstructionist Jacques Derrida with reference to the univocal predication of transcendentals.[118]

Ward sees *analogia entis* as the natural end of contemporary reflections on metaphysical subjects. He is particularly interested in the so-called contemporary linguistic turn, and how it might provide an opportunity today for what he describes as a "new analogical world-view."[119] This is his operating vision for the correction of the secular city as it stands today. A return to analogy, therefore, requires a present-state appropriation of another form of paradigmatic vision. It is here that we can insert the Scotus Story as portrayed in the work of Ward's colleagues. This narrative provides the counterpoint to Ward's insistent call for a return to analogy. This is seen not only in *Cities of God*, but as a looming theme throughout his work.[120]

While Ward does not contribute to the further development of the Scotus Story per se, he has bestowed his blessing on Radical Orthodoxy's Scotus Story. It is in part for this reason that others, following the model of Ward, have taken to the construction of

---

117. At the time of Ward's writing, Cunningham's text had not yet been completed or accessible in its present form. However, Ward does reference Cunningham's unpublished dissertation on the same subject, suggesting a consistency in ideology and an influence of theory. See Conor Cunningham, "Philosophies of Nothing: Reconstructing Metaphysics," (PhD dissertation, University of Cambridge, 2000); and Cunningham," The Difference *of* Theology and Some Philosophies of Nothing," *Modern Theology* 17 (2001): 289–312.

118. Ward, *Cities of God*, 155.

119. Ibid., 9.

120. For examples, see "Introduction, or, A Guide to Theological Thinking in Cyberspace," in *The Postmodern God: A Theological Reader*, ed. Graham Ward (Oxford: Blackwell, 1997), xv–xlvii; "Introduction: 'Where we Stand,'" and "Suffering and Incarnation," in *The Blackwell Companion to Postmodern Theology*, ed. Graham Ward (Oxford: Blackwell, 2001), xii–xxvii and 192–208; "Radical Orthodoxy and/as Cultural Politics," in *Radical Orthodoxy? A Catholic Enquiry*, ed. Laurence Paul Hemming (Burlington: Ashgate, 2000), 97–111; among others.

theological edifices built on the foundation of Scotus as protomodern antagonist.

Gavin Hyman

Perhaps no other Radical Orthodoxy theologian follows the prescribed Scotus Story as closely as Gavin Hyman. In his book *The Predicament of Postmodern Theology*, Hyman reiterates the Scotus as protomodernist narrative verbatim as it is found in the earlier work of Milbank and Pickstock. This should come as no surprise because, as was the case with Cunningham's text, *The Predicament of Postmodern Theology* originated as a doctoral dissertation under the direction of Graham Ward.[121] As we have already seen, while Ward is himself less overt in recapitulating the Scotus Story as the explicit foundation of his own work, Hyman adopts the previously developed narrative script wholesale. He draws on the same sources as Milbank, while also noting the more nuanced references that ground Pickstock's contribution.[122] Hyman's rhetoric is imbued with the tone of early Radical Orthodoxy antimodernist/anti-Scotist polemics. His integration of Milbank and Pickstock's narrative into the foundational chapter of his own project is overt. It is worth citing a portion of his text at length to sense the degree to which the adoption of the Scotus Story is clearly marked.

> The implications of this fundamental shift [away from analogy and toward univocity] occasioned by Duns Scotus and his successors were wide and far-reaching. For one thing, the dissolution of God's ontological transcendence and the establishment of a univocal concept of Being resulted in a "desymbolization" of the universe. For not only

---

121. Hyman, *The Predicament of Postmodern Theology*, ix–x.
122. See his especially heavy reliance on the work of Éric Alliez, a trademark of Catherine Pickstock's argument and a key source that appears after her in the work of Cunningham and Hyman among others.

was God said to "exist" univocally, but God was also said to be "good" and "true" univocally. Thus, God came to be spoken of in terms of "clear and distinct" ideas. This, in turn, resulted in an increased emphasis on representation, for if we know what it means to say that God "exists," and if we can use "clear and distinct" ideas to refer to God, then it appears that God can be referred to in much the same way as other "things." Thus, liturgical performance, narrative, and analogy give way to reference, science and representation.[123]

The indebtedness to Milbank and Pickstock is remarkable. The identification of Scotus with the proceeding members of the Scotist school and the later emergence of "modern" philosophers is characteristic of Milbank. The conflation of transcendentals to a degree that suggests their coextensiveness in univocal predication is also reminiscent of the nascent Scotus Story. The proposed anticipation of and association with Descartes ("clear and distinct ideas") comes right out of Pickstock's work, as does the emphasis on the diminished liturgical ethos symptomatic of modernity's disinterest in mystery and repugnant disposition toward narrative and analogy.

Hyman's work is, as one might guess, similar to that of Cunningham. Although Hyman does not cite Cunningham explicitly (perhaps due to the concurrent publication of their works), there is no doubt that a similar view of the Scotus Story is operative in his writing. This is made clear in the subsection of his fifth chapter, titled "The Advent of Nihilism," in which Hyman reviews his position as follows: "We saw that they [Milbank and Pickstock] maintain that it was Duns Scotus's turn to univocity that laid the foundations for the philosophical project of modernity, a project that masks a nihilist metaphysics."[124] This parallel to Cunningham's work is uncanny until one recalls that Cunningham, who had originally

123. Hyman, *The Predicament of Postmodern Theology*, 37.
124. Ibid., 96.

began his doctoral research under the direction of John Milbank, finished his dissertation under the direction of Graham Ward, after Milbank took up an academic position at the University of Virginia. Here is yet another example of both the cross-pollination of Radical Orthodoxy ideas and the influence of Ward in both Radical Orthodoxy circles specifically and postmodern theology study in general.

These observations are not to suggest that Hyman does not offer original contributions to the Scotus Story. While of seemingly minor importance, he does leave his own imprint on the narrative in two interesting ways. The first is his association of theologians and philosophers such as John Hick and Don Cupitt with the thought of John Duns Scotus.[125] Additionally, Hyman is unrelenting in his assertion that Scotus is the cause par excellence of modernity. While Milbank, and even Pickstock to a lesser extent, exercise caution in their assignment of blame, noting that Scotus is one among many (although the subtle doctor always remains the most significant), Hyman is overtly polemical in his indictment of Scotus. He is fond of referring to Scotus's work as "heretical."[126] Hyman's reading of Milbank results in a conclusive statement that Scotus is solely to blame for modernity, which is a statement Milbank might be hesitant to endorse. Hyman writes, "For Milbank, because the whole project of modernity (philosophical, cultural, economic) is founded on this Scotistic move, modernity itself cannot be other than heretical, idolatrous and secular."[127] The deprecatory terms describing Scotus and his works continue with notable remarks, including the following: "the antitheological moment of Duns Scotus."[128]

---

125. See ibid., 38–49 and passim.
126. Ibid., 5, 49 and passim.
127. Ibid., 49.
128. Ibid.

It is evident that Hyman's work has been clearly influenced by those Radical Orthodoxy thinkers that have gone before him, mentored him, and with whose thought he engages in his own work. The adoption and recasting of the Scotus Story is of paramount importance for Hyman's thesis, as it has been for others following in a similar vein.

Radical Orthodoxy and the Proliferation of the Scotus Story

From its inchoate stage as a lightly sketched theory through the overtly polemic and caustic invocation as the supreme impetus of modernity, the Scotus Story has developed into a narrative that has been adopted by many and continues to be presupposed with the veracity of an axiomatic principle. Milbank is certainly the preeminent figure and first narrator of this movement to establish Scotus as the protomodern antagonist. His early work in this area paved a path for Catherine Pickstock to follow. Their combined efforts orchestrated a convincing vision of a chronologically conceivable genealogy that begins with John Duns Scotus and continues through Descartes, Kant, and the rest of the modern philosophical schools. The medieval Franciscan thinker is, according to Milbank and Pickstock, ultimately responsible for planting the seed of "revolution" that would germinate completely in first Descartes and then Kant's so-called turn to the subject, earning Kant the title "the last Scotist" from Gavin Hyman and Éric Alliez.[129] The cause of this shift is almost completely the result of the doctrine of univocity that has made Scotus so famous. While Milbank essentially stops there, Pickstock sees the associated concept of the formal distinction

129. Ibid.

and Scotus's alleged elevation of possibility over actuality as instrumental in the launch of modernity too. Several Radical Orthodoxy interlocutors have appropriated the early work on the Scotus Story and in some cases applied this interpretation of the subtle doctor's thought to other theological and philosophical themes (such is the case with Cunningham).

I have sought in this chapter to present an overview of the origins and development of the Scotus Story. The significance of this anti-Scotist narrative should not be underestimated. While those interlocutors of the Radical Orthodoxy movement may be properly limited, there appears to be a general sentiment of acceptance among some contemporary theologians sympathetic to the genealogy outlined in the Scotus Story. The impact of Radical Orthodoxy's reading of Scotus specifically and the history of modernity generally has not been mitigated by the few voices that have spoken out against such a consideration of the subtle doctor. For the most part, the Scotus Story goes unquestioned, and is presumed to be legitimate. The prominence of the figures examined in this chapter has to date overshadowed the minority voices that have spoken out against such a reading of univocity and the formal distinction. The Scotus Story, as developed by those within and sympathetic to the Radical Orthodoxy movement, has become ubiquitous and granted uncritical acceptance by many, and it is this reception that we will survey in the next chapter.

2

———

The Reach of Radical Orthodoxy's Influence

One of the more interesting aspects of Radical Orthodoxy's interpretation of John Duns Scotus has been the unexpected and at times unattributed influence that it has had on so many other thinkers and their projects, particularly in the English-speaking world. Whereas one might naturally anticipate that some academic theologians would appropriate the thought of their Radical Orthodoxy colleagues, what is surprising is the way in which the Scotus Story has made its way into the work of historians, philosophers, and popular religious writers beyond the confines of the academic theological guild. As early as ten years after the launch of the key text of the movement, *Radical Orthodoxy: A New Theology*, John Milbank confidently acknowledged the impact Radical Orthodoxy was having in manifold ways. In the afterword to *The Radical Orthodoxy Reader*, which he coedited with Simon Oliver, Milbank wrote,

> Within ten years Radical Orthodoxy has succeeded in transforming the face of Anglo-Saxon theology and today helps to shape most of its serious agendas. Its international influence also increases at a rapid rate. But it remains a project that has scarcely begun and whose boundaries are fortunately fuzzy; many who are "close" to the movement are not necessarily "in" the movement and this is a fundamentally healthy thing. Uniquely, it was an ecumenical theology from the outset: fundamentally Catholic in its orientation, yet attracting many who would consider themselves as "post-Protestants." Uniquely also, it is a collectively undertaken project not dominated by any one person, even if there are certain texts that can be regarded as "foundational."[1]

The hubristic overtones and false humility notwithstanding, Milbank is correct in his assessment that the boundaries of the Radical Orthodoxy project are indeed fuzzy, allowing for an ideological bleed over into several perhaps unanticipated territories. Additionally, those who have cited, relied upon, or have been influenced by Radical Orthodoxy since its emergence during the last decade of the preceding century constitute a diverse collection of thinkers and writers. While an exploration of the various Radical Orthodoxy themes that have gained currency in other academic and popular venues is beyond the scope of this current project, it is likely not an overreach to suggest that the most appropriated topic has been Radical Orthodoxy's Scotus Story.

This brief chapter offers a survey of how the Scotus Story has been appropriated and adaptively used by several contemporary scholars and more popular authors. Rather than attempt an exhaustive exposition of Radical Orthodoxy's contemporary influence, which is a formidable project in its own right, this chapter is presented in an effort simply to illustrate the Scotus Story's reach and intellectual impact. The reception and engagement of the Scotus Story has not

---

1. John Milbank, "The Grandeur of Reason and the Perversity of Rationalism: Radical Orthodoxy's First Decade," in *The Radical Orthodoxy Reader*, ed. John Milbank and Simon Oliver (London: Routledge, 2009), 367.

been uniform. Some have appropriated the story wholesale from Milbank and Pickstock, relying entirely on the early narrators of the Scotus Story in their own representation. Others have followed the Radical Orthodoxy theologians' early work, citing Milbank and Pickstock, while also highlighting the limited primary and secondary sources upon which the first Radical Orthodoxy contributors relied. Still some, by far the least common among the group, like Conor Cunningham before them, have appropriated the Scotus Story as handed down by Milbank, Pickstock, and the rest, and attempted to further the argument. From among this last group, the work of Pickstock's former student Adrian Pabst is the most notable.

The structure of this chapter is organized in a tripartite manner, with the intention of grouping the different inheritors of the Radical Orthodoxy Scotus Story according to admittedly imperfect and rather loosely defined categories based on thematic considerations, publication date, and audience. First is the category of *theology*, including Stanley Hauerwas, Robert Barron, and Adrian Pabst. Second is the category of *philosophy, literary theory, and history*, including Charles Taylor, Terry Eagleton, and Brad Gregory. Third is the category of *popular presentations*, including Karen Armstrong and Francis Cardinal George.

The Scotus Story in Theology

Given the origin of the Scotus Story in the theological work of John Milbank and Catherine Pickstock, it logically follows that the academic field most likely to be shaped by and subsequently appropriate this narrative is that of theology. In this section we consider the pervasive influence of Radical Orthodoxy in contemporary theological reflection. Though not exhaustive, the work of Stanley Hauerwas, Robert Barron, and Adrian Pabst offers us three representative examples of this phenomenon.

Stanley Hauerwas:
The Church, Ethics, and Radical Orthodoxy

The well-known American ethicist Stanley Hauerwas, while not an official member of the Radical Orthodoxy movement (inasmuch as anyone can be an "official member" of a collective that eschews the terms *school, movement,* and the like), has nevertheless been a longstanding interlocutor of key Radical Orthodoxy figures, including John Milbank and Graham Ward. The contemporary concerns about which Hauerwas often writes—nationalism, faith, violence, church, postmodernism, and so on—are themes that have been perennial foci for those who associate with Radical Orthodoxy. It should come as no surprise, then, that parts of his 2000 book on ecclesiology, postmodernity, and ethics, titled *A Better Hope: Resources for a Church Confronting Capitalism, Democracy, and Postmodernity*, draw heavily on the work of Milbank, Pickstock, and Philip Blond in diagnosing what he sees as the problematic of postmodernity for Christians.[2]

Hauerwas appropriates the Radical Orthodoxy Scotus Story most directly in the second chapter of the book, titled "The Christian Difference: Or, Surviving Postmodernism." Drawing first on Nicholas Boyle's critical judgment about postmodernism, Hauerwas offers his take on the respective blessings and curses of the age denominated "postmodern."[3] While he is wary of the ostensible

2. Stanley Hauerwas, *A Better Hope: Resources for a Church Confronting Capitalism, Democracy, and Postmodernity* (Grand Rapids: Brazos, 2000).
3. See Nicholas Boyle, *Who Are We Now? Christian Humanism and the Global Market from Hegel to Heaney* (Notre Dame: University of Notre Dame Press, 1998).

nihilistic tendencies found in many of the so-called postmodernists, and incredulous about the delineation of an age described as such, he does recognize the value in the work of some so-called postmodernists like Michel Foucault. He writes, "Postmodernism seems, in other words, to call into question the Enlightenment project, and surely that is a good thing. Yet I am not convinced that postmodernism, either as an intellectual position or as a cultural style, is post-anything."[4] This doubt about the efficaciousness of postmodern thinking centers on Hauerwas's kindred concern with that of many Radical Orthodoxy theologians; namely, these thinkers believe that the only answer to the problems that face Christians in this age (or any age for that matter) is *Christianity itself.* "Christians must be able to narrate postmodernism in a manner that postmodernism cannot narrate Christianity. Or more adequately: we must show how Christianity provides the resources for a critique of its own mistakes in a way that modernity or postmodernity cannot provide."[5]

While clearly sympathetic to the founding concerns of Milbank and his followers, Hauerwas's issue is not primarily with the entire world as such, but with the ostensible demise of the church. He believes that "postmodernism, in short, is the outworking of mistakes in Christian theology correlative to the attempt to make Christianity 'true' apart from faithful witness."[6] In other words, Hauerwas believes that the real problem for Christianity arose from the desire of its adherents to justify or make sensible the tradition apart from the particularity of living the gospel. Those familiar with Hauerwas's other work, especially his earliest projects *A Community of Character* and *The Peaceable Kingdom,* will sense immediately the consistent

---

4. Hauerwas, *A Better Hope*, 37.
5. Ibid.
6. Ibid., 38.

refrain echoed here that Christians must be *radical,* insofar as radical is understood as a return to the *roots* of Christian living: gospel nonviolence.[7] Christian ethical action arises from the well-formed character of individuals who have appropriated the gospel story and made it their own. In seeking to ground the validity of Christianity outside the gospel, Hauerwas asserts that Christians have inaugurated the subject-centered, autonomous, and "nihilistic" trajectory that we have subsequently termed *modern* and *postmodern.* How did this happen?

Here enters the Radical Orthodoxy Scotus Story. Without invoking the name *Radical Orthodoxy,* Hauerwas nevertheless attributes the key to understanding this shift in Christian theological and philosophical history to "that extraordinary group of theologians recently clustered at or around Cambridge University."[8] The narrative of the "surrender of theology to secular reason's account of nature" that follows draws entirely from the scholarly repository of Radical Orthodox thought. Drawing on Philip Blond's account of the Scotus Story, Hauerwas first asserts that this shift occurred between the work of Henry of Ghent (1217–1293) and John Duns Scotus (1266–1308). While Hauerwas rightly features Henry as the most proximate interlocutor for Scotus, what follows is repeated verbatim from the Radical Orthodoxy Scotus Story:

> For Scotus the distinction between knowing God in himself and knowing him in a creature was not important. For this reason, according to Blond, when considering the universal science of metaphysics Scotus elevated being (*ens*) to a station over God in order that being could be distributed both to God and to his creatures. Scotus

---

7. See Stanley Hauerwas, *A Community of Character: Toward a Constructive Christian Social Ethics* (Notre Dame: University of Notre Dame Press, 1991); and Hauerwas, *The Peaceable Kingdom: A Primer in Christian Ethics* (Notre Dame: University of Notre Dame Press, 1991).
8. Hauerwas, *A Better Hope,* 38.

did this because God could not be known naturally unless being is univocal (*univocum*) to the created and uncreated.[9]

What Hauerwas presents here is the Scotus Story most distilled. It expresses the central, if mistaken (as we will see in the remaining chapters), tenet of the Radical Orthodoxy interpretation of Scotus's thought: Scotus advocated for being to be understood as a genus, thereby elevating being to a place under which both God and creatures could be considered. The single footnote that Hauerwas includes to support his account of Scotus's view of being is telling. It is a citation of Pickstock's *After Writing*, and includes the following comment:

> Pickstock's book is an extraordinary account of the theological and philosophical developments that created the possibility of modernity and postmodernity correlated with social and political developments. Anyone acquainted with her work will recognize how much I have learned from her as well as her and Blond's teacher, John Milbank. *I confess I am insufficiently schooled to evaluate their claims about Scotus.*[10]

In a way refreshingly honest, yet intellectually disappointing, Hauerwas clearly states his inadequate familiarity with the claims contained within the Scotus Story narrated by Pickstock, Blond, and Milbank. This scholarly lacuna does not prevent him from adopting the whole of their narrative in regard to Scotus.[11]

Presupposing the validity of the Scotus Story, Hauerwas continues to follow the lead of Radical Orthodoxy in concluding that Thomas Aquinas's view of the *analogia entis* is the only appropriate corrective

9. Ibid.
10. Ibid., 224n11. Emphasis added. The Pickstock text cited is *After Writing: On the Liturgical Consummation of Philosophy* (Oxford: Blackwell, 1998), 121–40.
11. This caveat is repeated in his subsequent text, *With the Grain of the Universe: The Church's Witness and Natural Theology* (Grand Rapids: Baker Academic, 2001), 34–41, and 34n49, in which Hauerwas maintains his reliance on and association with the Radical Orthodoxy Scotus Story, but appears more cautious, citing studies that have raised concerns about the way Milbank, Pickstock, and others have read Scotus.

to the "idolatry" Scotus's advocacy of the univocity of being inaugurated. Hauerwas concludes his representation of the Scotus Story with the argument that because modernity and postmodernity arose as the result of "the mistakes of Christian theology" (i.e., Scotus's philosophical innovations), one cannot correct the course by means of the error (i.e., modern and postmodern thinking). Put simply, Hauerwas, after the model of Radical Orthodoxy, believes that one cannot fight fire with fire; therefore, another course of action and set of resources beyond modern proposals are in order. It is only *true* or *authentic* Christianity, which is perhaps best exhibited prior to the turn of the fourteenth century, that serves as the icon of this answer to the problems of modernity and that which follows.

Robert Barron:
A Roman Catholic Appropriation of the Scotus Story

"The trouble began with Duns Scotus's option for a univocal concept of being in contradistinction to Thomas Aquinas's analogical understanding," writes Robert Barron early in the introduction of his book *The Priority of Christ: Toward a Postliberal Catholicism*.[12] Like Hauerwas, Barron's outlook on the origin and development of modernity arises entirely from the Radical Orthodoxy Scotus Story. Twice in his introductory remarks does Barron acknowledge his indebtedness to John Milbank for his view that "liberal modernity can best be seen as an energetic reaction to a particular and problematic version of nominalist Christianity" that finds its origins in the philosophical thought of Scotus.[13]

---

12. Robert Barron, *The Priority of Christ: Toward a Postliberal Catholicism* (Grand Rapids: Brazos, 2007), 13.
13. Barron, *The Priority of Christ*, 13. In addition to n10 on p. 13, which cites Milbank's *Theology and Social Theory*, and is the only reference Barron uses when referring to Scotus, Barron also acknowledges Milbank when he writes, "I follow Colin Gunton and John Milbank's suggestion

Barron, the president of Mundelein Seminary in Illinois and best known for his popular *Word on Fire* and *Catholicism* series, represents a Roman Catholic appropriation of the Radical Orthodoxy Scotus Story. While most of the interlocutors are self-identified Anglo-Catholics, Barron's opening remarks in *The Priority of Christ* illustrate the uniquely Latin foundation of his project. The scene of his text is set with a retelling of a Flannery O'Connor story, which itself is signals the catholicity of what follows, presented by Barron as a "particularly apt metaphor for the relationship between modernity and the late-medieval form of Christianity that gave rise to it."[14] What he refers to here as "the late-medieval form of Christianity" is what Radical Orthodoxy presents as that which emerged in Scotus's work, a paradigm that radically departs from Aquinas's participatory metaphysics and the absolute primacy of *analogia entis*. There are several common presuppositions that are found in nearly all of the texts of those who have adopted the Scotus Story, but come through with particular force in Barron's book. The most notable is the belief that Scotus holds that being per se is a genus under which both God and creatures exist in a way akin to species. Barron explains, "Whereas Aquinas insisted that God is categorizable in no genus whatsoever, Scotus held that God and creatures do belong together to a logical category that, in a real sense, transcends and includes

---

that the modern can be viewed as a sharp reaction to precisely the elements in late-medieval Christianity that I have been highlighting" (15).

14. Barron, *The Priority of Christ*, 12.

them."[15] This position, as was seen in the last chapter, can be traced back to Milbank.

Another common presupposition in Barron's text is the view that Scotus distinguishes God and creatures only in terms of quantitative infinity and finitude. "Though God is infinite and therefore quantitatively superior to any creature or collectivity of creatures, there is nevertheless no qualitative difference, in the metaphysical sense, between the supreme being, God, and finite beings."[16] This is a position that was largely developed in the work of Catherine Pickstock.

One other common presupposition is what Milbank describes as the flattening of being, which results in an "ontology of violence." Here Barron asserts that a natural result of holding God and creatures as existing "side by side, as beings of varying types and degrees of intensity," is the disassociation of creation from the Creator.[17] In other words, rather than participating in the being of God, as Aquinas is understood to affirm, God and creatures alongside each other form an oppositional nonrelationship. Barron writes, "A consequence of this conception is that God and finite things have to be rivals, since the individualities are contrastive and mutually exclusive."[18] This is somehow tied to Scotus's Franciscan confrere and intellectual heir, William of Ockham, who Barron ties—like Milbank before him—more closely to Scotus than most historical philosophers or

---

15. Ibid., 13. While this position will be addressed in greater detail in chapters 3 and 4, it is important to note that this is not at all true with regard to Scotus's view. The subtle doctor *did not* believe that being was a genus, and went to great pains to preclude that interpretation, anticipating precisely this sort of misunderstanding. Furthermore, what exactly Barron means by "a logical category" and, more importantly, "in a real sense," is unclear to me. This sort of obfuscation appears commonly in Pickstock's *After Writing* and might be traced back to her assertions about Scotus. Scotus carefully distinguishes between what is logical concerning concept and what is "real" in the absolute present order.

16. Barron, *The Priority of Christ*, 13. Again, this claim will be addressed in the next chapter.

17. Ibid., 14.

18. Ibid., 14.

medievalists would. There is an assumed inextricable connection between the "voluntarism" of Scotus and the "nominalism" of Ockham that accounts for the monadic metaphysics that Barron describes as "individualistic ontology."

Barron offers his own summary genealogical narrative of the emergence of modernity, tracing this "individualistic ontology" as originating with Scotus and bolstered by Ockham and carried forward by Descartes, Kant, and Rousseau through the Protestant reformers Martin Luther and John Calvin.[19] The mildly anti-Protestant undertone notwithstanding, Barron's project is offered as a positive return to "authentic Christianity" against the claims of modernity. The Scotus Story borrowed in whole from Radical Orthodoxy serves as the foundational problematic for Barron. What follows his cursory replication of the Scotus Story is his attempt to respond to both modernity and the inauthentic Christianity that began with Scotus. Barron returns, or at least makes reference, to the Scotus Story several times in the rest of the book, at times referencing Ockham too.[20] What is striking about both Barron's and Hauerwas's presentations of the Scotus Story in their respective theological projects is the lack of primary sources or secondary sources outside the Radical Orthodoxy corpus. Barron, who is otherwise especially good at citing original texts of Anselm or Aquinas in this book, never refers to a primary text of Scotus or Ockham. Instead, the reader is left to infer that he is relying completely on the Scotus Story he has received from Milbank, Pickstock, and other Radical Orthodoxy theologians. However, this is not the case with our next theologian.

19. Ibid., 14–16.
20. For example, see ibid., 193–95; 204–29; 262–64; 341–42.

Adrian Pabst:
Radical Orthodoxy and The Return to Scotus

According to the final publication date of his *Metaphysics: The Creation of Hierarchy*, Adrian Pabst is a relative latecomer to the Radical Orthodoxy movement.[21] By 2012, one might rightly question whether or not the theological school founded in Cambridge still stands as a proper academic force, and therefore doubt the possibility of the admittance of additional Radical Orthodoxy members. Regardless of whether or not one can still become an "official member" of Radical Orthodoxy as such, Pabst is surely the most recent heir and contributor to the Scotus Story. A student of Pickstock, Pabst first wrote *Metaphysics* as his doctoral dissertation at Cambridge in 2006, and revised it for publication under the direction of Milbank at the Centre of Theology and Philosophy at the University of Nottingham. It is, by and large, a masterful and interesting project. At the heart of Pabst's thesis stands the contention that, in contrast to many contemporary theological assessments, the Neoplatonic and other Hellenistic dimensions of the Christian theological tradition are correct and offer the most formidable resource for responding to the ill effects of modernity manifest in both contemporary theological reflection and politics. He argues that "overcoming metaphysics," that modern and then postmodern project most closely associated with Heidegger and his followers, is a ruse. One can never escape metaphysics.[22] The attempt to dismiss metaphysics in fact re-creates a metaphysic to take its place. Pabst is concerned with making sure the *right* metaphysic ultimately takes its place.

21. Adrian Pabst, *Metaphysics: The Creation of Hierarchy* (Grand Rapids: Eerdmans, 2012).
22. Ibid., xxviii.

Unlike Hauerwas or Barron, Pabst is not content simply to appropriate the Scotus Story wholesale, but rather incorporates it into his project as a starting point and referent as he attempts to engage the distinct, albeit related, theme of individuation. Pabst sees Scotus's proposed principle of individuation as insufficient and even problematic on scale with Aristotle's material individuation theory. In contrast to these, Pabst argues that "the Christian Neo-Platonic theology of creation *ex nihilo* and the Trinity offers an account of individuation that avoids both Aristotle's theo-ontology and the idolatry of onto-theology inaugurated by John Duns Scotus."[23] While there is much to say about the medieval debates surrounding theories of individuation, particularly as it concerns Scotus's principle of *haecceitas*, it is beyond the scope of this present book to engage and respond to Pabst's treatment of this subject.[24] Our interest here is to look at *how* Pabst has been influenced by the Radical Orthodoxy Scotus Story and, unique to his case, contributes to the proliferation of this narrative.

Pabst presupposes the veracity of the Scotus Story, frequently alluding to Scotus's culpability in inaugurating the genealogy of modernity and the eventual dissolution of the unity of theology and philosophy (Pabst, like Milbank and other Radical Orthodoxy thinkers, believes that Scotus held metaphysics to be independent from theology as the *scientia Dei*). In addition to the key texts of Milbank and Pickstock, requisite references in the representation of the Scotus Story, Pabst also cites the essential secondary literature upon which Milbank, Pickstock, and other Radical Orthodoxy theologians have relied in the establishment of the narrative of Scotus

---

23. Ibid., xxix.
24. In contrast to Pabst's reticence about the value of Scotus's concept of *haecceitas* for contemporary theological and philosophical reflection, see Daniel Horan, "Beyond Essentialism and Complementarity: Toward a Theological Anthropology Rooted in *Haecceitas*," *Theological Studies* 75 (March 2014): 94–117.

as protomodernist.[25] While he does not effectively alter the Scotus Story, Pabst approaches the Radical Orthodoxy thesis concerning Scotus's historical, philosophical, and theological significance from a different angle.

It is through Scotus's principle of individuation (*haecceitas*) that Pabst reinscribes a number of the now-classic Radical Orthodoxy theses. Among these is the view that Scotus's metaphysical outlook necessitates a break from creation's dependence and relation to the Divine. Like his Radical Orthodoxy predecessors, Pabst presents his reading of Scotus on this point in contradistinction to Aquinas:

> Scotus dismisses Thomas's argument that the divine act of being is the cause of individuation and divinely created matter its principle. This rejection of Aquinas's proposed solution to the problem of what individuates different species within a genus means that for the Subtle Doctor, the metaphysical link between God and creation is irrelevant for the individuation of material substances.[26]

Pabst asserts that somehow, according to Scotus, creatures (material beings) individuate *themselves* independently from God. Although Pabst affirms that Scotus maintains all creatures are dependent on God, a point that is not made by his predecessors as clearly, he notes that Scotus rejects relationality, which is a move that "seeks to preserve the absolute character of a creature."[27] Following Pickstock, Pabst ties this to Scotus's unique concept of the formal distinction, claiming that "this reinforces the primacy of formal essence over actual existence and deepens the divide between metaphysics and theology."[28] Like Pickstock, Pabst interprets the "formal" of Scotus's "formal distinction" to represent something like a philosophical antonym to "real." Later, Pabst explains further,

25. Among these are texts by Boulnois, Honnefelder, Gilson, Funkenstein, and others.
26. Pabst, *Metaphysics*, 283.
27. Ibid.
28. Ibid., 286.

Duns Scotus defends a variant of realism but introduced a formal distinction between the foundation of things and their relation to God. The formality of this distinction relativizes the ontological link between creatures and the Creator. The dependence of all created things on God is real, but (contrary to Augustine, Boethius, and Aquinas) creatures are purely substantial and not relational. This is so because the relation to God does not enter into the essential definition of a creature. Nor does it add any perfection to it.[29]

In this way, Pabst echoes the work of his Radical Orthodoxy mentors and predecessors. While he admirably includes references to Scotist primary sources, these texts are largely invoked to defend his reading of Scotus's principle of individuation and discussion of universals rather than justifying his (Radical Orthodoxy) view of univocity as the cause of modernity. For this, one is left to presume that he uncritically accepts the Scotus Story as he has received it.

One related contribution Pabst makes to the Scotus Story, however, is his attention to Ockham. In a way that rightly distances Scotus from his Franciscan successor, Pabst treats them individually. Pabst appears to pick up the baton from his mentor, Pickstock, with regard to Ockham's complicity in the genealogy of modernity. If, according to Pabst, Scotus severs the participatory and relational link between God and creatures, theology and philosophy, then Ockham establishes the insurmountable chasm between. Pabst explains,

By denying the reality of transcendent universals in immanent things, Ockham restricts human knowledge of divine self-revelation in the world to uncertain intuition and experience. And by subordinating divine intellect to divine will, he also separates God's volition from the incarnate *Logos* and natural law. The combined result of univocal being and the unreality of universals is to introduce a split between creator and creation and to privilege divine intervention in the world through God's omnipotent will at the expense of nature infused by divine grace and wisdom (as for much of patristic and medieval theology).[30]

29. Ibid., 301.

This original shift signals for Pabst the emergence of what will become "the dominant modern model of sovereign power" according to the primacy of the individual or particular over the universal (which, Pabst argues, does not exist for Ockham). One can see clearly the political implications tied to the Scotus Story for Pabst. Scotus (and a fortiori Ockham after him) is not only the harbinger of the philosophical and theological malaise of modernity, but the source of political problems in the ensuing centuries. Pabst's contribution to the Scotus Story is to expand it beyond the immediate concern with the restoration of theology as the "Queen of the Sciences," although he affirms that too. In appropriating the Scotus Story, Pabst broadens the list of those things for which the subtle doctor and his Franciscan inheritor are culpable.

It is clear that the Scotus Story has a strong appeal for Hauerwas, Barron, Pabst, and other theologians in narrating how we have arrived at our present age. The phenomenon of the wholesale appropriation of Radical Orthodoxy's interpretation of Scotus, especially in the work of Hauerwas and Barron, is interesting for its presumed veracity. None of the theologians examined in this section of the chapter offer even a hint that the historical and philosophical reading they repeat might be contestable. Rather, one of the successes of Radical Orthodoxy's Scotus Story has been the lack of critical examination of the proposed interpretation and subsequent usage.

The Scotus Story in Philosophy, Literary Theory, and History

This largely uncontested repetition of the Scotus Story seen in the work of theologians is not limited to the field theology alone, but

30. Ibid., 291.

has instead extended to other academic fields, among which are philosophy, literary theory, and history. In this section we look at the way in which philosopher Charles Taylor, literary theorist Terry Eagleton, and historian Brad Gregory have appropriated and contributed to the Scotus Story in their respective works.

Charles Taylor and Terry Eagleton: Secularity and Literary Theory

The way in which the Scotus Story appears in the work of Charles Taylor and Terry Eagleton varies in at least one significant way from the manner in which it appears in the other thinkers surveyed in this chapter, hence their unlikely pairing in this subsection. Whereas the Scotus Story appears in Hauerwas, Barron, and Pabst as explicitly appropriated (re)iterations of the Radical Orthodoxy account, it appears in more oblique yet nevertheless recognizable ways in Taylor and Eagleton.

The explicit references to John Duns Scotus in Taylor's magnum opus *A Secular Age* are few.[31] However, there is a kindred sensibility in the way Taylor presents the emergence of the secular and the way Radical Orthodoxy narrates their Scotus Story. To begin, both view the emergence of secularity as the result of religion and shifts in philosophical worldviews.[32] This is a position that is universally accepted by those who adopt the Radical Orthodox position or otherwise model it in their respective retelling of the Scotus Story.

---

31. Charles Taylor, *A Secular Age* (Cambridge: Belknap, 2007).
32. This is, of course, not limited to Taylor and Radical Orthodoxy; for another view, see Michael Allen Gillespie, *The Theological Origins of Modernity* (Chicago: University of Chicago Press, 2008). Although Gillespie maintains a theological impetus for modernity, his critique begins with William of Ockham and the emergence of nominalism, rather than with Scotus. Louis Dupré, to whom Taylor is admittedly indebted for his own views concerning religion and modernity, does feature Scotus prominently in his narrative. See *Passage to Modernity: An Essay in the Hermeneutics of Nature and Culture* (New Haven: Yale University Press, 1993).

Taylor famously describes the axial development of the secular in terms of the disenchantment of the universe, which in part provides the conditions for "modern secular society" and accompanies a newly founded prioritization of the natural and, secondarily, the social sciences.[33] These epistemological shifts that Taylor believes most aptly describe the secular age are tied to changing conditions for "belief and unbelief," which are rooted in what Radical Orthodox thinkers posit as the separation of philosophy from theology concomitant with the emergence of autonomy, subjectivity, and self-sufficient existence that reaches its pinnacle with the Western Enlightenment.

Taylor first mentions Scotus in a passing reference to the "great Franciscan thinkers" of the medieval period, including "Bonaventure, Duns Scotus, [and] Occam."[34] The context here is an anticipatory remark, drawing on the work of Louis Dupré, that what the Franciscan theologians and philosophers were doing, by way of systematizing the new *forma vitae* of Francis of Assisi and the emergent mendicant tradition, was inaugurating the trajectory toward what would later be dubbed modernity. Unlike most of the contributors to Radical Orthodoxy who overtly express their umbrage with Scotus and those who come after him, Taylor is typically subtle in his narration. His version of the Scotus Story, which does not depart in any substantial way from that of Radical Orthodoxy, is woven into his broader metanarrative of the onset of secularity in the North Atlantic region. For example, after naming Scotus among the other Franciscans, Taylor writes,

> Though it couldn't be clear at the time, we with hindsight can recognize this as a major turning point in the history of Western civilization, an important step towards that primacy of the individual which defines our

33. Taylor, *A Secular Age*, 59.
34. Ibid., 94.

culture. But of course, it could only have this significance because it was more than a mere intellectual shift, reflected in the invention of new unpronounceable scholastic terms. It was primarily a revolution in devotion, in the focus of prayer and love: the paradigm human individual, the God-man, in relation to whom alone humanity of all the others can be truly known, begins to emerge more into the light.[35]

While Milbank and his colleagues presuppose the wide-reaching effect of Scotus's philosophical innovations—the univocal concept of being, *haecceitas*, the formal distinction, and so on—it is Taylor who, like a master storyteller, presents the Scotus Story latently within the winding and verbose metanarrative of secularity. The almost hypnotic casting of *A Secular Age* often leaves readers overwhelmed by its force and, even if it is not quite subliminal, the subtlety of Taylor's iteration of the Scotus Story portends to offer an apodictic answer to the question "Whence the secular?" Taylor's answer is radical epistemological and social shifts inaugurated by changing religiosity, theological reflection, metaphysics, and philosophy in the late middle ages, one of the, if not the primary, figures behind this axial shift being John Duns Scotus. Taylor adds his own touch to the Scotus Story that the direct manner of Radical Orthodoxy's presentation could not offer, namely, the practical implications of the Scotus Story in terms of the "everyday people" of ages past. Taylor ties the Scotus Story to the narrative of changing devotionalism and affective religiosity, thereby highlighting the ways in which the seemingly arcane thought of a medieval schoolman could influence the entire Western world.

All of this is not to suggest that Taylor does not provide Radical Orthodoxy with its due credit, albeit of a minimal sort. Like Hauerwas, whom Taylor cites as similarly presupposing dimensions of the Scotus Story in his Gifford Lectures later published as *With the*

---

35. Ibid.

Grain of the Universe, Taylor acknowledges that he has not sufficiently examined the Radical Orthodox interpretation of Scotus's thought and his role in the inauguration of the long trajectory toward modernity. However, he recognizes that what he is presenting in *A Secular Age* offers a complementary narrative. This is expressed most clearly at the end of part 2 of *A Secular Age*, where Taylor writes,

> Hence the importance of studies which show how the subject was changed through a series of steps involving late Scholasticism, Duns Scotus, nominalism, "possibilism," Occam, Cajetan and Suarez, Descartes, where each stage appeared to be addressing the same issues as the predecessors it criticized, while in fact the whole framework slid away and came to be replaced by another. Buckley has contributed to this critique of this unconscious distortion of the medieval sources, as have Hauerwas, MacIntyre, Milbank, Pickstock, Kerr, and Burrell. I haven't been able to do justice to this work here, but the story I have been telling is in a sense complementary to theirs. I have been trying to understand some of the changes in social practice and hence also social imaginary that helped bring about the shift of horizon.[36]

However, it is not until the epilogue of *A Secular Age* that Taylor fully shows his cards and expresses his sympathy with and appreciation of the Radical Orthodoxy account of the emergence of modernity and the complicity of Scotus.

At the end of this project, Taylor writes, "There is one such current today, with which I have a great deal of sympathy. I'm thinking of the scholarship which links the critique of mediaeval 'realism' (as with Aquinas), and the rise of nominalism, possibilism, and a more voluntarist theology in Scotus, Occam, and others with the thrust towards a secular world."[37] It is here that Taylor cites Milbank, Pickstock, and the Radical Orthodox movement most explicitly. He even summarizes his own view, implying the veracity of Radical

36. Ibid., 295.
37. Ibid., 773.

78

Orthodoxy's Scotus Story and genealogy of modernity, with a nod to the "father" of the movement: "Indeed, we might following John Milbank see this new 'univocal' understanding of being, predicated alike of God and of creatures, as the crucial shift from which other changes flow."[38] While Taylor avoids naming the precise degree to which he is indebted to Radical Orthodoxy for his own views of the emergence of modernity and secularity, readers are left to assume at least a kindred appreciation, if not an unacknowledged complete reliance, given the unmistakable parallels in their respective presentations, and the attention he finally pays to Milbank and his followers.

Whereas Charles Taylor incorporates the Scotus Story into his magisterial, if somewhat idiosyncratic, narrative account of the emergence of the secular, Terry Eagleton opens one of his recent books on the state of literary theory with a straightforward presentation of how he understands the late medieval debates between the so-called realists and nominalists as relating to contemporary concerns in the shifting academic landscape of literary criticism. Specifically, Eagleton is interested in assessing the question of whether or not something called "literature" actually exists. The renowned Marxist and literary theorist warns the readers of *The Event of Literature* that they "will be surprised, perhaps dismayed, to find themselves plunged at the outset [of the book] into a discussion of medieval scholasticism."[39] He spends the entirety of his opening chapter exploring a theme already quite familiar to readers of this current book; namely, the significance of John Duns Scotus's innovative thought for the establishment of nominalism in his successor William of Ockham and others as the progenitive force for the later emergence of modernity.

38. Ibid., 774.
39. Terry Eagleton, *The Event of Literature* (New Haven: Yale University Press, 2012), xi.

Eagleton is direct and to the point on this subject: loosely defined, there is a continuum of metaphysical perspectives, each end of which is constituted by the "realist" and "nominalist" camps. John Duns Scotus enters immediately in Eagleton's overview because the literary theorist sees in the subtle doctor's work a midway proposal somewhere between the two extremes. "The great Franciscan theologian Duns Scotus proposed a moderate or qualified form of realism for which natures have a real existence outside the mind, but become completely universal only through the intellect."[40] At first Eagleton appears, like Pabst, to be primarily concerned with Scotus's principle of individuation or *haecceitas*. Eagleton asserts that Scotus's approach to individuation, in contrast to a more strict realist view like that of Aquinas, will eventually lead to an extreme form of nominalism that approaches all possible categories and universals with incredulity. Before discussing Scotus and modernity, Eagleton leaps ahead to suggest that this hostile approach to "categorical thought," represented by Nietzsche and a fortiori in Deleuze after him, is a Scotist trademark of postmodernity.[41] Like Milbank and others, Eagleton sees postmodernity as a concern to be addressed.[42]

After his brief discussion of *haecceitas*, Eagleton picks up the Scotus Story in a manner reminiscent of Charles Taylor's account, claiming after the example of Frank Farrell that nominalism and the modern era that follows "represents a kind of disenchantment with the world."[43] This disenchantment, as we might already anticipate, can be

---

40. Eagleton, *The Event of Literature*, 2. To his credit, it should be noted that Eagleton's sources here—Mary Beth Ingham, Mechthild Dreyer, Antonie Vos, among others—are generally sound secondary literature for Scotist studies. However, as with all of the aforementioned scholars with the partial exception of Pabst, Eagleton does not consult *any* primary literature of Scotus.
41. Eagleton, *The Event of Literature*, 9.
42. For more, see Terry Eagleton, *The Illusions of Postmodernism* (Oxford: Blackwell, 1996).
43. Eagleton, *The Event of Literature*, 10. Earlier in the chapter, Eagleton cites *A Secular Age* explicitly; see Eagleton, *The Event of Literature*, 3n7.

traced back to a particular reading of Scotus's notion of the univocity of being.

> Duns Scotus, by contrast with Aquinas, sees God as a being in the same sense that snails and oboes are, but infinitely different and superior. This then has the paradoxical effect of shoving the Creator away from the world in the act of claiming a certain kinship between the two. God is on the same ontological scale as ourselves, but inconceivably further up. A split accordingly opens between the sublimely remote deity and his actual Creation.[44]

There is hardly anything new in this narration of the Scotus Story. Citing Conor Cunningham, Eagleton connects the Scotus Story to a view that "God exerts absolute sovereignty over creation" and therefore "crushes the independent life out of it and leaves it unable to bear witness to his glory," thereby emptying the world of God's very presence.[45]

Eagleton's accounting of the shift from a "sacramental worldview" (presumably represented in the thought of Aquinas) to one that is scientific and autonomous (in the post-Enlightenment sense) mirrors Milbank's earliest assertion of this thesis in his *Theology and Social Theory*. Like Milbank and the other Radical Orthodoxy theologians that followed him, Eagleton holds that Scotus paved the way for the ills of nominalism, which find their natural "modern terminus in the Nietzschean will-to-power," which characterizes Milbank's view that Scotus's thought represents an incipient "ontology of violence."[46]

Although the Scotus Story remains largely untouched and merely replicated with a more accessible literary flair in Eagleton's version, he does make one interesting qualitative addition to the narration.

---

44. Eagleton, *The Event of Literature*, 11.
45. Ibid.
46. Ibid., 12–13. It is important to note that Eagleton, while offering no responses to the contrary, at least acknowledges the contested interpretation of the Radical Orthodoxy movement, stating in a footnote that this view of Scotus "has been strongly challenged by other scholars" (227n17).

Rather than suggesting that Scotus and everything that follows the subtle doctor's late medieval innovations is catastrophic (on which side, to be sure, Eagleton does appear to fall ultimately), Eagleton offers a brief pro and contra presentation of the Scotus Story's implications. On one side of the univocity-nominalist coin, there appears to be "an exhilarating emancipation" from those intellectual, social, and ecclesiastical barriers that would prevent philosophical and scientific inquiry. This, in the spirit of the Western Enlightenment, is viewed positively. However, on the other side of the coin, there appears to be negatively consequential shift: "The arbitrarily absolute God of some late medieval thought becomes a model for the self-determining will of the modern epoch."[47] Whereas Milbank and his colleagues see the first side of the coin as an irrevocably negative result of Scotus's thought, Eagleton remains ambivalent. It would seem highly implausible that his own work, especially influenced by Marxist thought as it is, could be possible without the Enlightenment ideals put to action. However, as noted above, Eagleton nevertheless appears to hold close to the Radical Orthodoxy view that what Scotus is ultimately responsible for has been and remains a problem.

> There is an extraordinary irony at stake here. Postmodernist theory casts a jaundiced eye on the science, rationalism, empiricism and individualism of the modern age. But it remains deeply indebted to that epoch in its rampant nominalism, however ignorant it may be of the history of that doctrine. In this sense, it signifies only a partial break with what it imagines it has left behind.[48]

Perhaps more than anything else, Eagleton is concerned with the future of literature, and whether or not there remains any categorical or universal approach to conceptualizing what that form of literature means. What bothers him is not as such directly tied to the restoration

47. Ibid., 12.
48. Ibid., 16.

of theology as the "Queen of the Sciences" or reconciling philosophy with theology within a context of faith. Rather, he wishes to present an explanation about how the state of the meaning of "literature" has become so confused. Those sympathetic to Radical Orthodoxy's genealogy of modernity and account of the secular might hail Eagleton's project as an illustration of the indeed wide-ranging effects of what is portrayed in their Scotus Story.

Brad Gregory:
A New History Beginning with Scotus

In a way similar to Charles Taylor's metanarrative form, and Terry Eagleton's historiography of literature, Brad Gregory offers an alternative description of what set the stage for the Protestant Reformation in an effort to form a narrative foundation for his historical reading of what has happened since. Gregory's *The Unintended Reformation: How a Religious Revolution Secularized Society,* is an incredibly ambitious project.[49] Early in his introduction, Gregory succinctly states his overarching thesis: "This book's principal argument is that the Western world today is an extraordinarily complex, tangled product of rejections, retentions, and transformations of medieval Western Christianity, in which the Reformation era constitutes the critical watershed."[50] The project is admirable, for it seeks to reexamine the converging factors, those hitherto recognized as well as many that Gregory argues have been overlooked, that form the constellation of our contemporary social setting. Like Charles Taylor's metanarration of secularity, Gregory's historical subject matter is necessarily limited to the European/North

---

49. Brad Gregory, *The Unintended Reformation: How a Religious Revolution Secularized Society* (Cambridge: Harvard University Press, 2012).
50. Ibid., 2.

American world, which is inexorably shaped by the one-time pervasiveness of medieval Christianity, and has since experienced a number of, as Gregory puts it, "rejections, retentions, and transformations." The method with which he proceeds is curious, even by his own admittance: "As a matter of deliberate intellectual strategy and not simply practical necessity, then, this book's experimental analysis of the past is highly targeted. It is self-consciously selective and, one might say, *extractive*."[51] To assess the validity of such a historical method, one that is—like the Radical Orthodox modus operandi—genealogical and selective, is far beyond the scope of this present book. However, it is worth noting that Gregory, while forthright regarding his methodological procedure, nevertheless begins his study with an extraordinarily bold claim that this text is "intended for anyone who wants to understand how Europe and North America today came to be as they are."[52] In so doing, Gregory invites critical inquiry, which is indeed a formidable project that will have to be left for others to pursue in greater detail. As with the previous authors and their texts, my aim here is to highlight some of the ways in which the Scotus Story has influenced and has been appropriated by Gregory in *The Unintended Reformation*. However, this is no easy task.

Gregory's text makes a succinct overview of his use of Scotus challenging. The primary reason has to do with the pervasiveness of the subnarrative grounded in the assumption of Scotus's culpability throughout the book. Although Gregory's most thorough and sustained engagement with the Scotus Story is found in his introduction and first chapter (aptly, if predictably, titled "Excluding God"), each chapter frequently refers back to the Middle Ages as a touchstone for illustrating the "rejections, retentions, and

51. Ibid., 4.
52. Ibid., 2.

transformations" of Christianity that have unfolded over time, ultimately leading to our "secularized society." Because of this, an examination of his preliminary presentation of the Scotus Story and its indebtedness to Radical Orthodoxy will have to suffice for our present purposes.

There are several striking evidences that signal Gregory's appropriation of Radical Orthodoxy's Scotus Story. The first, and perhaps most obvious, connection is the expressed reliance on the movement's earlier work on this front. In a telling footnote, Gregory writes,

> The so-called Radical Orthodoxy theologians (including John Milbank, Catherine Pickstock, and Graham Ward) have emphasized the importance of Scotist univocity in the formation of modern ideologies but they take their cues from postmodern philosophical perspectivalism. The most important and influential among their works is Milbank's *Theology and Social Theory: Beyond Secular Reason*, to some of the critical aspects of which I am indebted.[53]

A second connection is closely aligned with Gregory's admitted reliance on the Radical Orthodoxy precedential development of the Scotus Story. Readers of *The Unintended Reformation* familiar with the work of Milbank, Pickstock, and the other Radical Orthodoxy theologians will immediately recognize that one of the key texts upon which Gregory relies for his assessment of the thought of Scotus, and its role in the inauguration of the genealogy of modernity, is also highly influential in Radical Orthodoxy's early formation of the Scotus Story. What I am referring to here is Amos Funkenstein's 1986 text *Theology and the Scientific Imagination: From the Middle Ages to the Seventeenth Century*.[54] Gregory, like his Radical

---

53. Ibid., 400n26.
54. Amos Funkenstein, *Theology and the Scientific Imagination from the Middle Ages to the Seventeenth Century* (Princeton: Princeton University Press, 1986).

Orthodoxy predecessors, relies heavily on this text in establishing Scotus as a protomodern antagonist. Gregory asserts that "the metaphysical and epistemological assumptions of modern science and of antireligious, scientistic ideologies are clearly indebted to the emergence of metaphysical univocity that Funkenstein identified in medieval scholasticism beginning with John Duns Scotus."[55] A third connection is the genealogical approach to historical study that Gregory admittedly embraces and contributors to the Radical Orthodoxy movement tacitly pursue. The selective model of primary and secondary sourcing that results from this genealogical approach allows Gregory, like the Radical Orthodoxy theologians before him, to narrate the Scotus Story in a way that serves his particular thesis. Gregory spends several pages of his introduction defending this approach in contradistinction to the way he believes most histories of the Reformation or the emergence of secularity have been researched and written.

In addition to these three signals or illustrations of Gregory's kindred alliance with and indebtedness to the Radical Orthodoxy approach, he—like the other scholars surveyed in this chapter—offers his own presentation of the Scotus Story. His depiction of Scotus's thought exactly follows that which was narrated by Radical Orthodoxy and subsequently reiterated by those scholars surveyed so far. It begins with the claim that Scotus had "a different idea regarding what can be said about God and how it can be said" than did Aquinas.[56] Gregory rightly notes that it was in response to the views of Henry of Ghent on analogy that Scotus offers his own examination of the possibility of religious language and the conception of being.[57] Gregory summarizes what he understands the

55. Gregory, *The Unintended Reformation*, 5.
56. Ibid., 36.
57. To his credit, Gregory cites in a footnote a number of very reliable sources on the relationship and difference between Henry of Ghent and John Duns Scotus, including an important study

subtle doctor to have done in departing from Henry's argument on behalf of *analogia entis*:

> [Scotus] predicated of God something that he thought God *had* to share with everything else in the same sense, simply by virtue of existing, namely *being*. The eleventh century Muslim philosopher Ibn Sīnā (Avicenna; c. 980–1037) had argued that being is conceptually prior to and common to God and creatures. Insofar as God's existence is considered in itself and in its most general sense, Scotus agreed that God's being does not differ from that of everything else that exists. This is Scotus's univocal concept of being—"univocal" because it is predicated in conceptually equivalent terms of everything that exists, including God.[58]

This is precisely the interpretation of Scotus's theory of univocity that is shared among subscribers of the Radical Orthodoxy Scotus Story. Furthermore, in reiterating this view, Gregory actually cites Robert Barron, whose own perspective is *entirely* informed by Radical Orthodoxy, as we have already seen above. Gregory writes, "Scotus's move made God, in Robert Barron's phrase, 'mappable on the same set of coordinates as creatures.'"[59]

Gregory believes that Scotus effectively established a genus that was above and prior to God, under which both God and creatures would fall as like species, one infinite the others finite. Our contemporary historian argues that Scotus therefore inaugurated the "first step toward the eventual domestication of God's transcendence, a process in which the seventeenth-century revolutions in philosophy and science would participate."[60] This is not novel, but rather a

by Cyril Shircel on Scotus and univocity that, to date, *no other* narrator of the Scotus Story has referenced. However, what is extraordinarily curious is that many of the sources that Gregory names *outright refute* his claims and the Scotus Story as such, yet this does not seem to faze Gregory at all in proceeding with the relating of the Scotus Story. This is especially true in Shircel, *The Univocity of the Concept of Being in the Philosophy of John Duns Scotus* (Washington: Catholic University of America Press, 1942).

58. Gregory, *The Unintended Reformation*, 37. Emphasis original.

59. Ibid. Gregory is citing Barron, *The Priority of Christ*, 193.

reinscription of the Radical Orthodoxy contention that the emergence of modern philosophy can be, without a doubt, traced back to the subtle doctor and his advocacy on behalf of a univocal concept of being. For Gregory, as for his predecessors in this line of thought, univocity was not something limited to semantic, epistemological, or logical argumentation (as we will see in the next two chapters it properly should be), but was a "metaphysical univocity" that contained ontological claims and bore doctrinal consequences. Furthermore, like Milbank, Pickstock, and others before him, Gregory also holds that what began with Scotus was developed more potently in the nominalist movement attributed to William of Ockham. According to this view, Ockham can be attributed with having solidified the reification of the divine into "some *thing*, some discrete, real entity, an *ens*."[61] For Gregory, this helps set the stage for the theological problems at the dawn of the Protestant Reformation: "At the outset of the sixteenth century, the dominant scholastic view of God was not *esse* but an *ens*—not the incomprehensible act of to-be, but a highest being among other beings."[62]

While Gregory prefers to link this interpretation to the emergence of modern science more than the flattening or collapsing of a participatory metaphysics as Milbank and others have preferred to express it, the same point is expressed: Scotus's unique rejection of Henry's *analogia entis* sets in motion the cause of modernity, the Western Enlightenment and, as Gregory, following Funkenstein, prioritizes, the natural and social sciences.[63] "Metaphysical univocity in conjunction with Occam's razor are the two presuppositions that

60. Gregory, *The Unintended Reformation*, 37–38.
61. Ibid., 38.
62. Ibid.
63. Ibid., 55 and passim.

govern the thought of those intellectuals whose contributions are usually taken to be so critical for the formation of modern, secular views," Gregory firmly asserts.[64]

Before moving on, I want to highlight one additional aspect of Gregory's presentation of the Scotus Story. As with all of the other surveyed scholars, with the exception of Adrian Pabst and Karen Armstrong (as we will see below), Gregory does not reference a single primary text of Scotus. His reliance on admittedly limited and selective secondary literature further confirms the proximity of his account to that of the Radical Orthodoxy movement. What is especially striking about this possible oversight or intentional omission is that Gregory is otherwise very careful to cite the primary literature of Aquinas, Anselm, Dante, Meno Simons, Zwingli, Descartes and the other modern philosophers, among others. When referencing Scotus and his views on univocity, the most common citation is from Funkenstein.

The Scotus Story in Popular Presentations

Having examined the influence of the Scotus Story on the work of theologians, historians, philosophers, and literary theorists within the academy, this section explores the reach of the Radical Orthodoxy narrative in the realm of texts aimed at a more popular audience. Here we look at the work of Karen Armstrong and Francis Cardinal George.

64. Ibid., 64.

Karen Armstrong:
Responding to the Problem of Atheism

With the rise of the so-called new atheists, public intellectuals like Richard Dawkins, the late Christopher Hitchens, and Sam Harris, there has been an abundance of counterpointed writing seeking to set the record straight on what theists, especially Christians (who, perhaps by virtue of sheer numbers in the global West, have been the primary target of these figures), *actually* believe. Among the popular books of this sort, Karen Armstrong's *The Case for God* includes an interlude in her historical overview of the concept of *God* that rehearses the Scotus Story without explicit reference to Radical Orthodoxy.[65] While Milbank, Pickstock, and others associated with the movement are not explicitly mentioned, several of Armstrong's key citations come from the limited pool of secondary literature that forms the foundation of the Scotus Story.

Although her audience is presumably broader than the previous authors, given the major North American publisher that printed her book, she is one of the few storytellers surveyed in this chapter that attempts to offer primary sourcing for her claims. Nevertheless, the content of her argument lacks appropriate nuance and can be misleading from the start. For example, whereas most of those who appropriate the Scotus Story after Milbank and Pickstock have acknowledged Henry of Ghent as Scotus's primary interlocutor on the subjects of analogy and univocity, Armstrong only ever juxtaposes Scotus and Thomas Aquinas. She writes,

> Scotus criticized Thomas's theology, which in his view made it impossible to say anything meaningful about God. He was convinced that reason could demonstrate the existence of anything. It must be possible to arrive at an adequate understanding of God by our natural

65. Karen Armstrong, *The Case for God* (New York: Alfred Knopf, 2009).

powers alone. This was the governing principle of Scotus's philosophy, the criterion that determined the truth or falsity of his ideas. But this "natural theology" was feasible only if we knew what we meant when we said that "God exists." Scotus, therefore, insisted that the word "existence" was *univocal*; that is, it "had the same basic meaning," whether it applied to God or to men, women, mountains, animals, or trees.[66]

There are a number of issues with Armstrong's presentation of the Scotus Story already surfacing at the fore of her presentation, the analysis of which, while important, nevertheless exceeds the scope of this present book. Suffice it to say that, although she departs in the *didactic form* of the Scotus Story otherwise held intact by others influenced by this reading of Scotus (albeit with occasional and peripheral modifications), the major points reflect her general concurrence with the Radical Orthodoxy movement's view. Key among these is the contention that Scotus's thought marks a decisive and significant break with the Christian philosophical tradition and inaugurates a number of problematic outcomes, both acutely experienced and distantly affecting. For Armstrong, what is most important about Scotus's role in the history of Christianity generally, and theology specifically, is that his advocacy of univocity in contradistinction to Thomistic *analogia entis*, as she understands it, prepares the way for an idolatrous conception of God as *ens*. Here Armstrong mirrors one of the major critiques of the Radical Orthodoxy movement, in that she likewise asserts that Scotus's claims can only result in God becoming a creature, even if God is somehow

66. Ibid., 149. In all fairness to Armstrong, it is *somewhat* true that Scotus "criticized Thomas's theology," which he did on various occasions and about many themes in his *Lectura*, *Ordinatio*, and *Reportatio*. However, the way that this is so simply presented in Armstrong's text seems to suggest that Thomas Aquinas was the primary counterview to which Scotus wished to respond. This was not the case. Additionally, "the word 'existence'" was not what Scotus argued was univocal, but rather the *concept* of *being*. This is an important distinction, one that the Radical Orthodoxy movement and its sympathizers get wrong, and one that is made even more unclear in Armstrong's popular presentation.

conceived of as the biggest, best, and most supreme being. One can anticipate where she is going in her casting of Scotus in this role. For Armstrong, the subtle doctor anticipates the problematic and distorted conception of God that is later the object of cynical rejection, which is found in academic and popular discourse from the Enlightenment thinkers of centuries past to the "new atheists" of today.

Given the rather straightforward account of Scotus's historical place in Armstrong's project, it might be most beneficial to take a quick look at her sourcing. As mentioned above, she does not cite Milbank, Pickstock, or other central Radical Orthodoxy figures in her references to Scotus. However, Armstrong's key secondary sources are precisely those upon which the Radical Orthodoxy Scotus Story are founded; namely, Eric Alliez's *Capital Times: Tales from the Concept of Time* and Amos Funkenstein's *Theology and the Scientific Imagination: From the Middle Ages to the Seventeenth Century.* In this regard, a close comparative examination of Armstrong's source material reveals the vestigial presence of the Radical Orthodoxy project. The overt dependence on these specific secondary sources, the idiosyncratic quality of which will become clearer in the next chapter, can be read as something akin to Radical Orthodoxy's intellectual fingerprint left in Armstrong's work. Armstrong does depart, however, from her likeminded predecessors in that she offers a handful of references to Scotus's *Ordinatio* and one citation of a *Quodlibet*. Despite these references, Armstrong ultimately aligns herself with the Scotus Story as it has influenced others with kindred concerns.

Francis Cardinal George:
The Scotus Story and the Catholic Hierarchy

Our last contemporary illustration of the reach of Radical Orthodoxy's influence concerning the appropriation of the Scotus Story is a unique instance. Francis Cardinal George is the Roman Catholic Archbishop of Chicago and likely the most (ecclesiastically) powerful religious figure surveyed in this chapter. Although his book, *The Difference God Makes: A Catholic Vision of Faith, Communion, and Culture*, falls somewhere between a collection of academic essays and a popular book, I have included it in this third and final section of the chapter primarily because of George's popular, cultural, and ecclesial reach and influence.[67]

There are several similarities between Barron's book and that of George. First, like Barron, George is a Catholic cleric who is interested in addressing what he recognizes as pressing cultural and theological concerns.[68] Second, like Barron, George has been deeply influenced by the Scotus Story as portrayed by Radical Orthodoxy, to such a degree that the archbishop has uncritically appropriated this interpretation of Scotus's thought and its ostensible place at the origin of modernity. Finally, like Barron, George offers no primary sourcing to support his presentation of the Scotus Story. He cites only Milbank and Pickstock when advancing his view that there has been "a breakdown of classical Christian participation metaphysics" that has inexorably led to "the consequent emergence of a secular arena."[69]

---

67. Francis Cardinal George, *The Difference God Makes: A Catholic Vision of Faith, Communion, and Culture* (New York: Herder and Herder, 2009).

68. Furthermore, at present, Barron is the rector and president of the seminary to which the Archdiocese of Chicago sends its seminarians preparing for ordained ministry. Both of their respective books were published prior to Barron assuming this leadership position, yet it is perhaps not merely coincidental that both clerics see the contemporary world, the emergence of modernity, and the contours of secularity through similar lenses.

69. George, *The Difference God Makes*, 10.

George's representation of the Scotus Story bears all the usual marks of Radical Orthodoxy's influence. For example, George summarizes the standard narrative as follows:

> The loss of the *communio* ontology in Western thought begins, perhaps surprisingly, just after Aquinas, in the writings of Duns Scotus. Scotus consciously repudiates the Thomistic analogy of being—predicated upon participation—and adopts a univocal conception of being. . . . In maintaining that God and the world can be described with a univocal concept of being, Scotus implied that the divine and the nondivine are both instances of some greater and commonly shared power of existence. But in so doing, he radically separated God from the world, rendering the former a supreme being (however infinite) and the latter a collectivity of beings. In opting for the univocity of the idea of existence, Scotus set God and world alongside each other, thereby separating "nature" and "grace" far more definitively than Aquinas or Augustine ever had and effectively undermining a metaphysics of creation and participation. God is no longer that generous power in which all things exist but rather that supreme being next to whom or apart from whom all other beings exist.[70]

As with other iterations of the Scotus Story, the same narrative structure unfolds, which ultimately implicates Scotus as the cause of a metaphysical catastrophe that, as George goes on to note, irrevocably sets the world on a path toward modernity and the establishment of the secular, a space that can be conceived as apart from God.

Unlike Gregory's concern, centered on the unacknowledged history of the Protestant Reformation and its subsequent effects, or Armstrong's concern, focused as it is on responding to atheism in contemporary society, George's concern is the renewal of Christianity, particularly in its Roman Catholic form, in the United States of America. George appropriates the Scotus Story, following Radical Orthodoxy, and recognizes that this might help answer some of what he sees as pressing questions today, especially given that the

70. Ibid., 11.

philosophical foundations of the "American way of life" enshrined in the Declaration of Independence and the Constitution of the United States of America, which were so influenced by Western Enlightenment thinking and modern philosophers. In this respect, Scotus serves as a cultural scapegoat for George in a way hitherto unseen. His appropriation of the Scotus Story serves as the foundation for a theological-cultural narrative that can then be adapted to diagnose society's ills. As with others (one might recall Hauerwas, for example) George does not believe that modern thinking or postmodern theory offers any promising antidote. Rather, only a restored metaphysical view of the world rooted in *analogia entis*, one in which creation depends on and participates in the divine *esse*, can offer contemporary Christians a way forward in responding to the problems resulting from the late-thirteenth-century Franciscan's philosophical innovations.

The Breadth of the Scotus Story's Reach

This chapter aimed to offer a cursory survey of some of the ways the Radical Orthodoxy Scotus Story has been appropriated or mirrored in a variety of theological, philosophical, critical, historical, and popular texts. Regardless of what one thinks of the veracity of the Scotus Story as presented by Radical Orthodoxy theologians, or as it appears in its manifold replication, the truth is that the narrative has been widely accepted and repeated, often without the slightest bit of critical engagement. One of the most disturbing dimensions of this widespread dissemination of the Scotus Story is the lack of scholarly depth that should accompany such a repetition. Nearly all of the authors examined in this chapter relied *entirely* on secondary sources to justify their appropriated reading of Scotus and his historical significance. Additionally, the secondary literature upon which nearly all those who maintain the Scotus Story rely comes from a very narrow pool of authors. The two scholars that did offer primary source references, Pabst and Armstrong, did so in only the most cursory way. As we will see in the next chapter, this scholarly oversight—the limited use of secondary literature and widespread lack of engagement with primary sources—has aided in the unchecked repetition of Radical Orthodoxy's misreading and misrepresentation of Scotus's thought. Clearly, there is a need for a critical assessment and response to the Radical Orthodoxy Scotus Story, as well as a corrective reading of Scotus's actual thought. The next two chapters seek to offer my attempt at both of these.

3

Major Critiques and Analysis of Radical Orthodoxy's Use of Scotus

In the previous two chapters, we explored the genesis and subsequent development of what I have termed the Scotus Story in Radical Orthodoxy and beyond. Tracing the scripting of the Scotus as protomodern antagonist narrative, we came to see the increasing degree of influence and ubiquity the story has gained. Through the work of John Milbank, Catherine Pickstock, and others, many contemporary theologians have adopted the Scotus Story. As we saw in chapter 2, this influential narrative has gone largely unquestioned and unanalyzed, especially by those who have adopted it in their own work. There exists little opposition to the increasingly widespread adoption of this interpretation of Scotus's thought. The primary exception to this has appeared in the occasional responses offered by the small cadre of philosophers representing the contemporary guild of Scotist scholars. Two figures emerge as overtly critical of Radical Orthodoxy's reading of the subtle doctor's work, striving in large part to call attention to what they consider to be a misreading of Scotus's doctrine of the univocity of being.

The leading Scotus apologist is Richard Cross, the former Oxford theologian and current faculty member in the philosophy department at the University of Notre Dame. A widely respected authority on the philosophy of John Duns Scotus, especially in the English-speaking world, Cross has been the most vocal critic of the Radical Orthodox reading of Scotus and its presentation of the subtle doctor's approach to univocity. Concerning himself with explicit correction, Cross has seen his role as one to assess the "accuracy of the various accounts" of Radical Orthodoxy's use of Scotus.[1] This is a role he does not take lightly, noting that Milbank and Pickstock are clearly mistaken in their understanding of Scotus's intention, method, and aim.

In addition to Richard Cross, Thomas Williams, a professor at the University of South Florida, has provided elucidating commentary on what he sees as problematic in the work of Radical Orthodoxy vis-à-vis Scotus. Williams coined the phrase "univocity is true and salutary" in the title of his most visible critique of the Radical Orthodoxy reading of Scotus's doctrine of univocity.[2] Invited to respond to Catherine Pickstock's article "Duns Scotus: His Historical and Contemporary Significance" published in the same issue of *Modern Theology*, Williams is keen to highlight the "notably careless" treatment of Scotus by Pickstock and others.[3] As the title of his essay implies, Williams focuses on the ways in which the doctrine of univocity, as outlined by Scotus, is in fact valid and praiseworthy. Additionally, Williams has delivered less visible responses to the

---

1. Richard Cross, "'Where Angels Fear to Tread': Duns Scotus and Radical Orthodoxy," *Antonianum* 76 (2001): 7.
2. See Thomas Williams, "The Doctrine of Univocity is True and Salutary," *Modern Theology* 21 (2005): 575–85.
3. Ibid., 575.

Radical Orthodoxy version of the Scotus Story in the form of conference papers and colloquia presentations.

In addition to Cross and Williams, there are few North American scholars that have publicly taken notice of the inherent problems latent in the Scotus Story as crafted by members of the Radical Orthodoxy movement. Even fewer have responded to the mistaken interpretations and claims made by Milbank, Pickstock, and those who have followed them. One additional exception to this rule, beyond Cross and Williams, is Mary Beth Ingham. Ingham, a well-known Scotus scholar whose interest focuses primarily on Scotus's ethics, participated in the roundtable-like symposium in the special issue of *Modern Theology*, along with Williams. In her short text, Ingham is forthcoming about her desire to leave the details of critique concerning univocity to Cross and others, thinkers she views as solid in their assessment and already vocal about their criticism of Radical Orthodoxy. Instead, Ingham's contribution is largely historical and contextual, focused on how Radical Orthodoxy in general (and Pickstock in particular) has "moved from interpretations about Scotus to affirmations about his thought" and has neglected to consider Scotist thought within the context of his "Franciscan assumptions."[4] Ingham's contribution is significant by way of refocusing attention to the importance of historical and philosophical context for interpreting a thinker.

There are several European thinkers that have actively engaged Radical Orthodoxy's position on Scotus. A notable contributor to the ongoing Scotus conversation regarding Radical Orthodoxy and authentic *ressourcement* is the French Dominican Emmanuel Perrier. He too contributed to the special issue of *Modern Theology*, with an article that supports Ingham's call for accurate contextualization, and

---

4. Mary Beth Ingham, "Re-Situating Scotist Thought," *Modern Theology* 21 (2005): 609.

a demarcation of Scotus's thought per se from "Scotist thought" and its subsequent interpretation(s).[5]

Isidoro Manzano, Orlando Todisco, and Javier Andonegui, all Franciscan friars, have also responded to recent claims made about and against Scotus within Radical Orthodoxy. Their works have approached the subject from a variety of angles. Manzano is particularly interested in the function Scotus serves in Pickstock's political agenda. He seeks to reevaluate the claim that Scotus's philosophical work prepares a path for destructive political thought, in turn positing that Scotus's thought is richly fecund with positive ethical and social implications, most of which are found in texts not familiar to Pickstock.[6] Todisco is less concerned with refuting the claim that Scotus is the originator of modernity than asserting the positive nature of such a development, in contradistinction to the negative and more polemical view offered by Radical Orthodoxy.[7] Andonegui is well aware of the same trend emerging in contemporary theology that Cross notes in his work, namely the viral transmission of the Scotus Story and the increasing unquestioned adoption of the narrative among many scholars. Andonegui's primary observation is that the scholars responsible for advancing the Scotus Story are simply mistaken in their reading of the subtle doctor because they are not sufficiently familiar with the Scotus corpus. He is also interested, like Ingham and Perrier, in the recontextualization of Scotus's thought.[8]

Curiously, several scholars whose works are frequently invoked by Radical Orthodoxy writers in support or defense of the Scotus Story

5. See Emmanuel Perrier, "Duns Scotus Facing Reality: Between Absolute Contingency and Unquestionable Consistency," *Modern Theology* 21 (2005): 619–43.

6. See Isidoro Manzano, "Individuo Y Sociedad en Duns Escoto," *Antonianum* 76 (2001): 43–78.

7. Orlando Todisco, "L'Univocita Scotista Dell'Ente E La Svolta Moderna," *Antonianum* 76 (2001): 79–110.

8. Javier Andonegui, "Escoto en el Punto De Mira," *Antonianum* 76 (2001): 145–91.

have responded with an apparently cautious, if not quite a critical, voice. Here one might look to Olivier Boulnois, for example, who is a favorite source for Milbank and Pickstock. His important work, *Etre et Représentation: Une genealogie de la métaphysique moderne a l'époque de Duns Scot,*[9] is cited by Radical Orthodoxy thinkers. This is not without cause, for Boulnois is generally a supporter of the view that Scotus's thought lends a significant contribution to the onset of what would become the long road to modernity. However, Boulnois has also noted the presence of several so-called "ruptures" in philosophical history that have contributed to this alleged genealogy as a whole, forming something of a constellation of responsibility, thereby not limiting culpability just to Scotus.[10] Additionally, Boulnois's work strengthens the connection of dependence between the Radical Orthodoxy movement, and their likeminded fellows, and the interpretation of Scotus presented in the early twentieth century by Étienne Gilson, whose reading of the subtle doctor is largely contested by Scotus scholars. Ludger Honnefelder is another important figure for Radical Orthodoxy in the casting of the Scotus Story. His work, especially *Scientia Transcendens: Die Formale Bestimmung der Seiendheit und Realität in der Metaphysik des Mittelalters und der Neuzeit,*[11] is referenced in passing in the work of both Milbank and Pickstock.[12] It is important to note the frequently

---

9. Olivier Boulnois, *Etre et Représentation: Une genealogie de la métaphysique moderne a l'époque de Duns Scot* (Paris: Presses Universitaires de France, 1999).

10. Boulnois has nevertheless maintained an unapologetic position that Scotus's so-called philosophical rupture is directly linked to the onset of the trajectory that led to the emergence of modernity, a view rooted in the thought of Étienne Gilson.

11. Ludger Honnefelder, *Scientia Transcendens: Die Formale Bestimmung der Seiendheit und Realität in der Metaphysik des Mittelalters und der Neuzeit,* Paradeigmata 9 (Hamburg: Felix Meiner GmbH, 1990).

12. While this work appears in the bibliographies and footnotes of both thinkers, the thought of Honnefelder is largely unexplored by either thinker. Nearly all the references to Honnefelder's work are vague and do not include specific referential pagination, leaving the reader to ask *what precisely* of Honnefelder's work is informing this or that part of their arguments. Milbank, for example, finds it sufficient—among a list of other allegedly sympathetic thinkers including

indirect referential dimension of Radical Orthodoxy's engagement with Honnefelder's work, which suggests a less proximate relationship between Honnefleder and the Scotus Story than Radical Orthodoxy thinkers would have readers believe. Serious engagement with Honnefelder's scholarship offers a more nuanced reading of Honnefelder's view of the subtle doctor's work. While Honnefelder, like Boulnois, does not seem interested in challenging the possibility that certain later interpretations of Scotus's work could have contributed to the axial shifts in the history of philosophy and theology, the German scholar is more careful in his reading of Scotus qua Scotus than Milbank, Pickstock, and others have been subsequently.

In this chapter, I will present a tripartite examination of Radical Orthodoxy's use of Scotus. The first section focuses on Richard Cross's response to the Scotus Story. Cross offers a succinct and direct attack of what he calls a "profound misunderstanding" of Scotus's theory of univocity based on a "deeply flawed analysis" of the subtle doctor's work.[13] The second section follows where Cross leaves off and Thomas Williams picks up. Williams's work seeks to elevate univocity as an argument of value and something to be praised rather than condemned as the harbinger of modern and secular ills. Finally, the last section of this chapter includes my own contribution to the critique of Radical Orthodoxy's use of Scotus. Complementing the work begun by Cross and Williams, I offer additional critical points of consideration, including the following: (a) a brief examination of Radical Orthodoxy's unique form of Thomism as a response to Scotus's alleged errors; (b) an analysis of the primary and secondary

---

Courtine, Boulnois, Marion, et al.—only to cite Honnefelder's text without explanation, interpretation, or page. Of the veritable litany of so-called elaborators of Gilson's work on the subject (see list above), only Honnefelder earns a book reference, leaving the others simply mentioned in passing without even the general textual reference.

13. Cross, "Where Angels Fear to Tread," 11n9.

source material that grounds the Radical Orthodoxy Scotus Story; and (c) an evaluation of the theological content and Christian confessional quality of the Scotus Story as the Radical Orthodoxy movements presents it.

Richard Cross:
The Authenticity of Tradition

Interestingly, Richard Cross begins his treatment of Radical Orthodoxy's use of John Duns Scotus not too far from John Milbank's own beginning. Both thinkers emphasize the importance and place of tradition and the history of ideas in the development of doctrine, theology, and philosophy. Cross holds this dimension of Radical Orthodoxy's method up to be lauded as its greatest strength.[14] However, the celebration of Radical Orthodoxy's methodological asset is short-lived for Cross also believes that it is precisely this aspect of the movement's approach to theology and philosophy that is flawed. He explains that such a method necessarily entails the construction of a master or metanarrative (or what Cross calls "the grand narrative") that consists of smaller narratives to support and explain the larger one.[15] This dependence on these smaller stories mandates a degree of veracity for each in order to maintain the truthfulness of the whole system. Cross's concern, as he clearly states, is not with the so-called grand narrative of the Radical Orthodoxy movement, but simply with one of the smaller stories—the Scotus Story.

Cross keenly observes that there are inconsistencies within the rhetoric and explanation of the Radical Orthodox method from the start. Radical Orthodox theologians defend their engagement with

14. Ibid., 7.
15. Ibid.

thinkers such as Aquinas and Scotus as appropriate "conversations with the past" within the "space of abstract philosophical debate." However, Cross reminds us that the work of these past thinkers is in fact used by Radical Orthodoxy to "provide an explanation of the origins of a specific intellectual phenomenon that has been the mark of Western society for a greater or lesser part of the last millennium: modernity."[16] The claims made and the defense given by Radical Orthodoxy do not stand under the weight of their mode of invocation. In other words, Cross's brief recapitulation of Radical Orthodoxy's agenda and modus operandi reveals the *post factum* and anachronistic quality of their reading *into* Scotus rather than their accurate exegesis of the medieval thinker's thought.

This examination of Cross's contribution proceeds in four sections. First, we look at three methodological presuppositions that Cross identifies at the heart of Radical Orthodoxy's presentation of Scotus. Second, we examine the importance of considering Scotus's inherently semantic argument for adequately interpreting the subtle doctor's thought. Third, we explore Cross's view that Scotus's nuanced understanding of infinity also shapes Scotus's arguments in significant ways. Finally, we consider several other aspects of Cross's critique of Radical Orthodoxy's use of Scotus, including the movement's claims that Scotus's thought leads to idolatry and is the progenitor of modernity.

Radical Orthodoxy's Problematic Methodological Presuppositions

As we have already seen in the first chapter, there are a few notable contributors to the Scotus Story inaugurated by Milbank, and still more that follow suit. However, as also noted, these contributors

16. Ibid., 8.

never depart from the Scotus Story's inchoate form as originally sketched out by Milbank and later expanded by Pickstock, but rather they adopt, adapt, and repurpose the narrative in their own projects. Cross also recognizes this shaping of the Scotus Story's history, observing the general consistencies of the narrative at all stages with that of Milbank's original interpretation and narrative proposal. Cross sees three methodological presuppositions operating in the Scotus Story's construction that are subsequently shared by all who likewise appropriate or are influenced by it. These assumptions are viewed by Cross as highly problematic and contribute significantly to the misreading and misrepresentation of the subtle doctor's work.

The first methodological presupposition is that those scholastic thinkers who appear in the grand narrative of Radical Orthodoxy can be viewed as doxographical figures.[17] Cross believes that the thought of theologians like Aquinas, Henry of Ghent, and Scotus are ultimately reduced to a set of opinions within the Radical Orthodoxy corpus.[18] In other words, Milbank, Pickstock, and others do not present arguments or reasons for the claims they ascribe to the medieval thinkers they examine. Rather, they posit only *doxa*. In its classical Greek origin, the term *doxa* referred to a commonly held opinion, belief, or view. The description of Scotus or Aquinas as doxographical figures in the Radical Orthodoxy corpus suggests that a popularized opinion, belief, or view about what Scotus or Aquinas allegedly holds to be the case is identified and transmitted in place of adequate consideration of the respective thinker's actual work, thereby bypassing the primary sources for a more generalized perspective. In framing the discussion as a difference in *doxa*, Aquinas's thought becomes reduced to "advice that comes after" and

---

17. Ibid., 9.
18. Ibid. For more, again see Simon Blackburn, "Doxography," in *Oxford Dictionary of Philosophy* (New York: Oxford University Press, 2005), 105: "The practice of recording the opinions of other philosophers, practiced by classical philosophers and historians."

Scotus's work is seen as "simply ignoring" the wisdom put forward decades prior by the angelic doctor.[19] As Cross summarizes, "This way of treating Aquinas and Scotus is far removed from the reality of their thought-patterns. Aquinas offers *reasons* for his conclusion, and Scotus offers further *reasons* for wanting to reject it in favor of his own theory."[20] What is at stake here is the context of the work of these medieval thinkers. Cross's accusation suggests that these medieval schoolmen are not read or interpreted in light of their own contexts, dispositions, and intentions, but are read instead in a manner alien to their own way of thinking. The result of this is, in short, an eisegetical accounting of a given historical figure's position. In this way, Radical Orthodoxy commits a form of hermeneutical violence to the thought of both Aquinas and Scotus, to name but two figures.

Cross sees the second methodological presuppostion as closely related to the first. I have termed this second methodological problem *consequentialism*, an expression not found in Cross's argument, but one that I believe accurately describes the critique. Cross explains his concern as follows: "On the sort of analysis presented in [Radical Orthodoxy] accounts of the history of ideas, opinions are naturally assessed in terms of their supposed historical consequences—and not, for example, in terms of whether they might be coherent, or in terms of their possible truth-value."[21] In other words, the theories posited by each medieval figure are not weighed or even considered according to their own coherency or on their own merit, but, rather, on the real (or imagined) historical consequences of such a position. Additionally, these theories are reduced to doxographical statements and treated in light of their apparent and subsequent impact. As

19. Cross, "Where Angels Fear to Tread," 9.
20. Ibid.
21. Ibid.

such, this methodological presupposition is closely allied to the first, rendering yet another violation of accurate contextual analysis.

The third methodological presupposition Cross highlights in his examination of Radical Orthodoxy is related to the movement's sources. As intimated in the first chapter, Radical Orthodox theologians use a very restricted set of scholarly sources to support their claims. Perhaps the most astonishing dimension of this is the extremely austere treatment of Scotus's primary texts in Radical Orthodoxy's development of the Scotus Story. Whereas the ongoing project to critically edit Scotus's corpus has produced more than twenty-five large tomes, and several other uncritical editions of his work are readily accessible (here I think of the Wadding edition in twenty-four volumes, for example), one is hard pressed to find a reference to one of Scotus's works not found in the small Hackett Publishers' volume of translated excerpts edited by Allan Wolter in 1987.[22] The ostensible lack of familiarity with Scotus's writings is troubling and can suggest a poor scholarly approach to the subject.[23] Additionally, Radical Orthodoxy's use of secondary sources is idiosyncratic and limited. As noted earlier, Milbank and Pickstock are largely indebted to Étienne Gilson's *Jean Duns Scot*. Cross and others see this as highly troublesome. So as not to appear partial in this assessment of Gilson's work, Cross cites Gilson's ("extremely sympathetic") biographer who notes that this work on Scotus is

---

22. See Duns Scotus, *Philosophical Writings*, ed. and trans. Allan Wolter (Indianapolis: Hackett, 1987).

23. As will be made clear below, the Radical Orthodoxy interpretation of Scotus's work that renders an account of infinite difference between God and creatures (see my section in the first chapter, "Univocity, Formal Distinction and the Distant Divine") is primarily the result of unfamiliarity with the Scotistic corpus in general. See Cross, "Where Angels Fear to Tread," 23: "But at any rate, a wider reading of pertinent Scotist texts would have revealed how misleading it is to assert that the difference between God and creatures is just quantitative, that 'the distance between the infinite and the finite becomes an undifferentiated and *quantified* (though unquantifiable) abyss.'" Cross cites Pickstock, *After Writing: On the Liturgical Consummation of Philosophy* (Oxford: Blackwell, 1998), 123.

generally accepted to be flawed.[24] Gilson's work is, as Cross notes, more than half century old. Ironically, one of the two names that Cross suggests that would have been a more recent and helpful source is none other than Ludger Honnefelder, someone Milbank and Pickstock have frequently invoked and claim for themselves, without perhaps closely examining his reading of the subtle doctor. The other recommended source is, of course, Allan Wolter.

These three methodological presuppositions succinctly capture the lack of secure footing with which the Radical Orthodoxy thinkers begin their inquiry, while also anticipating the eventual problems to be faced in sustaining such claims about Scotus and his work.

The Importance of Semantic Argument

After outlining his methodological concerns with the Radical Orthodoxy approach to reading and interpreting Scotus, Cross sets out to clarify where Milbank, Pickstock, and those who follow them have gone wrong in the establishment and repetition of the Scotus Story. His attention is particularly focused on how Radical Orthodoxy portrays Scotus's doctrine of univocity and, by extension, God's infinity. Cross finds it important to begin with what appears to be a shared starting point between Aquinas and Scotus, namely the subject of metaphysics as *ens*, with the object of such a science being the arrival, by natural reason, of some knowledge of God. The similarity does not extend much further than this. As Cross observes, "A crucial difference lies in their assessment of the notion of *ens*. For Scotus, there is a sense of *ens*—and other key concepts—which is univocal to God and creatures; for Aquinas there is not."[25] This is

24. See Cross, "Where Angels Fear to Tread," 10n7.
25. Ibid., 12. For the primary sources, see Thomas Aquinas, *Summa Theologica* 1.13.5 (I/I, 67–68) and John Duns Scotus, *Ordinatio* 1.3.1.1 (Vatican III, 1–48).

precisely the breakdown in agreement that Radical Orthodoxy finds so repugnant.

What we are dealing with here is a difference in understanding the meaning and purpose of concepts. For Thomas, concepts are instantiated in a variety of different ways (e.g., properly, improperly, primarily, derivatively).[26] For Aquinas, it is a distinction between the *res significata* and the *modus significandi* (i.e., the thing signified and the way in which the term signifies). The *res significata* remains the same, but the *modus significandi* is different.[27] In light of this distinction, using Aquinas's philosophical system, we can say that God and creatures both come under the extension of the concept of *being* in terms of the *res significata*, but the concept of *being* belongs properly to God and derivatively (i.e., *per participationem*) to creatures. As such, *being* has different *modi significandi* for both God and creatures.[28] For Scotus, however, the concept of *being* applies properly to *neither* God nor creatures (something Radical Orthodoxy has overlooked or mistaken).[29] Being, then, does not apply to any real *extramental* property of a thing, but instead remains a concept understood in terms of a "vicious abstraction."[30] This is a clear departure from the Thomistic understanding of *being* as applied in itself (properly) to God, and by derivation, to creatures.

Cross is correct to point out that Milbank, Pickstock, and the rest of the Radical Orthodox theologians find this understanding of the concept of being to be theologically damaging, as outlined in the first chapter. Furthermore, Radical Orthodoxy understands Scotus's

---

26. Cross, "Where Angels Fear to Tread," 13. See also Richard Cross, "Scotus and Suárez at the Origins of Modernity," in *Deconstructing Radical Orthodoxy: Postmodern Theology, Rhetoric and Truth*, ed. Wayne Hankey and Douglas Hedley (Burlington: Ashgate, 2005), 66–67.

27. Cross, "Where Angels Fear to Tread," 13.

28. Ibid.; and Cross, "Scotus and Suárez at the Origins of Modernity," 68.

29. See Richard Cross, *Duns Scotus* (New York: Oxford University Press, 1999), 38–39.

30. Cross, "Where Angels Fear to Tread," 13; and Cross, "Scotus and Suárez at the Origins of Modernity," 69.

distinction between God and creatures, with regard to being, to be problematic. The claim is that the fundamental difference between God and creatures is a matter of degree in terms of *infinite* versus *finite* being. One can begin to see the problems such a reading would naturally imply. Univocity of this sort suggests God and creatures are basically the same kinds of *thing* differing only in terms of degree.[31] This reading of univocity flies in the face of the Thomistic understanding that all concepts predicated of both God and creatures must *necessarily* refer to God in the proper sense and to creatures derivatively, that is *analogously*. Radical Orthodox theologians appear, at first, justified in their concern. However, there are aspects of this argument that are overlooked. Cross introduces these observations as follows:

> The [Radical Orthodox] theologians are right to spot that there is a radical difference between Aquinas and Scotus. For Aquinas, after all, the analogy between God and creatures is grounded in creaturely participation in a divine attribute, a participation that is intended to guarantee at once both qualitative difference and real resemblance; for Scotus, the notion of participation in the divine attributes is wholly extra-theoretical to the doctrine of univocity. . . . As I hope to show, the [Radical Orthodox] presentation of Scotus on univocity and infinity is highly misleading.[32]

Fundamentally, Aquinas and Scotus are dealing with two different understandings of *concept*, and because of that, *being*. This is most clearly revealed in the application of the concept. On one level, there is the basic adjudication concomitant with difference in predication: one *analogously* and the other *univocally*. On another level, there is the understanding of the concept that is predicated: one *properly attributed to God* and the other *properly attributed to neither God nor creatures*.

31. Cross, "Where Angels Fear to Tread," 13–14.
32. Ibid., 14.

110

As such, to hold Aquinas's analogous predication of being beside Scotus's univocal predication of being is, in some sense, "comparing apples and oranges." Nevertheless, this is the foundational approach to understanding univocity from the perspective of the Radical Orthodoxy movement. Without clearly understanding what *Scotus* intends and defines by the concept of being or its univocal predication, Milbank, Pickstock, and those who follow them treat his terms as though they emerge from a Thomistic lexicon.[33]

Cross explains the necessary starting point for authentic appreciation of Scotus's doctrine of univocity: "The key to understanding Scotus's theory is his claim that univocal concepts are vicious abstractions: they are *general* terms."[34] This is, first and foremost, the most serious interpretive error committed by Radical Orthodoxy in its reading of Scotus's univocity of being. While Scotus does not hold that these concepts qua vicious abstractions are classifiable as *genera*, he does allude to their understanding as *analogous* to genera. Conceptualizing being as if it were a genus does help illustrate what it is Scotus is suggesting.[35] Comparing being to the genus *animal*, Cross offers the example of the species of *dog* and *cat* to demonstrate Scotus's point. "Dogs and cats are animals in just the same sense—just as God and creatures are beings in just the same sense. But these claims, of course, tell us nothing about the properties had by real objects, dogs, cats, God, creatures."[36] Like *animal*, *being* is just a concept that does not tell us anything about the real properties

---

33. This is a point that I will address in greater detail below in the first part of the third section of this chapter.

34. Cross, "Where Angels Fear to Tread," 15.

35. As will be made clear in chapter 4, Scotus anticipates the possibility that some might misunderstand his argument and mistake his univocal concept of being in terms of a genus, and explicitly makes clear that this is not what he means. It cannot be overstated that Scotus *does not* hold that being is a *genus* under which God and creatures fall as *species*. Rather, being *is like* a genus under which we might *conceive* of God and creatures falling under such a genus as *species*. The illustration is simply analogous.

36. Cross, "Where Angels Fear to Tread," 15.

POSTMODERNITY AND UNIVOCITY

of things. Likewise, these concepts do not tell us anything about what is different about the things of which they are predicated. Cross goes so far as to suggest that this dimension of Scotus's theological language is "as apophatic as Aquinas's." He writes, "All that it tells us is that there is a concept under whose extension both God and creatures fall, just as there is a concept under whose extension both cats and dogs fall."[37]

This understanding of being is radically different from the concept as understood by Aquinas. Scotus's rejection of Aquinas's view is replaced by this genus-*like* conceptualization (albeit admittedly, it is *not* a genus), a move about which the Radical Orthodox theologians appear unaware or, at least, with which they seem unconcerned. The importance of the shift is such that any negligence in clearly adjudicating the intent of the medieval Franciscan from that of his Dominican predecessor ultimately misconstrues his philosophical system. It then becomes clear that the doctrine of univocity as interpreted and understood by Radical Orthodoxy is absolutely alien to the concept intended and expressed by Scotus. Given the gravity of this point, it is worth returning to Cross's explanation to further clarify an authentic reading of Scotus's thesis:

> In Scotus's theory, to say that things "are" in the same sense is to tell us nothing about the things under discussion, because nothing just "is" at all. In reality, things "are" in as many different ways as there are kinds of things. There is no extramental property, *being*, shared by all beings, just as there is no extramental property, *being an animal*, shared by all animals. To say that a dog, or a cat, is an animal, is just a way of saying that in virtue of instantiating respectively the extramental properties of

37. Ibid. See also Cross, "Scotus and Suárez at the Origins of Modernity," 72: "For claiming that God falls under the extension of a concept—*being*—is very different from claiming that God somehow requires Being for his existence, as it were. In general, claiming that something falls under the extension of a concept does not entail that the reality of the concept is in any sense necessary for the existence of the thing that falls under it. That there is a concept *being* may well be necessary for the truth of the *statement* 'God is.'"

being a dog or *being a cat*, they fall under the concept of *being an animal*; and it is likewise with the concept of *being*. When we claim things "are" in the same way, we are saying no more than they fall under the same vicious abstraction.[38]

To interpret Scotus as advocating for any sort of *real* extramental correlate to *being* in his usage that is a univocal concept predicated of both God and creatures is simply erroneous. Additionally, contrary to the proponents of Radical Orthodoxy, Scotus's *being as vicious abstraction* does *not* tell us anything about God *or* creatures. In other words, the metaphysical implications (and there are some) do *not* entail descriptive attributes, qualities, or clarifications about the way things (God, creatures, etc.) *are*. Cross believes that in this sense, Milbank's following assertion is flawed: "Being [Scotus] argued, could be either finite or infinite, and possessed in the same simple meaning of existence when applied to either. The term 'exists,' in the sentence 'God exists,' has therefore the same fundamental meaning (at both a logical and a metaphysical level) as in the sentence, 'this woman exists.'"[39] Cross notes well that, in light of Scotus's conceptualization of *being as vicious abstraction* noted above, Milbank is highly misleading to assert that existence in this sense—predicated of God and creatures—maintains the same "fundamental meaning" at a metaphysical level.[40] Scotus's doctrine of the univocity of being in no way "entails that there is an unmodified 'common essence of being' between God and creatures. It means that there is a sense in which God and creatures fall under the extension of one and the same concept—though even then in radically different ways."[41]

---

38. Cross, "Where Angels Fear to Tread," 15. See also Cross, "Scotus and Suárez at the Origins of Modernity," 69–80.
39. Milbank, *Theology and Social Theory: Beyond Secular Reason*, 2nd ed. (Oxford: Blackwell, 2006), 302–3.
40. Cross, "Where Angels Fear to Tread," 15.
41. Ibid., 22.

The Importance of Scotus's Infinity

In addition to the lack of an accurate interpretation of Scotus's understanding of the concept of being in his doctrine of univocity that results in misleading assertions, Radical Orthodox theologians appear to have misunderstood the intrinsic modes of being in Scotus's thought. More specifically, it is the disjunctive intrinsic modes (*infinite* or *finite*) that Radical Orthodox thinkers have exhibited a failure to accurately comprehend. Cross believes that the source of the problem is a "very impoverished understanding of Scotus's account of the intensive infinite."[42] When Scotus speaks of "infinite being," he is not speaking of degree in a proper sense, but rather a mere abstraction (again, it is modifying what Cross describes as a "vicious abstraction"). According to Cross, Scotus does not posit *infinite or finite* (i.e., degree) as the sole way of specifying a transcendental (in this case, *being*). Rather, there are in fact many disjunctive transcendentals that are coextensive with being.[43] For some reason, Radical Orthodoxy exclusively focuses its gaze on infinity as the primary means of distinction between God and creatures. As explained above, such a qualification (that of an abstract transcendental) tells us *nothing* about God or creatures in themselves, beyond the existence of a genus-like concept under which both God and creatures fall. Additionally, the qualitative modification (e.g., infinity) also tells us nearly nothing. Cross again compares Scotus to Aquinas, observing that "the precise nature of the qualitative modifications remain nearly as obscure in Scotus's account as it is in

---

42. Ibid., 22–23.
43. For example: necessary or contingent, actual or potential, cause or caused, prior or posterior, and so forth. For a more extensive treatment of disjunctive transcendentals in Scotus, see Allan Wolter, *The Transcendentals and Their Function in the Metaphysics of Duns Scotus* (St. Bonaventure, NY: Franciscan Institute, 1946), esp. 138–61. Cross also gives a succinct overview in his *Duns Scotus*, 147–148.

Aquinas's."[44] The suggestion that Scotus's modification of *ens* with *infinity* is descriptive of some concrete extramental reality is misleading. A more accurate understanding of the modification of *ens* with *infinity* reveals that there are disjunctive transcendentals that simply cannot apply to God (e.g., contingent or posterior).

So why infinity? It is true that in his *Ordinatio* Scotus asserts a belief that the most perfect concept we have of God is that of *infinite being*. That is to say, we (human beings) cannot conceptualize any better a concept of God, *in this life*, than God as infinite being.[45] The reason why infinite being is our most precise concept of God is because *infinity* is the only disjunctive transcendental that cannot, in any way, be applied to creatures. Cross is keen to caution us against misinterpreting this reason or reading too much into it, which is precisely what the Radical Orthodoxy movement has done. What in turn results is a misguided emphasis on and misleading interpretation of the relationship of *infinity* to *ens*. Additionally, Radical Orthodoxy has not grasped the nuance of Scotus's understanding of infinity. Cross explains, "Scotus takes great pains to show that the intensive infinite is not at all quantitative, and should not ultimately be conceived of in quantitative terms—even though the *analogy* to a quantity can help us conceive of the nature of the intensive infinite."[46] The reason that Scotus would be appalled to learn of Radical Orthodoxy's assertion that his concept of infinite being is somehow understood as quantitative is that Scotus understands any quantitative infinity to be divisible. As such, it would remain imperfect. However, an *intensive infinity* is perfect and, therefore, is not divisible.[47] Returning to the Radical Orthodoxy claim that the modification of

44. Cross, "Where Angels Fear to Tread," 23.
45. Ibid., 24.
46. Ibid. See also Cross, *Duns Scotus*, 40–41.
47. Cross, "Where Angels Fear to Tread," 24.

POSTMODERNITY AND UNIVOCITY

ens with *infinity* leads to an impassable abyss that separates God and creatures, Cross responds, "Something that is indivisible cannot in an Aristotelian universe be in any real sense quantitative: quite the contrary, that which is indivisible is not meaningfully *distant* from everything at all."[48]

Idolatry, Formal Distinction, and the (Mis)attribution of Modernity

Having established the importance of understanding Scotus's project as deeply indebted to a semantic theory, thereby restoring the proper understanding of univocity from the misinterpretations present in Radical Orthodoxy, Cross addresses several particular aspects of erroneous positions concerning Scotus. Three important themes he examines include the following: (a) the accusation that Scotist univocity leads to a form of idolatry; (b) the highly misleading account of Scotus's formal distinction; and (c) the general (mis)attribution of modernity, at least in its most inchoate form, to the philosophical innovations of Scotus.

Idolatry is a harsh accusation. This claim is found frequently in the Radical Orthodoxy corpus, but it is traced by Cross to Philip Blond in the latter's introduction to a collection of essays he edited while he was a student of Milbank.[49] For the most part, Cross leaves Blond's argument untouched, because Cross sees the argument as essentially an adoption of the previously established Scotus Story,[50] something

48. Ibid.
49. See Philip Blond, "Introduction: Theology Before Philosophy," in *Post-Secular Philosophy: Between Philosophy and Theology*, ed. Philip Blond (London: Routledge, 1998), 1–66.
50. By way of chronological clarification, it would seem that Blond was writing his introduction around the same time Catherine Pickstock drafted her *After Writing*. A student of Milbank and colleague of Pickstock, Blond is undoubtedly indebted to both for the content of his Scotus narrative. Therefore I attribute the true authorship of the Scotus Story to Milbank and Pickstock, even though the influential *After Writing* volume had not been published prior to Blond's text.

he has already attempted (in large part) to dismantle in his treatment of univocity.

What most interests Cross, then, is addressing the accusation that Scotus's philosophical system somehow constitutes a form of idolatry. Blond explains, "It appears that a discourse about God, philosophical or theological, is idolatrous in nature when it understands the ground of objects as being utterly synonymous, and hence exchangeable with, the ground of God."[51] Like Milbank and Pickstock, Blond sees Scotus's univocity of being as necessitating something *prior* to both God and creatures, namely *being*. It is idolatrous because *being* somehow is elevated over and above the divine. Cross addresses this charge in two ways. The first is simply to reiterate what he had laid out before. For Scotus, being is *not* something prior to God in any extramental or proper way. For Scotus, *ens* is *analogous* to a genus under which both God and creatures fall. It is a purely semantic theory, one that does not say *anything* about God or creatures, other than that both *are*.

The second response to the charge of idolatry comes in the form of Cross's observation of the possible Heideggerian lens through which Blond (and others) read Scotus. In this context, *being* is understood as the Heideggerian *Grund* upon which all is grounded. This arises from Heidegger's critique of what he terms *ontotheology*, something for which Scotus is also indicted by Radical Orthodoxy. In this approach, Scotus is seen as elevating being in an idolatrous fashion, because such a claim about the universal applicability of being ostensibly implies that there is something that grounds both God and creatures alike.[52] Cross points out that this is not what Scotus means. It is a distinction Blond and his Radical Orthodox fellows do not seem to make, "for

51. Blond, "Introduction: Theology Before Philosophy," 6.
52. Cross, "Where Angels Fear to Tread," 26.

claiming that God falls under the extension of a concept—*being*—is very different from claiming that God somehow requires being for his existence, as it were."[53] In this sense to posit idolatry is, again, a misconstrual of the subtle doctor's work.[54]

Cross's direct response to Pickstock is nothing less than trenchant. Taking aim at nearly every one of her propositions and interpretations found in *After Writing*, Cross relentlessly dismisses almost everything she does associated with Scotus and the subtle doctor's work. At the onset of his response, he writes, "The final account of Scotus that I consider here, that proposed by Catherine Pickstock, is vitiated by a series of misunderstandings and straightforward factual errors."[55] Cross is meticulous with his detailed critique of Pickstock's attempt at implicating Scotus in such a manner. Chief among her problematic interpretations of the subtle doctor's argument is her take on Scotus's formal distinction.

Invoked as part of her discourse on the manner in which Scotus understands the relationship between *being* and its *modes*, Pickstock's understanding of the formal distinction is vague at best and, as Cross suggests, more likely erroneous. Pickstock makes the claim "that the formal distinction is at once both real and logical and neither real nor logical."[56] Cross is perplexed by this claim, as perhaps most readers would be. What exactly is Pickstock trying to say? Cross, before addressing the "content" of such a statement, notes, "This degree of

53. Ibid., 26–27.
54. Interestingly, Cross takes this opportunity to elaborate on the Heideggerian theme of *ontotheology* in an effort to refute claims made accusing Scotus of such a charge. Cross writes, "The concept *being* is in no sense necessary for God to exist. If onto-theo-logy is understood such that being somehow grounds the existence of God, then Scotus's claims about the concept *being* do not amount to onto-theo-logy. Conversely, if onto-theo-logy is that God and creatures fall undert the extension of the concept *being*, then Scotus's claims do amount to onto-theology, but onto-theo-logy does not entail that there is any sense in which being grounds God" (ibid., 27).
55. Ibid., 31.
56. Pickstock, *After Writing*, 124.

rhetorical hesitancy is often a sign of misunderstanding and so it is here."[57] Cross then addresses Pickstock's reading of the theory: "The basic flaw is to suppose that the point of the formal distinction is to distinguish items that are somehow neither real things nor merely rational objects, or items that are somehow indifferently either real things or merely rational things."[58] Beyond this foundational misreading stands the possibility that Pickstock perhaps does have a clearer conceptualization of the formal distinction, yet does not articulate this view in her text—this is Cross's way of offering her a benefit of the doubt. On that note, granting the muddled and "rhetorically hesitant" delivery of her reading of the formal distinction, Cross observes that one will never know what she really thinks because such an articulation necessitates clear definitions, the likes of which are never offered by Pickstock.[59] Pickstock is the Radical Orthodoxy theologian who engages the formal distinction with the most attention, which leaves us to conclude that her reading of this theory remains representative of the rest of the movement's reading.

Finally, Cross makes passing reference to the general (mis)attribution of the nascent founding of modernity to Scotus. Cross's initial response to claims made by Radical Orthodoxy that Scotus's ontology and metaphysics allows for the establishment of a place apart from God, and therefore launches the trajectory to modernity and the secular, is worth citing at length.

> It is false to claim (by an implied contrast with Aquinas) that for Scotus creatures have some kind of ground in themselves—whether being, or the possibility of being. Both being and the possibility of being are radically dependent on God in Scotus's understanding of the creative act. While it is true that Scotus makes little use of the language of

57. Cross, "Where Angels Fear to Tread," 33.
58. Ibid.
59. Ibid., 34.

participation, it is not true that he abandons the underlying claim that things owe their perfections to God, and that they in important respects resemble him. . . . Neither is it true that the alleged abandonment of participation "encouraged the establishment of *contractual* relations [between] the creature and God." Scotus certainly does believe that there is now a contract or *pactum* between God and his people: it is the New Covenant, brought about by the salvific work of Christ and enacted in the Eucharist. But this is the only context in which Scotus talks of a contractual relationship between God and creation, and its precedents are Biblical, not philosophical.[60]

While Cross is specifically addressing Pickstock's work here, his critique of Radical Orthodoxy's reading of Scotus's philosophy in such a way as to claim Scotus established a space outside of the divine within which creatures are able to assert themselves, having their own subsistence and autonomy, applies equally (if not more so) to the writing of Milbank.[61] This has been stated more clearly elsewhere in the work of Cross. For example, in addressing Milbank's assertion that Scotus is the inaugurator of modernity, Cross writes, "I have tried to argue that Milbank's worries about onto-theology do not really stand up to scrutiny, for the simple reason that he mistakenly understands a merely semantic claim to have certain ontological consequences that it manifestly does not have."[62]

What remains clear is that the antecedent claims Milbank and Pickstock make in the preliminary development and later defense of the Scotus Story are misleading. Cross's work in illuminating some of the particular themes where this is made manifest has been done with great service to those trying to understand better the thought of John Duns Scotus, while at the same time process the arguments leveled against him by Radical Orthodoxy. For Cross, the primary problem with Radical Orthodoxy's interpretations is the apparent

---

60. Ibid., 36.
61. See my section "The Problem with Scotus's Philosophical Vision," above in the first chapter.
62. Cross, "Scotus and Suárez at the Origins of Modernity," 77.

disregard for authentic scholarship and adherence to the philosophical and theological tradition it seeks to study.[63] While Cross is certainly the most authoritative voice to speak out against Radical Orthodoxy's use of Scotus, he is not the only one, nor is he the last.

Thomas Williams:
A Proponent of Univocity

The response offered by Thomas Williams to Radical Orthodoxy's use of John Duns Scotus focuses on a twofold restoration of univocity. His approach begins with the presupposition that the doctrine of univocity, as interpreted correctly, is "true." Williams holds that regardless of the consequences (counterfactually assuming that the consequences Radical Orthodoxy advances are in fact correct), "it is not the job of the theologian or philosopher to shrink from uncomfortable truths."[64] The implication is that Radical Orthodoxy thinkers might be resistant to appreciate the truth-value of Scotus's claims on account of their retrospective interpretation of univocity, presented in support of their genealogical assertions about modernity. Williams believes that even if their final assertions concerning Scotus's anticipation of modernity *were* true, their attempt to dismiss or reject the doctrine of univocity in favor of a Thomist *analogia entis* is wrongheaded.

Naturally, Williams then takes up the issue of the consequences of univocity, suggesting that there are no deplorable logical consequences to Scotus's thought. He does acknowledge, however, that there might indeed be historical consequences stemming from

---

63. The most glaring example of this view is expressed in Cross's analysis of Pickstock's reading of Scotus. In a footnote, Cross writes: "Pickstock, *After Writing*, 130. Needless to say, the passage referred to by Pickstock (Scotus, *In Metaph.* 8.18, n.11) does not exist." In Cross, "Where Angels Fear to Tread," 37.

64. Williams, "The Doctrine of Univocity is True and Salutary," 575.

misunderstanding of univocity that remain open to interpretation. He notes, "What historical consequences the doctrine may have had are beside the point: if people have been led astray by false inferences from the doctrine of univocity, the proper remedy is to correct their inferences, not to reject univocity."[65] For Thomas Williams, the entirety of the problem with univocity as interpreted, expressed, and passed on by Radical Orthodoxy rests in the incorrect understanding of the thought of Scotus. Like Cross, Williams sees in Radical Orthodoxy's account a theology rooted in an inaccurate reading of Scotus, which ultimately results in the creation and dissemination of the Scotus Story as it stands today.

The Truth of Univocity

Williams begins his presentation of the doctrine of univocity as true with the assertion that in order to argue for or against the correctness of a given philosophical view, one must authentically show what the philosophical view actually is.[66] This is the first case in which Williams believes that the Radical Orthodoxy movement is notably careless. Perhaps above all else, Williams—much like Cross before him—is concerned with restoring the semantic context within which the doctrine of univocity was born and developed. Williams, also like Cross, admits that Scotus's position does necessarily entail certain ontological claims as a consequence of the primarily epistemological theory. However, to assert, as many within the Radical Orthodoxy movement do, that the Scotus doctrine of univocity is a "univocalist ontology" is clearly fallacious.

In addition to the misunderstanding and factual misrepresentation in Radical Orthodoxy's attempt to grapple with the subtle doctor's

65. Ibid.
66. Ibid.

work, Williams notes that the lack of critical scholarship on the part of the movement's foundational thinkers like Milbank and Pickstock helps explain the misconstruals found in their texts. His primary target is Pickstock. Williams notes that among the problematic aspects of Pickstock's scholarship is the lack of both primary and secondary source references to support her reading of Scotus. On the rare occasion that Pickstock (or any of the other Radical Orthodoxy thinkers) offers an interpretation of some primary source, it is usually incomprehensible, which leads Williams to describe one such instance from Pickstock as "unintelligible."[67] This lack of sources is a persistent problem in Radical Orthodoxy scholarship and will be addressed in greater detail in the last subsection of this chapter.

Williams's primary approach in his assertion of univocity as true comes in the form of reclaiming Scotus's doctrine as a semantic theory. He notes that every reliable interpreter recognizes the distinction the subtle doctor makes between ontology and semantics. He observes that Pickstock either simply does not understand the semantic argumentation Scotus is engaged in, or has chosen to disregard it. Williams expresses his concern about Pickstock's reading as follows:

> But the whole point, the very core, of Scotus's separation of the semantic from the metaphysical is precisely the claim that our possession of a concept under whose extension both God and creatures fall does *not* imply that there is any feature at all in extramental reality that is a common component of both God and creatures—let alone that there is such a thing as "purely punctiliar essential univocal being *in quid*," whatever that would be. Scotus has a number of exceedingly complex

---

67. Ibid., 576. This is a common criticism of the Radical Orthodoxy movement in general. Milbank, and to a lesser extent Pickstock, appear to be intentionally complicated in their explanations and more often than not obfuscate their texts. For an example of such an observation, see Paul Griffiths, "Either/Or: A Review of *The Monstrosity of Christ*," *Commonweal* 136 (June 19, 2009): 22–24.

and subtle arguments to show that such an inference from univocal concept to ontological overlap is invalid.[68]

What becomes clear throughout Williams's examination of Radical Orthodoxy's misinterpretation of univocity is that Milbank and Pickstock appear unfamiliar with the nuances and argumentative details of Scotus's theory as the subtle doctor presented it. In an effort to put to rest this misreading and help establish a sounder foundation upon which to construct an argument in favor of univocity, Williams summarizes the doctrine in this way:

> *Univocity*: Notwithstanding the irreducible ontological diversity between God and creatures, there are concepts under whose extension both God and creatures fall, so that the corresponding predicate expressions are used with exactly the same sense in predications about God as in predications about creatures.[69]

The argument that Williams puts forward, after summarizing what he believes to be an accurate understanding of Scotus's doctrine of univocity, is that univocity must be true in order to have an intelligible theological language. In other words, like Scotus, who does not begin his project with an ontological question but an epistemological one, Williams begins his presentation with a linguistic elucidation, not a metaphysical one.

In exploring the meaning of any given term predicated of two subjects, Williams explains, using *wisdom* as an example, there might be three different ways to interpret the distinct meanings in the predications of the term. These ways include equivocity (used entirely differently), analogy (different, but related senses), and univocity (used in exactly the same sense). Following the argument Scotus himself makes, Williams argues that these three options

68. Williams, "The Doctrine of Univocity is True and Salutary," 577.
69. Ibid., 578.

ultimately reduce to two, "either unintelligibility or univocity."[70] Concerning the option of equivocity, Williams insists that such a route would be unhelpful. If we claim that the term *wise* is predicated of God and creatures equivocally, then our language of God would have no meaning at all. It would be equally justified to say that God is "unwise" as "wise" if it were equivocal and devoid of intelligible content.[71] Furthermore, if the terms themselves are devoid of intelligibility, because of our incapability to talk of God, then we fall into a seemingly infinite regress of deferred meaning. Williams explains it as such: "By 'God is wise' I mean that God is *F*, by which I mean that God is *G*, by which I mean that God is *H* [etc.]."[72] Instead, we draw from the variety of expressions we use in reference to creatures to predicate of God. It would appear that univocal predication is the logical option to prevent such a regress, while at the same time maintaining some sort of intelligible theological language.

Radical Orthodoxy thinkers might respond to such a conclusion with the objection that analogical predication has not been considered and would be a legitimate approach to such a dilemma. Williams addresses this objection with a brief analysis of analogy. Returning to the dual predication of *wise* in the cases of God and creatures, he asks whether or not we can decipher the sense *wise* is predicated in the case of God, and its subsequent relationship to *wise* as predicated of creatures. He concludes that we simply do not know the sense of the former and its relationship to the latter, and neither

---

70. Ibid. Elsewhere Williams summarizes this as the following: "There is no middle ground for theological language between univocity, on the one hand, and complete unintelligibility, on the other." See Thomas Williams, "Radical Orthodoxy, Univocity and the New Apophaticism," unpublished paper presented at the International Congress for Medieval Studies, Kalamazoo, Michigan (2006), 2.
71. Williams, "The Doctrine of Univocity is True and Salutary," 578.
72. Ibid., 579.

do Milbank and Pickstock.[73] Williams summarizes his conclusion on this point:

> Strictly speaking, if my argument is successful, it does not show that the doctrine of univocity is true, but rather that *either* the doctrine of univocity is true *or* that everything we say about God is in the most straightforward sense unintelligible—that is, that we literally do not know what we are saying when we say of God that he is good, just, wise, loving, or what have you. Now I take it that an acknowledgement of the unintelligibility of all language about God is simply not a live option, and so I am convinced that the doctrine of univocity is true.[74]

It is worth noting here that Scotus himself does not dismiss or devalue analogy per se, but rather holds to the necessity of univocal predication in order to make sense of an analogical statement. Likewise, while Williams does not expressly concur with the subtle doctor's position on this matter, I presume he would acknowledge the importance of analogy as a veritable exercise built upon a foundation of univocal predication. Ultimately, as Williams has indeed noted, analogous language not founded on univocal terms is simple reduced to unintelligible discourse.

While he does not address the matter of apophatic versus kataphatic theology in his article "The Doctrine of Univocity is True and Salutary," Williams does take this matter up in a 2006 conference presentation. Any attempt to argue for the elevation of analogy by dismissing univocity ultimately makes a claim that language about God is always necessarily apophatic. Williams sees a direct correlation between the two claims (those concerning apophatic/kataphatic language and those concerning analogy/univocity), observing that perhaps the protection of apophaticism is one of the more central, if not more noble, impetuses that launches the Radical Orthodoxy

73. Ibid.
74. Ibid., 579–580.

condemnation of Scotus. The problem, however, as Williams sees it, is that there is a place and a value in kataphatic discourse about God that is both true and praiseworthy. A restoration of the dignity of kataphaticism is part of Williams's defense of the truth of univocity.

Williams introduces his position in the following way: "So I need to offer some considerations in favor of an unabashedly kataphatic theology and, correspondingly, some reasons to resist the current apophatic rage."[75] Returning to the problem of ultimate equivocity stemming from a form of analogy not rooted in univocal predication, Williams sees a parallel in the rejection of kataphasis by Radical Orthodoxy thinkers. The root of the problem is the lack of a clear understanding of the difference between the "insufficiency" of theological language and the "unintelligibility" of theological language.[76] In other words, kataphatic discourse does not presume sufficiency when it comes to describing God or God's attributes. On the contrary, there is a necessary and admitted *insufficiency* that haunts any kataphatic theology. What is possible, however, is intelligible theological language, grounded in a discursive grammar that makes theo-*logos* (God talk) possible in the first place. The absolute transcendence of the divine will forever prohibits the invocation of sufficient language, but necessarily insufficient theological language should not be misconstrued as inappropriate, heretical, or the like for that reason. Williams elaborates,

> The proponent of univocity need not say, and typically does not say, that our language about God is fully adequate to reveal the very nature of God, to tell us what God is in himself [*sic*]. Indeed, the proponent of univocity can go quite far not merely acknowledging the ways in which our language about God is partial and misleading, but even explaining precisely why and how it is misleading. Indeed, it is only if we can say

75. Williams, "Radical Orthodoxy, Univocity and the New Apophaticism," 3.
76. Ibid.

to some extent what God is that we have any basis for saying that our language about God fails to express what he is.[77]

Herein lies the problem with an exclusively apophatic approach to theological language. If one adheres to apophaticism at the expense of univocity, the result is unintelligibility. Williams holds that we cannot say what something *is not* unless we have some intelligible sense of what that something *is*. In this respect, how can we say that "God is not ____" (fill in the blank), unless we have some concept of what God *is* first. In order to form such a concept, we must rely on the truth of univocal predication in order to ground our theological language.[78]

As is made clear by Williams's argument, the doctrine of univocity is indeed *true* insofar as it is absolutely necessary to ground any theological discourse. Even the exercise of analogous predication necessitates foundational univocity. The admittance of this point and a clear appreciation for the distinction between insufficient and unintelligible language leaves the Scotus Story of Radical Orthodoxy seriously marred.

The Doctrine of Univocity is Praiseworthy

Williams's conclusion about the veracity of Scotus's doctrine of univocity leads him to explore the consequences of such a philosophical view. He keenly notes that proponents of Radical Orthodoxy rarely argue against the truth of univocity, but instead focus their attention and justify their subsequent condemnation of the view on the "various disastrous consequences for theology and philosophy, and for society and culture in general" that allegedly

77. Ibid.
78. Ibid., 5.

stem from Scotus's approach to univocity.[79] This is the centerpiece of the Radical Orthodoxy thesis: beyond that of Scotus's particular involvement in their narrative as conveyed in the Scotus Story, there are pernicious consequences that are made manifest in our contemporary context, otherwise described in terms of "the secular" or "modernity" or "nihilism." That there are wholly problematic dimensions to today's world, worship, and culture leads Milbank to trace the inchoate Scotus Story in an effort to explain how things happened to become what they are today. Williams sets out to examine the claims, at least in part, that Radical Orthodoxy makes based on the Scotus Story. In opposition to their assertions, Williams argues that univocity is not only true (as he previously outlined), but it is also salutary. As such it does not entail the negative effects that Radical Orthodoxy advocates. Rather, Williams claims, "The further doctrines it [univocity] entails are altogether wholesome and beneficial, and the disastrous effects that have been blamed on the doctrine of univocity do not in fact follow from it at all."[80]

He highlights two overtly positive aspects, effects, or consequences (depending on how you analyze the presentation) of the doctrine of univocity. The first is one that he introduced in his defense of the truth of univocity: that univocal predication is the condition for the possibility of intelligible (if inadequate) language about God.[81] Williams finds it sufficient not to elaborate further on the subject, given his previous exploration of the matter. Likewise, I find no need to examine this effect further, given the explication above. Suffice it to say that Williams sees in the Radical Orthodoxy denial of univocity a clear impediment to intelligible speaking of God. The second overtly positive consequence of univocity that Williams

79. Williams, "The Doctrine of Univocity is True and Salutary," 580.
80. Ibid.
81. Ibid. See also Williams, "Radical Orthodoxy, Univocity and the New Apophaticism," 3–4.

explores is something that Scotus explicitly affirms. "Univocity allows for the possibility of a demonstrative argument for the existence of God."[82] This is something for which Pickstock accidentally advocates as she (mistakenly) claims that Aquinas regards arguments for God's existence as dialectical and not demonstrative (as Scotus and Aquinas *actually* hold), in her effort to distance the angelic doctor from the subtle doctor.

One of Williams's most helpful contributions to the conversation about Radical Orthodoxy's use of John Duns Scotus is his assessment of the validity of the "unwelcome" or "worrisome" consequences of univocity.[83] He makes this move in the form of strong statement that Cross has been much less committed to asserting:[84] that the conclusions or consequences that Radical Orthodoxy thinkers have inferred from their reading of Scotus are simply errant and do not follow from the actual doctrine. Williams begins his investigation into the veracity of these consequences with a brief discussion about argumentative method. He does this in order to establish what is and is not sufficient to prove or disprove a given claim. His outline is helpful, succinct, and worth citing at length to contextualize what follows.

> Suppose someone says that p entails q. How do I go about showing otherwise? That is, how do I establish that p does not entail q, but is consistent with the denial of q? The only decisive way is one that is seldom available, namely, to show that p in fact entails not-q. The second best way is to show, empirically or in some other way, a case in which p and not-q are both true together. Least satisfactorily, the best one can usually manage is to establish that the arguments that purport to derive q from p are unsound. Strictly speaking, of course, this last approach establishes only that one's opponent has not proved that p entails q, not

---

82. Williams, "The Doctrine of Univocity is True and Salutary," 581.
83. Ibid.
84. Cross only makes passing reference to these concerns. See my "Idolatry, Formal Distinction, and the (Mis)attribution of Modernity," section above.

that p does not in fact entail q. But the burden of proof certainly falls on the person who has attempted to show that p entails q, and if it can be shown that the burden of proof has not been met, one is entitled to continue to hold p and deny q.[85]

Williams believes that the first two types of argumentation are not useful in his effort to debunk the Radical Orthodoxy position on the consequences of Scotus's doctrine of univocity. The first approach is immediately dismissed because, in Williams's view, the consequences have little to do with the actual doctrine of univocity. Therefore, it seems impossible to prove that the doctrine of univocity actually entails the opposite of the consequences that Milbank and Pickstock assert.[86] Similarly, the second point is not useful because, as Williams observes, "it is also hard to see how one could point to a case in which univocity is true but its purported consequences are not."[87] The only remaining course of action is to demonstrate that the arguments used by Radical Orthodoxy thinkers are unsound.

Williams develops three points where he finds the argument presented by Pickstock on behalf of Radical Orthodoxy to be unsound. The first argument addressed is that of the correlation articulated in Pickstock's assessment of univocity, which suggests that "univocity underlies a shift to a view of knowledge as representation."[88] Williams reminds us that Pickstock never presents an argument to support her claim or trace the alleged consequence from its correlative foundation. In some sense, Williams adopts a form of Richard Cross's earlier assertion that Radical Orthodoxy effectively evacuates argument from theology.[89] In doing so, the reader is left to either speculate the relationship between the claimed

85. Williams, "The Doctrine of Univocity is True and Salutary," 581.
86. Ibid.
87. Ibid., 582.
88. Ibid.
89. See Cross, "Where Angels Fear to Tread," 22.

cause and effect, or simply take Radical Orthodoxy's word for the claim's veracity. Either option proves unacceptable. Without explicitly demonstrating the correlative connection, Pickstock and the rest fail to provide a legitimately sound argument.

The second aspect of Williams's critique is focused on the claim that Scotus is either a voluntarist, or that he anticipated voluntarism, in such a manner as to make the subtle doctor the founder of that system of thought.[90] Coincidentally, Williams actually professes to be an adamant proponent of both univocity and voluntarism, yet does not find a connection between the two. In fact, in his article, he laments the fact that such a connection does not actually exist. However, no such connection seems feasible, nor does Pickstock make any argument that might bolster this correlation. We are led to conclude again that Pickstock does not effectively advocate Radical Orthodoxy's opinion, but instead offers yet another unsound argument.

The final point of dispute for Williams, at least the last of the features of the Radical Orthodoxy argument he found noteworthy to examine, centers on Pickstock's argument "from univocity to epistemological and political atomism."[91] Pickstock's entire argument in this matter extends from her assertion that "univocity requires that God and creatures 'are' in the same albeit spectral ontic fashion."[92] Williams notes that this is a faulty premise. Scotus does not, in fact, hold this position, but instead outrightly rejects it.[93] Furthermore, Williams insightfully highlights the fact that even if there were indeed some "irreducible minimal common element" found among things, which included God and creatures, the argument that there

---

90. Williams, "The Doctrine of Univocity is True and Salutary," 582.
91. Ibid.
92. Pickstock, "Duns Scotus: His Historical and Contemporary Significance," *Modern Theology* 21 (October 2005): 553.
93. Williams, "The Doctrine of Univocity is True and Salutary," 583.

is in fact a resulting epistemological atomism (i.e., roughly, the knowing of an individual thing *in se*) makes little sense.[94] Williams suggests that the opposite would actually be more likely. In other words, if there was indeed an "irreducible minimal common element," then it would logically follow that this element would be the focus of one's reflection, thereby effectively requiring one to think about the other things that share that common element. Whereas Pickstock appears to be arguing for an "atomist" microcosmic perspective, her argument more logically implies a macrocosmic epistemology. There is no doubt that her "thin and unconvincing,"[95] to use Williams's words, argument in this case opens more questions than it provides answers.

Thomas Williams makes a significant contribution to the restoration of univocity, especially through his advocacy on behalf of the truth and value of the philosophical view. Whereas Cross is most concerned with the error of Radical Orthodoxy's ways, Williams believes that the doctrine of univocity should be free from critique by virtue of its sound development and logical construction. In the last section of this chapter, I will highlight yet a few more areas of concern with the Radical Orthodoxy reading of Scotus. What follows develops the work and assessments of Cross and Williams in an effort to continue what began in their initial critiques. Formidable as their responses are, Cross and Williams leave plenty of room to level further scholarly criticism against Radical Orthodoxy's Scotus Story. My observations seek to fill, at least in part, what remains of the lacunae of restorative scholarship on behalf of Scotus's doctrine of univocity.

94. Ibid.
95. Ibid., 582.

Further Analysis:
Continuing the Critique of Radical Orthodoxy's Use of Scotus

This section of the chapter is dedicated to briefly introducing three additional elements of Radical Orthodoxy's Scotus Story that merit further investigation. My intention here is not to offer a final word on all that is untenable about the Radical Orthodoxy Scotus Story, but rather provide something of a "beginning word" to highlight areas of research and investigation that can still be taken up in greater detail at a later time. In the first section, I will examine yet another facet of the methodological approach adopted by proponents of Radical Orthodoxy, illuminating the problematic and operative hermeneutic of the movement. The second section is a continuation of something to which Richard Cross first drew our attention; namely, the exclusive use of highly unreliable and selected sources engaged by Radical Orthodoxy thinkers. The final element is a brief excursus on the problem of the Radical Orthodox approach in light of its ostensible mission and goal.

The Cambridge Thomist Hermeneutic and the Problem of Reading Scotus

We all wear lenses. Each of us brings to a text a certain collection of presumptions, experiences, expectations, understanding, and methods of interpretation. For example, the seminal works of Hans-Georg Gadamer and Paul Ricoeur,[96] among others, have provided

---

96. For more, see Hans-Georg Gadamer, *Truth and Method*, trans. Joel Weinsheimer (New York: Continuum, 1975); Paul Ricoeur, *Interpretation Theory: Discourse and Surplus of Meaning* (Fort Worth: Texas Christian University Press, 1976); Paul Ricoeur, *Freud and Philosophy: An Essay in Interpretation*, trans. Dennis Savage (New Haven: Yale University Press, 1970); and Paul Ricoeur, *The Rule of Metaphor: Multi-Disciplinary Studies of the Creation of Meaning in Language*, trans. Robert Czerny (Toronto: University of Toronto Press, 1977).

us with studies that challenge the assumption of objective meaning. Awareness of such presuppositions and operative hermeneutics allows the reader to be cautious in interpretation, while at the same time acknowledging the lenses through which one views a given subject. Given what we have seen so far, we can argue that the Radical Orthodoxy movement has not been entirely forthcoming—neither to itself nor to its readers—about the lenses through which it reads the work of John Duns Scotus. This is an important oversight, for the lack of conscious admittance of one's operative hermeneutic can shape the emergent result of textual examination. In the case of Milbank and Pickstock, there is a clear and unabashed preference for the work of Thomas Aquinas as the standard bearer of authentic ontological discourse and theological method. Held up as the paragon of theology, Aquinas becomes more than iconic for Radical Orthodoxy in its quest to restore theology as the "Queen of the Sciences." Additionally, the Radical Orthodoxy Scotus Story is largely composed *in light of* Aquinas's theology (or, more accurately, the Radical Orthodoxy *version* of Aquinas's theology). The primary set of lenses donned by the Radical Orthodox thinkers is a version of Thomism. The question arises, however: Which type of Thomism?

There appear to be at least four major schools of Thomism that have remained influential over the course of the last century. The first form would be the explicitly historical-theological school of Thomism that attempts to examine the work of Aquinas from a historical perspective. Such an approach would entail textual and manuscript analysis, historical contextual reconstruction, and the study of sources that engage the influences on Aquinas's thought. This type of scholarship is most closely associated with the work of Étienne Gilson. While Gilson is often cited by those in the Radical Orthodoxy movement, this particular form of Thomism rarely results in contemporary application and does not appear to be of any great interest to Radical Orthodoxy theologians.[97] It is important to note that when it comes to Radical Orthodox engagement with scholastic texts and modern commentators, it is only within the context of Scotus that Gilson's work is so heavily relied upon and not, as one might expect, within the context of Aquinas. This is problematic, as stated earlier in the chapter, because Gilson's *Jean Duns Scot* is widely considered flawed and at times erroneous.

The second major school is the neo-Thomist camp of study. This movement gained significant ground in France during the early part of the twentieth century. Its origins can be traced to the important papal encyclical of Pope Leo XIII titled *Aeterni Patris*, which, in 1878, set forth a program that elevated the theology of Thomas Aquinas as the standard for "Catholic theology." This mandated that Aquinas be used as the primary resource for theological instruction and inquiry at all Catholic institutions of higher education. Some decades later, a movement had arisen that concluded "that in the interests of orthodoxy, Catholic theology must abandon the subjective starting points of post-Cartesian philosophical systems and return to the metaphysics of St. Thomas, grounded as this was on a grasp of finite being, attained through the cooperation of the lowly human senses and the agent, or abstractive intellect, of Aristotelean theory of knowledge."[98] One might see in this assessment the anticipation of the work of Radical Orthodoxy, particularly in Radical Orthodoxy's fear of modern philosophy and theology. However, this is not exactly the mode of scholarship espoused by the movement. Historically speaking, this form of theology quickly

97. A good example of how this approach is clearly neglected by Catherine Pickstock is Thomas Williams's assessment of her misreading of the angelic doctor. See Williams, "The Doctrine of Univocity is True and Salutary," 582–83. Also, see DeHart, *Aquinas and Radical Orthodoxy: A Critical Inquiry* (London: Routledge, 2012), 15–33 and passim.

98. Aidan Nichols, *The Shape of Catholic Theology* (Collegeville: Liturgical, 1991), 329–30. See also Richard McBrien, *Catholicism*, rev. ed. (San Francisco: HarperCollins, 1994), esp. 133–35 and 909.

devolved into antimodernism, the likes of which overshadowed original scholarship in place of reactionary apologetics. It seems unlikely that Radical Orthodoxy could fit into a category of neo-Thomism, at least as an exclusive means of categorization.

The third form of contemporary Thomism is most certainly not an approach Radical Orthodoxy is interested in adopting, namely transcendental Thomism. This form of theology is most commonly identified with the work of Karl Rahner.[99] It is an approach that critically engages the so-called late -modern period of philosophy, marked by the Kantian shift in thought and "turn to the subject." Drawing on the philosophical work of Heidegger, Hegel, Kant, and others, Rahner reinterpreted the thought of Thomas Aquinas as a way to develop a system of transcendental theology. Rahner is most certainly not the only transcendental Thomist of the twentieth century. Others, including Bernard Lonergan and Edward Schillebeeckx, also contributed to the *nouvelle théologie* of the day, critically engaging Aquinas in light of contemporary philosophical and theological concerns.[100] Milbank and Pickstock dismiss this form of Thomism, a version that has remained controversial among certain other "Thomists" to this day, as pandering to modernity in such a way that allows for the subordination of theology and the "blessing" of the secular. The transcendental Thomist agenda that entailed bringing Thomistic theology into conversation with modernity stands in stark contrast to the whole Radical Orthodoxy project.[101]

99. While developed throughout his entire corpus, for something of a succinct *summa*, see Karl Rahner, *Foundations of Christian Faith: An Introduction to the Idea of Christianity*, trans. William Dych (New York: Crossroads, 2002). See also Karen Kilby, "Karl Rahner," in *The Modern Theologians: An Introduction to Christian Theology Since 1918*, ed. David Ford, 3rd ed. (Oxford: Blackwell, 2005), 92–105.
100. For a helpful overview of this period and these figures, see Francis Schüssler Fiorenza, "The New Theology and Transcendental Thomism," in *Modern Christian Thought: The Twentieth Century*, ed. James Livingston and Francis Schüssler Fiorenza, 2nd ed. (Minneapolis: Fortress Press, 2006), 197–232.

The fourth form of contemporary Thomism is what I would call "Thomas after Wittgenstein," and has been alternatively associated with a movement called "Analytic Thomism."[102] This school of Thomism is alive and well today and, when compared with the others mentioned above, it remains the youngest of the lot. For this reason, it is difficult to pin down the precise characteristics of this camp, apart from the critical engagement some theologians (most, but not all, Roman or Anglo-Catholic) have pursued between analytic philosophy and the work of Thomas Aquinas. Explained in an understandably vague way, John Haldane notes that "analytic Thomism . . . seeks to deploy the methods and ideas of 20th century philosophy—of the sort dominant within the English speaking world—in connection with the broad framework of ideas introduced and developed by Aquinas."[103] There are many contemporary theologians that could be classified as post-Wittgenstein Thomists of this sort. Examples of some of the more prominent theologians in this camp include Fergus Kerr, David Burrell, and Stanley Hauerwas, to name just a few.[104] Kerr's most influential work in this regard is

---

101. See, for example, John Milbank, "The Grandeur of Reason and the Perversity of Rationalism: Radical Orthodoxy's First Decade," in *The Radical Orthodoxy Reader*, ed. John Milbank and Simon Oliver (London: Routledge, 2009), 367–404.

102. I am grateful to Professor Terrence Tilley for insights leading the to demarcation of this fourth form of Thomism. For an introduction to "analytical Thomism," see John Haldane, "Analytical Thomism: A Prefatory Note," *The Monist* 80 (1997): 485–86, and the remaining contents of the following topical issue; see also Craig Paterson and Matthew Pugh, eds., *Analytical Thomism: Traditions in Dialogue* (London: Ashgate, 2006).

103. Haldane, "Analytic Thomism," 485.

104. For an overview of one scholar's listing of theologians deeply influenced by Wittgenstein, see Bruce Ashford, "Wittgenstein's Theologians? A Survey of Ludwig Wittgenstein's Impact on Theology," *Journal of the Evangelical Theological Society* 50 (June 2007): 357–75. Among the theologians listed are Rowan Williams, David Burrell, Fergus Kerr, Stanley Hauerwas, James Wm. McClendon Jr., Brad Kallenberg, Paul Holmer, Donald McKinnon, Cornelius Ernst, Herbert McCabe, and Victor Preller. A less-known theologian, Terrance Klein, has also written on the influence of Wittgenstein on theology, particularly as it concerns the reception of Thomas Aquinas. See his *Wittgenstein and the Metaphysics of Grace* (New York: Oxford University Press, 2007); and *How Things Are in the World: Metaphysics and Theology in Wittgenstein and Rahner* (Milwaukee: Marquette University Press, 2003).

his *Theology After Wittgenstein*, in which he engages Wittgenstein as a philosophical guide across doctrinal subjects, such as theological anthropology, soteriology, and contemporary apologetics, among other themes.[105] David Burrell's work often bears a kindred sympathy to the project of Radical Orthodoxy, though his version of Thomism stands in discernible contrast to the idiosyncratic form of Radical Orthodoxy's Aquinas scholarship, as we will see below. Having written his dissertation on "Analogy and Philosophical Language," Burrell's implacable defense of *analogia entis* can be traced to his earliest scholarly work.[106] It is this metaphysical preference that would align Burrell sympathetically with the Radical Orthodoxy focus on Aquinas. Stanley Hauerwas, best known for his contributions to theological ethics, has also been deeply influenced by the thought of Wittgenstein.[107] Hauerwas's unique style of theological reflection draws on a restorative approach to the virtue ethics of Aquinas in a manner that follows Alasdair MacIntyre's seminal work on the subject.[108] The result of these two influences, Wittgenstein and Aquinas, appear in Hauerwas's emphases on character formation and narrative theology.[109]

While none of these four brands of Thomism fully articulates the form contained as the foundation of the Radical Orthodoxy agenda, the first two appear to lend some resources to the movement

---

105. Fergus Kerr, *Theology After Wittgenstein* (Oxford: Blackwell, 1986). Also, see Fergus Kerr, *After Aquinas: Versions of Thomism* (Oxford: Blackwell, 2002).

106. See David Burrell, "Analogy and Philosophical Language," (PhD dissertation, Yale University, 1973). Also, see David Burrell, *Aquinas: God and Action* (Notre Dame: University of Notre Dame Press, 1979); and David Burrell, *Knowing the Unknowable God: Ibn-Sina, Maimonides, Aquinas* (Notre Dame: University of Notre Dame Press, 1986).

107. For more on this influence on Hauerwas, see Brad Kallenberg, *Ethics as Grammar* (Notre Dame: University of Notre Dame Press, 2001).

108. See Alasdair MacIntyre, *After Virtue: A Study in Moral Theory*, 3rd ed. (Notre Dame: University of Notre Dame Press, 2007).

109. See Stanley Hauerwas, *A Community of Character: Toward a Constructive Christian Social Ethic* (Notre Dame: University of Notre Dame Press, 1981); and Stanley Hauerwas, *The Peaceable Kingdom: A Primer in Christian Ethics* (Notre Dame: University of Notre Dame Press, 1983).

by way of source and sympathy. The earliest historical Thomist movement represented by Gilson provides a resource that will later serve Radical Orthodoxy in its quest to vilify and dismiss the work of Scotus. Additionally, the neo-Thomistic rejection of modernity and modern philosophy further supports the Radical Orthodoxy attempt to likewise suppress such dialectical or correlative engagement. Nevertheless, neither of these approaches legitimately summarizes the Radical Orthodoxy approach to Aquinas, nor do Radical Orthodoxy theologians actively appropriate those schools of thought in an exclusive manner. Furthermore, while the post-Wittgenstein approach to the study of Aquinas characterized by the work of Fergus Kerr and David Burrell appears at times close to the Radical Orthodoxy approach, the latter two's form of Thomism departs significantly from what their sometimes sympathetic who appropriate this post-Wittgensteinian approach present. Nevertheless, there is clearly a preferential option (to say the least) for a theological system rooted in a particular reading of Aquinas that pervades Radical Orthodoxy.[110]

Given the unique and seemingly eclectic composition of Radical Orthodoxy's Thomism, I believe it is necessary to describe their reading and application of Aquinas with a new term. Such a term unexpectedly emerges in the work of the famous postmodern philosopher of religion John D. Caputo. In his book *The Weakness of*

---

110. Emblematic of this fact is the work of Radical Orthodoxy thinker D. Stephen Long, about whom this response is written: "Long views Thomistic thought as the definitive theology that most fully expresses the truth of the relationship between the human desire for the good and the goodness of God made available through the incarnation of Christ present in the sacraments of the Church. Everything about the theology of Thomas Aquinas is defended as giving us the correct view of creation's relation to God. He rejects what he sees as later Thomisms that allow a space for natural theology apart from supernatural revelation and redemption as misunderstanding Thomas," Rosemary Radford Ruether, "The Postmodern as Premodern: The Theology of D. Stephen Long," in *Interpreting the Postmodern: Responses to "Radical Orthodoxy,"* ed. Rosemary Radford Ruether and Marion Grau (New York: T & T Clark, 2006), 77.

God, Caputo makes a passing reference to Radical Orthodoxy in an endnote:

> Radical Orthodoxy is a movement that turns on the quaint and (self-)comforting idea that everything is either a Christian metaphysics of participation (that is, Radical Orthodoxy) or nihilism, by which they seem to mean variants of their version of Nietzsche or Derrida, which for them means that human existence is awash in an irrational flux. So Radical Orthodoxy, which gives us a choice between being *Cambridge Thomists* or nihilists, needs to expand its horizons.[111]

His rather succinct, yet incredibly applicative, term—*Cambridge Thomists*—appears to adequately capture the essence of the movement's appropriation of Aquinas in light of its particular reading of the angelic doctor. For this reason, following Caputo, I have adapted his term for the purpose of articulating the axiomatic or foundational character of Radical Orthodoxy's preferential treatment of Aquinas. We can therefore say that Radical Orthodoxy theologians are operating with a Cambridge Thomist hermeneutic.

On the surface, there is nothing particularly problematic with the choice to adopt this form of Cambridge Thomism. As surveyed above, various schools of interpretation and application inevitably rise and fall around a thinker as important as Aquinas. But some have strongly argued that Cambridge Thomism is flawed in several ways. For example, Cross writes, "It seems to me that the treatment of Aquinas is in many ways just as cavalier as that of Scotus: in an anxiety to find a hero, the Radical Orthodoxy theologians seem to construct an Aquinas more in their own image than in his."[112] It is

---

111. John Caputo, *The Weakness of God: A Theology of the Event* (Bloomington: Indiana University Press, 2006), 310. Emphasis added.

112. Cross, "Where Angels Fear to Tread," 10–11. Ironically, this is the same accusation leveled by Pickstock *against* John Duns Scotus. In this case, Scotus is accused of reading and appropriating sources in his own way. She suggests that Scotus achieves his particular brand of "representation" as the result of "reading Pseudo-Dionysius and Augustine in his own fashion."

beyond the scope of this current book to investigate the particular nuances of Cambridge Thomism, and others have already offered skilled analyses.[113] However, what makes this aspect of Radical Orthodoxy theology important with regard to this present study is the apparent lack of disclosure that would otherwise be necessary for a more accurate engagement with Scotus's work.

When Milbank and Pickstock read Scotus, they do not read his work in itself but always with an eye toward how it is *not* the work of Aquinas. In other words, there is rarely a sound exegetical or historical analysis of Scotus's thought. Instead, the Radical Orthodoxy theologians engage the Scotus corpus in an exclusively eisegetical manner. In place of the meaning that is found in Scotus's own explanation and elucidation of his philosophical and theological arguments, proponents of Radical Orthodoxy seem to project their own meaning into the texts in accord with its apparent Thomistic-privative dimension. Scotus then becomes the "not-Thomas" instead of simply being "Scotus" on his own terms. While there are clearly distinctions between the two, differences that are irreconcilable and worthy of investigation on their own merit, Thomas and Scotus need to first be treated individually, apart from one another, in order to glean the necessary nuances of each thinkers' respective arguments, which can then be examined comparatively with the other.

This leads to my belief that the effective result of such an approach to reading Scotus's work is "Scotist illiteracy." In other words, Radical Orthodoxy theologians appear to be inhibited by their operative Thomist hermeneutic from *reading* the work of Scotus in an accurate

See Catherine Pickstock, "Postmodernism," in *The Blackwell Companion to Political Theology*, ed. Peter Scott and William Cavanaugh (Oxford: Blackwell, 2004), 473.

113. For more on the Radical Orthodoxy approach to Thomas Aquinas, see DeHart, *Aquinas and Radical Orthodoxy*; Laurence Paul Hemming, "*Quod Impossibile Est!* Aquinas and Radical Orthodoxy," in *Radical Orthodoxy? A Catholic Enquiry*, ed. Laurence Paul Hemming(London: Ashgate, 2000), 76–93; and John Marenbon, "Aquinas, Radical Orthodoxy, and the Importance of Truth," in Hankey and Hedley, *Deconstructing Radical Orthodoxy*, 49–63.

manner. While this is clearly seen at various points in the corpus of those contributing to the Scotus Story, it is especially seen in the work of Milbank and Pickstock, dating to the earliest sketching of their anti-Scotist narrative. For example, in his *Word Made Strange*, Milbank does not examine Scotus in the subtle doctor's own right, but first outlines the ontological vision of Aquinas and only secondarily highlights how Scotus is therefore not like the angelic doctor.[114] Even in the foundational text of Radical Orthodoxy, *Theology and Social Theory*, one finds Milbank's ongoing parallel assessment, revealing a latent Scotist illiteracy:

> Duns Scotus, unlike Thomas Aquinas, already distinguished metaphysics as a philosophical science concerning Being, from theology as a science concerning God.[115] Being, he argued, could be either finite or infinite, and possessed the same simple meaning of existence when applied to either. . . . Aquinas, by contrast, had interpreted Aristotle's denial that Being is differentiated amongst beings in the way that a genus is differentiated by its species, or a species by individuals, to mean that the relationship between genus and genus or generically different species is of an analogical character.[116]

Nowhere in the Radical Orthodoxy corpus does one find an explicit analysis of Scotus or the subtle doctor's thought per se. Instead, each invocation of Scotus is prefaced with some polemical dialectic that takes the shape of a contrasting portrayal of Scotus vis-à-vis Aquinas.[117] What I am calling Scotus illiteracy becomes even more

---

114. See Milbank, *Word Made Strange: Theology, Language, Culture* (Oxford: Blackwell, 1997), 36–50; and Marenbon, "Aquinas, Radical Orthodoxy and the Importance of Truth," 54–55.

115. Interestingly, the famous theologian Karl Rahner offers an alternative and converse reading of the history of the dissolution of theological metaphysics, which, in place of Scotus, implicates Aquinas. He writes, "It was Thomas Aquinas who first recognized philosophy as an autonomous discipline, and its secularization, its emancipation, constitutes the first step in the legitimate process by which the world is allowed to become 'worldly,' a process which, ultimately speaking, is willed and has been set in motion by Christianity itself." Karl Rahner, "Philosophy and Theology," in *Theological Investigations*, trans. David Bourke, vol. 13 (New York: Crossroads, 1975), 77.

116. Milbank, *Theology and Social Theory*, 305.

starkly observable in the work of Pickstock. Take, for example, her *After Writing*, in which she begins her presentation of Scotus's role in the genealogy of secularity as follows:

> The theology of Duns Scotus (c. 1265–1308) is perhaps the first definite theoretical symptom of the destruction from within of the liturgical city. . . . His most celebrated doctrines—univocity of being and the "formal distinction"—are deliberately and consciously opposed to those of Aquinas, and spawn further anti-Thomistic ideas, such as the actual existence of matter, individuation through form (*haecceitas*), a new leaning towards voluntarism, and the priority of the possible over existential actuality.[118]

This style of rhetoric continues similarly throughout her text, and is not worth quoting at length here. There are basic errors in fact present in her argument (e.g., the assertion that Scotus's doctrines were "deliberately and consciously opposed to those of Aquinas," when in fact the arguments were developed more proximately in response to the analogical theory of Henry of Ghent, among others)[119] that a priori weaken the presentation, but, taken at face value, her presentation of Scotus is never removed from an exaltation of Aquinas.

Examples of the influence of Radical Orthodoxy's operative Cambridge Thomist hermeneutic are found throughout the Scotus Story. This Scotist illiteracy plays a significant, if at times latent, role in their reading of the work of Scotus. This problematic dimension

---

117. For more, see James K. A. Smith, *Introducing Radical Orthodoxy: Mapping a Post-Secular Theology* (Grand Rapids: Baker Academic, 2004), 96; and Steven Shakespeare, *Radical Orthodoxy: A Critical Introduction* (London: SPCK, 2007), 10–12.

118. Pickstock, *After Writing*, 121–22.

119. Mary Beth Ingham highlights this dimension of the argument well: "Pickstock presents Thomist analogy as the counter to Scotus's focus on univocity. Historians of Scotist thought know well that the Franciscan's discussion of being as a univocal *concept* (and not a term) was in direct response to Henry of Ghent's neo-Augustinian illumination theory. It was not a response to Aquinas's position on analogy and its key use in language about God." Ingham, "Re-Situating Scotist Thought," 611.

of Radical Orthodoxy's methodology is further heightened by the movement's selective use of primary and secondary sources.

The Myopia of Selective Sources:
Or, Reading What You Want

While the influence of Radical Orthodoxy's operative Cambridge Thomist hermeneutic lends itself to a severely compromised reading of the Scotist corpus, the sources cited by Radical Orthodoxy theologians betrays a more egregious and confusing scholarly approach. One might be exonerated from accusations of malicious intent or poor scholarship if that person's operative textual hermeneutic was the only problematic feature of an otherwise sincere effort to interpret a particular theologian's work. However, those engaged in the establishment and development of the Scotus Story seemingly fail to take into account the breadth and depth of the subtle doctor's work. Furthermore, Milbank and Pickstock rely on either significantly outdated or selected secondary sources, many of which are widely recognized as flawed.

The first matter is that of the primary sources consulted by Radical Orthodoxy theologians. The absence of significant consultation of the expansive work of John Duns Scotus throughout the development of the Radical Orthodoxy Scotus Story is a problem. Cross notes, "To judge from the references cited, the accounts of Scotus that we find in the grand narratives of the radical orthodoxy theologians seems to be based on a very restricted range of primary sources, and involve no discussion of anything other than a very small proportion of the relevant material."[120] By "relevant material" Cross means those few passages that Milbank, Pickstock, and others

---

120. Cross, "Where Angels Fear to Tread," 10.

have selected to reference as they saw fit to support their claims. The location of these references is found in a short collection of translated passages from Scotus.[121] This small volume includes passages from Scotus's *Ordinatio* and a few samples of his more philosophical works, in particular the commentary on Aristotle's *Metaphysics*. The exclusive use of this translation for primary source material suggests that Radical Orthodoxy thinkers are either unaware or uninterested in the available editions of Scotus's work. While not complete in critical edition, the full body of Scotus's work is accessible in a variety of forms, including some recent critical translations of his commentary on Aristotle's *Metaphysics* and the examined Parisian report, *Reportatio-1A*.[122]

What emerges from this selective body of primary sources is a particular, idiosyncratic, and perhaps even disingenuous presentation of Scotus's thought. A familiarity with the broader collection of his work might have yielded a clearer understanding of what he meant by the semantic theory of univocity, his conceptualization and role of the transcendentals, and the purpose and significance of his formal distinction. Instead, the Radical Orthodoxy theologians provide their own gloss of the subtle doctor's thought in the form of generalizations and Cambridge Thomist projections. For example, Milbank and Pickstock's reduction of Scotus's nuanced and complicated semantic theory of univocity to a simplistic ontological rendering as a quasi-pantheistic parody does not at all represent the

---

121. See Duns Scotus, *Philosophical Writings*, trans. and ed. Allan Wolter (Indianapolis: Hackett, 1987).

122. See John Duns Scotus, *The Examined Report of the Paris Lecture: Reportatio I-A*, ed. Allan Wolter and Oleg Bychkov, 2 vols. (St. Bonaventure, NY: Franciscan Institute, 2004–08); and John Duns Scotus, *Quaestiones Super Libros Metaphysicorum Aristotelis*, in *Opera Philosophica*, ed. Girard Etzkorn et al., 5 vols. (St. Bonaventure, NY: Franciscan Institute, 1997–06), see vols. 3 and 4 (for the English translation, see John Duns Scotus, *Questions on the Metaphysics of Aristotle*, ed. Girard Etzkorn and Allan Wolter, 2 vols. (St. Bonaventure, NY: Franciscan Institute, 1997–98)].

true meaning of Scotus's philosophical view. Furthermore, the lack of a diachronic historical approach to Scotus's written corpus does not sufficiently represent the development of his thought over the course of his short philosophical and theological career. It would seem, therefore, that Milbank and Pickstock are not interested in exploring how Scotus's theory of univocity originates and is then modified over the course of his lifetime, a task that is complicated, but nevertheless feasible given the accessibility of his early *Lectura,* the later *Ordinatio,* and his Paris *Reportatio,* to name a few of the major works. To pick and choose, seemingly without discretion, which texts one wishes to consult to form a critical assessment of such a complicated medieval thinker is simply indefensible. As Mary Beth Ingham keenly notes, "To isolate the univocity of being from all other aspects of Scotist thought and to use it to ground a philosophical perspective is to do something with a piece of Scotus's thought that Scotus did not do."[123] Simply put, Radical Orthodoxy thinkers fail to accurately depict the vision of Scotus as it is found in his writing and interpreted according to the best secondary literature.

The lack of familiarity with the primary sources can indeed be seen as a form of scholarly oversight, but we also find an additionally troubling dimension to the Scotus Story in the limited selection of secondary source material referenced by the Radical Orthodoxy thinkers. As Cross has pointed out, the most heavily relied-upon source among the Radical Orthodoxy movement's selected secondary literature is more than a half-century old and recognized as flawed, which is a fact admitted even by some of those sympathetic to the Radical Orthodoxy authors. Here I am referring to Radical Orthodoxy's dependence on Étienne Gilson's *Jean Duns Scot.*[124]

---

123. Ingham, "Re-Situating Scotist Thought," 611.
124. See Honnefelder, *Scientia Transcendens,* xi–xii and passim; and Cross, "Where Angels Fear to Tread," 10.

Perhaps the most significant problem with Gilson's work on Scotus is his reliance on spurious works wrongly attributed to the subtle doctor, a fact that Wolter has pointed out.[125] Given the lack of reliable editions of Scotus's texts at the time, it is understandable that a study published in 1952 might contain significant errors that have subsequently come to light in recent scholarship. However, relying as heavily as the Radical Orthodoxy theologians have on this text as a major source for their interpretation of Scotus remains an understandable source of controversy. Ironically, even Gilson himself warns of the need for scholars to carefully examine the corpus of the Scotus himself: "Of a hundred writers who have held Duns Scotus up to ridicule, not two of them have ever read him, and not even one has understood him."[126] Additionally, early in his major work, Gilson summarizes his experience of studying Scotus stating succinctly: "Duns Scot est un auteur difficile."[127]

Curiously, Gilson writes elsewhere about Scotus's methodology and consistency in thought. Even amid spurious texts, Gilson is firm in asserting the transdisciplinary nature of Scotus's "theological philosophy" (a term later developed by Allan Wolter). Had Milbank and Pickstock moved beyond the boundaries of the problematic *Jean Duns Scot* text to explore other publications of Gilson on Scotus, they might have discovered their assertion that Scotus separates metaphysics from theology would have been likely rejected by one of their most oft-cited references.[128]

---

125. See Allan Wolter, "The 'Theologism' of Duns Scotus," in *The Philosophical Theology of John Duns Scotus*, ed. Marilyn McCord Adams (Ithaca: Cornell University Press, 1990), 211.

126. Gilson as quoted in Bérard de Saint-Maurice, *John Duns Scotus: A Teacher for Our Times* (St. Bonaventure, NY: Franciscan Institute, 1955), 48.

127. Gilson, *Jean Duns Scot* (Paris: Vrin, 1952), 8.

128. See Étienne Gilson, "Les seize premiers Theoremata et la pensée de Duns Scot," *Archives d'histoire doctrinale et litteraire du Moyen Age* 12–13 (1937–38): 5–86. While in this article, Gilson asserts the theological consistency in Scotus's work, ranging from his *Quaestiones subtilissimae super libros metaphysicorum* to the *Ordinatio* and *Reportatio*, etc., he does name the *Theoremata* as perhaps the one exception to the rule, noting that it, unlike the other works, denies the

Although Gilson's work is largely considered to be an unreliable resource for contemporary Scotist research, it is perhaps not the most calamitous of the few key secondary sources cited in support of the Scotus Story. Even more than Gilson, the work of Éric Alliez, the French philosopher of art and former student of Gilles Deleuze, is used to bolster (if not, more accurately put, *found*) some of the axiomatic claims upon which the Scotus Story is based. Alliez's *Capital Times* plays an immensely important role in the development of the Scotus Story by Catherine Pickstock and, following her, Conor Cunningham. As we have also seen in the last chapter, Alliez's text also plays a significant role in Karen Armstrong's presentation of Scotus's understanding of God. To give a brief glimpse of the degree to which Pickstock is indebted to Alliez for her own reading of Scotus, in *After Writing*, she cites Alliez eleven times out of the forty-five footnotes in her major section on Scotus. Nearly a quarter of all her references are dedicated to the third section of Alliez's *Captial Times*.[129] Likewise, Cunningham also draws heavily on Alliez's text. Although proportionally less, his dependence on this source (as well as that of Gilson) is significant.[130]

The problems with Alliez's reading of Scotus are too numerous to address here in their entirety, but I will quickly highlight a few of the themes that are ultimately adopted by Radical Orthodoxy in the quest to advance the Scotus Story. The first theme of Alliez's approach to Scotus is his assertion that, according to Scotus, between God and

demonstrability of the existence of God. Nevertheless, Gilson sets out to prove that there is no contradiction between the *Theoremata* and the rest of his corpus. See pp. 60–67 of the above-named article. See also Felix Alluntis, "Demonstrability and Demonstration of the Existence of God," in *John Duns Scotus: 1265–1965*, ed. John Ryan and Bernardine Bonansea (Washington, DC: Catholic University of America Press, 1965), 133–70.

129. See Pickstock, *After Writing*, 120–35; and Éric Alliez, *Capital Times: Tales from the Conquest of Time*, trans. Georges Van Den Abbeele (Minneapolis: University of Minnesota Press, 1996), 197–239), 196–238.

130. See Conor Cunningham, *Genealogy of Nihilism: Philosophies of Nothing and the Difference of Theology* (London: Routledge, 2002), esp. 3–43.

creatures there exists an infinite and impassable divide resulting from univocal predication of being to both God and creatures.[131] As we saw in chapter 1, this is an assertion that is featured prominently in the work of Pickstock. While it is clear that this view is not original to Pickstock, it would appear that this concept is also not the result of Alliez's creative work. He takes his cue from Gilson's *Jean Duns Scot* (or at least claims Gilson as his source).[132] He also cites *Ordinatio* d. 2 q. 9 and suggests that "the univocity implicating God and creature excludes any resemblance between them (the same goes for Ockham)."[133] Scotus does not believe that there is an absence of a locus of encounter between the divine and creatures, nor would the subtle doctor claim that there exists no resemblance between them. Additionally, Alliez provides no reference for his parenthetical comment positing congruence between the thought of Scotus and Ockham on this matter. The most obvious contributing problem in Alliez's assessment comes in the form of a misunderstanding of Scotus's notion of *infinitas intensiva*. Alliez appears to understand this as a numerical conceptualization of infinite degree, something that Scotus is precisely denying. Scotus holds that to assert a mathematical infinity in this matter opens the door to divisibility, something that could not be attributed to God given God's simplicity (affirming God's simplicity is a move Scotus *does* make).

A second theme that is appropriated by the Radical Orthodoxy theologians is Alliez's claim that "the notion of univocal being supposes that being is a something 'real and common.'"[134] Drawing on the claim that Scotus asserts an actual "intensive foundation,"[135] Alliez somehow envisions a theory of being as univocal that is *real*

---

131. Alliez, *Capital Times*, 199.
132. See Gilson, *Jean Duns Scot*, 629–30.
133. Alliez, *Capital Times*, 199.
134. Ibid., 201.
135. Ibid., 203.

and not simply conceptual. As has been made clear in the analysis given by Cross and Williams, presented earlier in this chapter, Scotus is clearly opposed to such a notion. Alliez has, in this instance, made assertions completely foreign to the semantic theory of Scotus. If, like Philip Tonner, we return to the early work of Alliez's *Doktorvater* Deleuze, we might have a better appreciation for how Alliez arrives at this misreading of Scotus, which is then picked up by Pickstock and others.[136] Tonner explains that Deleuze mistakes Scotus's *conceptual* argument for the necessity of univocity for a "real" or more ontological theory. Tonner explains,

> But Scotus does not hold that there is an actually existing being that is neither finite nor infinite, neither contingent nor necessary, and so on. He believes, rather, that univocal being does exist, though only at the conceptual level. There is a *concept* of univocal being neutral to the alternatives of infinite and finite and so on, which can be predicated of both of them. Thus the doctrine of univocal being is a doctrine about predication, nothing more. The doctrine is therefore on the side of logic rather than metaphysics.[137]

That Deleuze took the ideas and arguments further than Scotus ever did, pushing them into the metaphysical and ontological realm beyond the conceptual, logical, and semantic plane on which they originated in Scotus's writing, suggests that those who follow Deleuze's reading of Scotus's univocity cannot presume to be appropriating the subtle doctor's actual position.[138] It is not unlikely that such was also the case with Deleuze's student Alliez.

---

136. Philip Tonner offers a skillful, if brief, examination of Scotus's *concept* of the univocity of being in light of the modern appropriation of Scotus ideas in Heidegger and especially Gilles Deleuze. See his "Duns Scotus's Concept of the Univocity of Being: Another Look," *Pli* 18 (2007): 129–46.

137. Ibid., 146. Emphasis orginal.

138. See Gilles Deleuze, *Difference & Repetition*, trans. Paul Patton (New York: Columbia University Press, 1968; 1994), esp. 35–69.

The third theme that I wish to briefly mention is that of the elevation of possibility over actuality.[139] This, like the previous two themes in Alliez's work, is a notion that captures the attention of Radical Orthodoxy theologians, especially Pickstock. There is little need to explore at length this misreading of the subtle doctor. As was shown earlier in this chapter, Cross has already drawn sufficient attention to this problem in the adopted version of Alliez's argument in the work of Pickstock. Suffice it to say that Alliez also appears confused about a great many other things vis-à-vis Scotus's authentic philosophical vision, including Scotus's formal distinction.[140]

It is clear that the heavy reliance on Alliez, Gilson, and others further narrows the interpretive vision of the Radical Orthodoxy movement. Without wider examination of the primary sources, namely, the available critical editions of Scotus's work or even those other editions currently available in translation beyond the small Wolter *Philosophical Works* volume, the Radical Orthodoxy interpretation of Scotus's univocity of being was sure to remain at least confused, if not misleading. Yet, that oversight matched with an overtly myopic reading of the selected secondary texts renders the primary source analysis in the Radical Orthodoxy Scotus Story largely inaccurate.

What's So "Orthodox" About Radical Orthodoxy?

Before concluding this chapter, I want to suggest one additional problem with the Radical Orthodoxy movement as such, and their engagement with Scotus in particular, though there are many additional avenues open to further exploration by way of Radical Orthodoxy criticism. David Ford writes,

139. Alliez, *Capital Times*, 202 and 209.
140. Ibid., 203–8.

Theology does at its best raise profound issues relevant to the whole of life and every discipline, but this is not usually recognized in our universities or churches, let alone the media. Radical Orthodoxy says boldly that it is a bad thing for theology to be marginalized in this way; Milbank in other writings argues that the social scientific disciplines, which have in many respects taken over from theology the role of constructing worldviews, values and forms of explanation, are in fact best understood as heretical forms of theology; and the program is therefore to rethink reality in orthodox theological terms and, in the academic sphere, to give every discipline a theological framework.[141]

In light of this summary of the Radical Orthodoxy agenda, my question is simply: What is *theological* about Radical Orthodoxy? More specifically, what is so *orthodox* about the movement that presents itself as both unapologetically Christian and ecumenical? This appears to be a concern shared by Ford, who finds that the so-called Radical Orthodoxy Manifesto, articulated in the introduction to the seminal essay collection *Radical Orthodoxy: A New Theology*, has been ultimately left unfulfilled.[142] R. R. Reno has an insightful observation that emphasizes this point: Radical Orthodoxy's agenda is such that it cannot be explicitly identified with any *particular* Christian tradition (perhaps this is what is meant by the assertion that Radical Orthodoxy is "ecumenical").[143] Because of this inability to identify with a particular tradition, Radical Orthodoxy seems to be left to "invent one."[144] What results from this innovative non/denominational creation is something of a Neoplatonic, quasi-Augustinianism that Reno explains as follows: "Radical Orthodoxy cannot invent the flesh and blood of a Christian culture, and so must be satisfied with describing its theoretical gestalt, gesturing,

---

141. David Ford, "Radical Orthodoxy and the Future of British Theology," *Scottish Journal of Theology* 54 (2001): 385.
142. Ibid., 388.
143. R. R. Reno, "The Radical Orthodoxy Project," *First Things* 100 (February 2000): 40.
144. Ford, "Radical Orthodoxy and the Future of British Theology," 393.

in postmodern fashion, toward that which was and might be."[145] In other words, whereas Radical Orthodoxy claims that the advent of modernity inaugurated the emergence of the secular and the subordination of theology to social sciences, Radical Orthodoxy itself has apparently evacuated theology of Christianity, or at least of some recognizably orthodox tradition. Furthermore, it is striking that this novel vision of Christianity—or, at least its accompanying theoretical *ecclesia*—is seen by some scholars as being more exclusive and less welcoming than the ostensibly troublesome and hostile space of the "secular" that Radical Orthodoxy theologians wish to overcome. Christopher Newell explains, "This is the paradox of Radical Orthodoxy: it seeks to challenge the overarching, overwhelming, grand narrative of rationalism and the capitalist endeavor of consumption, yet replaces it with a theology of church that is as equally overarching and exclusive of all other communities and narratives."[146]

So what does this have to do with Scotus?

The answer lies in the wonderfully succinct assessment offered by Emmanuel Perrier. Perrier writes, "The adoption of univocity by Scotus is a decision of the *theological order, specific to Christianity*, breaking with the reading of the Graeco-Latin metaphysical heritage, which prevailed before him and on which we still depend."[147] One of the most overlooked dimensions of Scotus's doctrine of the univocity of being is the primary impetus for the entire project. Scotus's motivation is largely theological in that his interest is in affirming humanity's ability to say anything and know anything, and therefore make truth claims, about God the Creator. The semantic theory of

---

145. Reno, "The Radical Orthodoxy Project," 43.
146. Christopher Newell, "Communities of Faith, Desire, and Resistance: A Response to Radical Orthodoxy's *Ecclesia*," in *The Poverty of Radical Orthodoxy*, ed. Lisa Isherwood and Marko Zlomislić (Eugene, OR: Pickwick, 2012), 182.
147. Perrier, "Duns Scotus Facing Reality," 625. Emphasis added.

univocity arises from an epistemological inquiry in the service of a theological dilemma that, logically, Scotus saw as unanswered in the preceding theories of analogous predication.[148] Scotus's project is deeply rooted in a Christian worldview that is both biblical and doctrinal. This further suggests that the Scotus Story presented by Radical Orthodoxy theologians stands in direct contrast to the authentic reading of the doctrine, its origin, and its aim. In this regard, one might confidently suggest, alongside Ford, Reno, Newell, and others, that the neo-Christianity that contextualizes Radical Orthodoxy's theological agenda is maybe more harmful than helpful. Additionally, one naturally wonders, what is the precise charge against Scotus concerning Christian theology that Radical Orthodoxy itself has not more gravely violated by virtue of its very project, sourcing, and method?

Reconsidering the Scotus Story in Light of Critical Assessment

This chapter has outlined the major sources of critique in the effort to restore John Duns Scotus and his doctrine of univocity to its rightful place unmarred by Radical Orthodoxy's narrative. The means to this end include critical reading, careful interpretation, and responsible transmission of the subtle doctor's philosophical and theological vision. Both Richard Cross and Thomas Williams have led the way in calling attention to the mistaken interpretation of Scotus's doctrine of univocity in Radical Orthodoxy. Cross's primary intention is to call

---

148. It is worth noting that some scholars, including Stephen Dumont and Alex Hall, suggest that Scotus himself might not have been entirely convinced by or comfortable with his own conceptual theory, but for the sake of theological integrity maintained and defended univocity against analogy reducible to equivocity. See Stephen Dumont, "The Notion of Univocity in Duns Scotus's Early Works," *Franciscan Studies* 43 (1983): 347–95; and Alex Hall, "Confused Univocity?" *Proceedings of the Society for Medieval Logic and Metaphysics* 7 (2007): 18–31.

attention to the seemingly negligent approach to Scotus scholarship exhibited in the genesis and development of the Scotus Story by Milbank, Pickstock, and those who come after them. Cross's desire is to encourage an accurate retrieval of the Scotist tradition, something almost completely ignored in the project and according to the method of the Radical Orthodoxy theologians. Williams, in some ways following Cross, sees univocity as both necessarily true and practically salutary. His primary method is a focused response to the claims advanced by Pickstock, while obliquely responding to the entire Radical Orthodoxy movement. The last critique in this chapter is to highlight three areas of problematic methodology and practice in the Radical Orthodoxy movement with the hope that others might engage these questions more deeply. All three of the concerns I raise tend to be overlooked by those who adopt the Scotus Story as foundational, such as we have seen in chapter 2. These areas include the role of Radical Orthodoxy's operative hermeneutic ("Cambridge Thomism"), the problem of sources in the development of the Radical Orthodoxy argument, and the questionable success (or failure) of the Radical Orthodoxy agenda in light of Scotus's own motivation and work. While this chapter does not exhaust the possible avenues of analysis open to those interested in evaluating the Radical Orthodoxy movement's use of John Duns Scotus and its subsequent understanding of univocity, it does provide ample evidence that calls into question the Scotus Story as such.

4

Toward A Correct Reading of Scotus's Univocity

Having examined the arguments put forward by the Radical Orthodox theologians in chapter 1, the ways in which the Scotus Story has been appropriated in chapter 2, and the critiques of that reading of John Duns Scotus in chapter 3, it is necessary for us to explore the doctrine of univocity as Scotus himself presents it. Following the substantial critique leveled against the Radical Orthodoxy reading and subsequent interpretation of this theory of univocity, it is important to present a reading of the subtle doctor's work that provides a more accurate account of Scotus's position in contrast to the Radical Orthodoxy position. While Richard Cross, Thomas Williams, and others have done exemplary work in the area of dismantling the positions generated and advanced by theologians like John Milbank and Catherine Pickstock, these critical responses have not necessarily provided a constructive alternative to the Scotus Story as posited by Radical Orthodoxy.

A presentation of Scotus's thought that offers a corrective to the Radical Orthodoxy narrative requires special attention to the primary sources. As we have seen in the preceding chapter, the limited use or absence of primary texts of Scotus has been one of the primary reasons for a compromised reading and interpretation of the subtle doctor. This restorative project will rely not only on the selections of the *Ordinatio* presented in Allan Wolter's translation of selected philosophical writings, but also examine and incorporate wider primary sources when necessary.[1] Elsewhere, for example in Scotus's later *Quaestiones Quodlibetales*, we see dimensions of the subtle doctor's work that bolster his theory of univocity.

In a variety of secondary sources and over the course of many years, several scholars have taken up the challenge of summarizing or highlighting the arguments advanced by Scotus. These previous readings offer an authoritative guide for my own reading of Scotus. These scholars include Allan Wolter, Richard Cross, Ludger Honnefelder, Mary Beth Ingham, Antonie Vos, Stephen Dumont, Philip Tonner, and others. The most significant texts consulted, although spanning a wide spectrum of authorship, are written primarily in English and German, the two languages in which Scotus study has been most explored.[2] Because the central focus of this project is an attempt at a more accurate reading of Scotus's work as such, the reliance on secondary sources, while necessary and important, remains supplementary and directive.

---

1. John Duns Scotus, *Philosophical Writings*, trans. and ed. Allan Wolter (Indiana: Hackett, 1987). The singular reliance on the texts selected for this publication was perhaps one of the greatest (but not only) points of critique leveled against Milbank and Pickstock.
2. One major exception to this is Etienne Gilson's French work. While I am familiar with his study *Jean Duns Scot*, I have opted to set it aside, given the problematic reputation it has and the compromised reliability that has been attributed to it since its publication. Furthermore, some minor publications in Italian have also appeared during the last century; while I am aware of their existence, I have not relied on them for this study.

In addition to the explicit emphasis on responsible reading of Scotus's texts and the consultation of authoritative secondary sources to guide my assessment, the establishment of the historical context and the acknowledgement of the antecedent sources will function as the preliminary launching point for a corrective reading of the doctrine of univocity. In so doing, I hope to fill the contextual lacuna left unaddressed in the Radical Orthodoxy narrative, although a fuller exploration of the thought of Henry of Ghent or Avicenna, for instance, is beyond the scope of this current project.

In this chapter, I will present a reading of Scotus's work on the univocal concept of being, in an effort to come to a proper understanding of the doctrine in light of the Radical Orthodoxy reading. The aim of this final chapter is to outline the basic principles Scotus presents in his work so as to provide an accurate and concise introduction to his theory, which might enable us to authentically retrieve the subtle doctor's insight for future theological inquiry. This chapter is divided into three sections. The first section focuses on the context out of which Scotus develops his work and the antecedent influences, particularly that of Henry of Ghent, that serve as the impetus and counterpoint to Scotus's vision. The second section is a concise examination of the major principles Scotus develops to form his understanding of the univocity of being. The final section is a brief conclusion that introduces a sampling of the metaphysical or ontological implications present in Scotus's semantic and logical position.

The Context and Antecedent Sources

The intellectual milieu of the period before Scotus significantly and indelibly shaped the arena within which the subtle doctor would craft his own philosophical and theological contributions. Steven Marrone summarizes the context of Scotus's work when he writes, "Although Duns was hardly shy about advancing novel or even idiosyncratic ideas in his endeavor to subject philosophy and theology to a penetrating critical analysis, most of his novelties found their roots in the debates of the generation or two preceding him."[3] It was a time of growth in formalized academic inquiry that both witnessed and nurtured the birth of the universities.[4] As is well known, two locations would become the dual foci of the thirteenth-century emergence of what would come to be called scholasticism.[5] These sites were Paris and Oxford.[6] The works of Aristotle became one of the centerpieces of the then-contemporary study and, although many of the theories and much of the work reliant on the ancient philosopher's texts were later condemned at Paris (1277), the influence of Aristotle on the philosophy and theology of the day cannot be overstated.[7] Prior to the 1277 condemnation, there was a period of several decades that represent a highly productive engagement with the Aristotelian commentators and texts. The then "modern," to use the term anachronistically, theology generally bore an Aristotelian mark. The politics of the condemnation of 1277 also

3. Steven Marrone, "The Notion of Univocity in Duns Scotus's Early Works," *Franciscan Studies* 43 (1983): 348.
4. For an overview of the milieu, see Stephen Brown, "The Intellectual Context of Later Medieval Philosophy: Universities, Aristotle, Arts, Theology," in *Medieval Philosophy*, ed. John Marenbon, Routledge History of Philosophy vol. 3 (London: Routledge, 2004), 188–203.
5. The term *scholasticism* as such did not develop until the middle of the nineteenth century. For more on this moniker, see Timothy Noone, "Scholasticism," in *A Companion to Philosophy in the Middle Ages*, ed. Jorge Gracia and Timothy Noone (Oxford: Blackwell, 2006), 55–64; and M. W. F. Stone, "Scholastic Schools and Early Modern Philosophy," in *The Cambridge Companion to Early Modern Philosophy*, ed. Donald Rutherford (New York: Cambridge University Press, 2006), 299–327.
6. For a helpful study of the emergence of scholasticism at these locations, see Edward Grant, *God & Reason in the Middle Ages* (New York: Cambridge University Press, 2001).
7. See Jan Aertsen, Kent Emery, and Adrian Speer, *Nach der Verurteilung von 1277: Philosophie und Theologie an der Universität von Paris im letzten Viertel des 13. Jahrhunderts*, Studien und Texte (Berlin: Walter de Gruyter, 2000).

influenced the decision of some to espouse an Aristotelian approach or react against it.[8]

Arguably, the most famous thinker of this age is Thomas Aquinas, although that was not always the case in his own time. Thomas, deeply indebted to the new philosophical rediscoveries of the age, worked out a system that would serve as a focal point and launching pad for many subsequent theological engagements. However, Thomas was not the only theologian of this era that would later serve as an interlocutor and as the subject of critique for Scotus.[9] Several major figures emerged after Thomas that would help shape the agenda taken up by Scotus. For example, Henry of Ghent, Godfrey of Fontaines, and Giles of Rome can be counted among such thinkers. Giles was a master at the University of Paris from 1285 to 1291 and had studied under the angelic doctor. Godfrey, another former student of Aquinas, was a strong proponent of Aristotle and followed Aquinas's model of theologizing. Henry of Ghent is, undoubtedly, the most influential when it comes to the setting of Scotus's philosophical and theological agenda, especially as it concerns analogy and univocity.[10] He was a regent master at the University of Paris from 1276 until 1293, and is remembered as a contributor to the so-called neo-Augustinian theological line and, as

8. John Wippel, "The Parisian Condemnations of 1270 and 1277," in Garcia and Noone, *A Companion to Philosophy in the Middle Ages*, 65–73; and J. M. M. Thijssen, *Censure and Heresy at the University of Paris 1200–1400* (Philadelphia: University of Pennsylvania Press, 1998). Also, see Stephen Brown, "Peter of Candia's Hundred-Year 'History' of the Theologian's Role," *Medieval Philosophy and Theology* 1 (1991): 156–90.

9. For a historical overview of the intellectual developments during the period from 1277 to 1300, the essential stage-setting timeframe for Scotus's work, see Richard Cross, *The Medieval Christian Philosophers: An Introduction* (London: I. B. Tauris, 2013), 131–62.

10. See Steven Marrone, "Henry of Ghent and Duns Scotus on the Knowledge of Being," *Speculum* 63 (1988): 22–57. See also Timothy Noone, "Universals and Individuation," in *The Cambridge Companion to Duns Scotus*, ed. Thomas Williams (New York: Cambridge University Press, 2003), 114–18; Richard Cross, *Duns Scotus* (New York: Oxford University Press, 1999), 5 and passim; Stephen Dumont, "Henry of Ghent and Duns Scotus," in Marnebon, *Medieval Philosophy*, 291–328; and Mary Beth Ingham and Mechthild Dreyer, *The Philosophical Vision of John Duns Scotus* (Washington, DC: Catholic University of America Press, 2004), 17

Cross asserts, "is arguably the most important philosopher in the years between Aquinas and Scotus."[11]

According to Ingham and Dreyer, the leading epistemological concerns during the era centered on the questions of the cognition of the particular and the constitution of the intellect.[12] Both of these issues arose as the result of the Aristotelian model of sense perception, the role of the agent intellect, and the formation of phantasms having been introduced into scholastic theology. Both issues are concerned with the relationship between the immaterial substance of the mind and the concrete, extramental world of material substances.[13] The academic conversation was shaped by the debate between the possibilities of Aristotelian agent intellection versus Augustinian illumination theory (or some variation of it). In between the respective periods of Aquinas and Scotus, a number of Franciscans had abandoned the long-held Augustinian tradition of illumination in favor of an Aristotelian approach.[14] Scotus will fall in line with these thinkers, although his own idiosyncratic approach will definitively shape his proposal, which included a harsh rejection of Henry's unique theory of divine illumination and its relationship to theology as a science.[15] The epistemological concerns of Scotus's day serve as the starting point for his reflection.[16]

---

11. Cross, *The Medieval Christian Philosophers*, 134.

12. Ingham and Dreyer, *The Philosophical Vision of John Duns Scotus*, 18.

13. Ibid., 18–19.

14. Some of these Franciscan thinkers included Richard of Middleton, William of Ware, and the famous Peter John Olivi. For more see Bonnie Kent, *Virtues of the Will: The Transformation of Ethics in the Late Thirteenth Century* (Washington, DC: Catholic University of America Press, 1995).

15. For more, see Raymond Macken, "La théroie de l'illumination divine dans la philosophie d'Henri de Gand," *Reserches de théologie ancienne et médiéval* 39 (1972): 82–112; and Jerome V. Brown, "Duns Scotus on Henry of Ghent's Arguments for Divine Illumination: The Statement of the Case," *Vivarium* 14 (1976): 94–113.

16. Ingham and Dreyer note well the difference in starting point between Scotus and Aquinas or Bonaventure: "In short, philosophers and theologians in Scotus's generation faced questions about scientific knowledge, necessity and contingency, mediated and immediate cognition, autonomy, and freedom that were not precisely those encountered by Bonaventure and

The Position of Henry of Ghent

While some like to juxtapose the univocal theory of predication of Scotus with the analogous theory of predication of Aquinas, such a positioning betrays a lack of appreciation for Scotus's most proximate interlocutor, Henry of Ghent.[17] While it is conceivable that one might be justified in analyzing the differences between Scotus and Aquinas, an understanding of Henry's position is more helpful in elucidating Scotus's approach.

Henry's own counterpoint is held to be Aquinas, to whom he directed his own response, shaping his understanding of analogy in contradistinction to the angelic doctor. Henry was critical of Aristotle on some fundamental points, which ultimately led him to "return" to a more Augustinian outlook. In addition to Augustine, Henry was strongly influenced by Avicenna.[18] "Where Aquinas argues 'according to Aristotle and truth' (*secundum Aristotelem et veritatem rei*), Henry will instead argue 'according to Augustine, Avicenna and the truth' (*secundum Avicennam et veritatem rei; secundum Augustinum et Avicennam*)."[19] Henry leveled a number of critiques against Aquinas's theology including the following:

> The concept of theology as a subalternated science, the exclusivity of faith and demonstrative reasoning, the definition of self-evidence and related criticism of Anselm's ontological argument, the pre-eminence given to Aristotle's argument for the unmoved mover, the denial of any

Aquinas before them. And, in a post-1277 world, these questions appeared as part of a single, coherent philosophical view of human nature and destiny that focused on the intellect and speculation." Ingham and Dreyer, *The Philosophical Vision of John Duns Scotus*, 21.

17. See Ludger Honnefelder, *Johannes Duns Scotus* (München: C. H. Beck, 2005), 59: "Die zuletzt genannten Schwierigkeiten lassen erkennen, warum sich Aristoteles gegen eine univoke Prädikation von 'Seiendem' entschieden hat und warum Scotus' vorrangiger Gesprächspartner Heinrich von Gent (wie auf andere Weise auch Thomas von Aquin) zu einer sog." Also, see Phillip Tonner, "Duns Scotus's Concept of the Univocity of Being: Another Look," *Pli* 18 (2007): 140.
18. Dumont, "Henry of Ghent and Duns Scotus," 296.
19. Ibid.

positive knowledge of God's essence (*quid est*) in the present life, the limitation of each Aristotelian separate form or angel to a species in itself, the real distinction of essence and existence (at least as defended by Giles of Rome), the indemonstrability of the temporal beginning of the world, and a variety of theses connected to the relationship of the intellect to the will.[20]

The distinctly neo-Augustinian approach of Henry later catches the attention of Scotus, who critically evaluates the former's position. The reason why Scotus focuses more on Henry and not Aquinas for his critique remains a debated subject. Scholars suggest that one reason is that when the Franciscans were restricted from reading Aquinas's *Summa Theologica* in 1282, the friars began reading Henry's *Summa*. Additionally, Scotus's alignment with those who would distance themselves from the neo-Augustinian divine illumination theories would also help explain why Henry was such a target for the subtle doctor. Regardless of the precise reason, Henry's work is, as Dumont so pointedly notes, "not just a source, but the source for Scotus's thought."[21] One caveat is needed here with regard to Henry's relationship to Scotus's work. While Scotus often critiques the work of Henry, it would be a distortion to consider Scotus's work simply as an abandonment or rejection of Henry's thought. Dumont observes that even when Scotus is clearly repudiating his predecessor, Scotus adopts much of Henry's philosophical presuppositions and framework, while also utilizing his technical vocabulary.[22]

20. Ibid. See also Henry of Ghent, *Quodlibeta Magistri Henrici Goethals a Gandavo Doctoris Solemnis*, ed. I. Badius, 2 vols. (Louvain: Bibliothéque SJ, 1961); and Henry of Ghent, *Summae quaestionum ordinariarum* (St. Bonaventure, NY: Franciscan Institute, 1953).

 Thanks to the work of faculty in the departments of philosophy and classics at the University of North Carolina Asheville, major selections of the *Opera Omnia* of Henry of Ghent, the complete editing of which remains ongoing and based at Leuven, have been made available online at http://philosophy.unca.edu/henry-ghent-series.

21. Dumont, "Henry of Ghent and Duns Scotus," 297. Dumont goes on, "This is in fact so true that Scotus appears to be the first major scholastic thinker to base his principal work explicitly on the systematic examination of a contemporary."

22. Ibid.

Of all the themes Henry explores, the one of interest to us for this project is his view of analogy. Henry's approach to analogous predication is innovative and differs from that of the position widely held before him (e.g., that of Aquinas). It is fair to say that Henry's innovation of analogy as he inherited it was an attempt, albeit a failed one, to transcend or respond to the difficulties he saw with the previously held views. As both Dumont and Tonner note, "Henry's position took the philosophy of analogy to its furthest-most point."[23] Subsequently, we can say that Scotus's response to Henry's view of analogy is the subtle doctor's attempt to respond to similar difficulties, ultimately resulting in the advocating of the necessity of univocally predicated concepts of transcendentals, rather than advocating for the fundamentally analogical quality of the concept of being with regard to creatures and the Creator, as Henry argued.

The starting point for Henry is the issue of our natural knowledge of God. As was the case for those in the latter part of the thirteenth century, epistemology served as a primary impetus for subsequent metaphysical inquiry. In speaking about God, the question arises concerning the relationship between our language and what it is we are actually describing, namely God. Scholastic theologians, drawing on the *Metaphysics* and other works of Aristotle, held that transcendentals could not be predicated of both God and creatures univocally, that is, with the same meaning.[24] Likewise, it would be absurd to suggest that we can only predicate concepts equivocally, that is with completely different meanings. Therefore, it follows that concepts that are predicated of both God and creatures must be done so analogously. This provided, it would seem, a middle ground between the extremes of univocity and equivocity. As such,

---

23. Tonner, "Duns Scotus's Concept of the Univocity of Being," 142. Also, see Dumont, "Henry of Ghent and Duns Scotus," 299.
24. See Aristotle, *The Metaphysics*, trans. and ed. Hugh Lawson-Tancred (New York: Penguin, 2009).

analogous predication applied a concept to God in a primary way and only secondarily to creatures, but in a related sense, so that there was no equation, yet some relationship, between the two. This is where Henry of Ghent begins his work.[25] However, it is not where Henry ends.

In addition to Aristotle, Henry is deeply influenced by the Aristotelian commentator and philosopher Avicenna (*ibn Sina*). Avicenna advocated for being (*ens*), and not God, as the subject of metaphysics. In this way, there appears to be a primacy of being that suggests an antecedent concept prior to both God and creatures.[26] Henry responded to this position in a manner that ultimately defends and bolsters his understanding of analogy:

> What is predicated of several things, but has an essential concept different from the concepts of those things [of which it is predicated], is something really common to them, for every concept is based upon some thing. Being is this sort, because according to Avicenna, "Being is imprinted on the mind by a first impression," even before the concept of God or creature are impressed on it. [Therefore, being is something really common to God and creatures.][27]

The implication of Avicenna's position is that there must exist something *really* common (i.e., not just conceptually common) to both God and creatures, suggesting therefore that being as such exists prior or antecedently even to God. Henry's objection lies in the widely held assertion that no reality can be admitted as common to God and creatures. In response to his reading of Avicenna, Henry asserts that any *real* concept of being must be proper to God *or*

---

25. See Henry of Ghent, *Summae quaestionum ordinariarum* a. 21, q. 2.

26. Dumont, "Henry of Ghent and Duns Scotus," 299.

27. Henry of Ghent, *Summae quaestionum ordinariarum* a. 21, q. 2., trans. as found in Dumont, "Henry of Ghent and Duns Scotus," 300. For a classic study on Henry's view, see Stephen Brown, "Avicenna and The Unity of the Concept of Being: The Interpretation of Henry of Ghent, Duns Scotus, Gerard of Bologna, and Peter Aureoli," *Franciscan Studies* 25 (1965): 117–50.

proper to creatures, but not to both. His proposed solution is again summarized well by Dumont:

> Henry concludes that at the transcendental level being forms two proper and distinct concepts corresponding to the two separate and diverse realities of divine and created being. These concepts, while proper and diverse, none the less have a community of analogy, the real foundation for which is the causal dependence of the creature on God.[28]

Henry moves a step further to suggest that when a concept *appears* to be predicable univocally of both God and creatures, it is only because one is conceiving of it in a vague or indistinct way, thereby neglecting the concept's true proper relationship to one (God) or the other (creatures). Another way to consider this is as a confused conceptualization. Henry holds that there is no absolutely undetermined concept of being that can be abstracted from both God and creatures. It only appears that such a concept exists when one confuses the different ways each concept of being is a priori undetermined (as concerns God and creatures *distinctly*). "What appears to be a simple, common notion of undetermined being is in fact a conflation of two proper notions of being, which resemble each other in their removal of determination."[29]

With regard to the previously held concept of analogy, Henry is initially in line with thinkers like Thomas Aquinas and Bonaventure. However, in light of the position advanced by Avicenna, Henry goes a step beyond, creating a two-tiered system of analogy. This second step results in Henry's belief that one could conceive of a transcendental (e.g., *being*) with sufficient indeterminacy so as to appear univocal, while insisting that there is in fact no such univocal concept.[30] Henry's position makes perfect sense in light of his

28. Dumont, "Henry of Ghent and Duns Scotus," 301.
29. Ibid., 302.
30. Ibid.

underlying motivation, which, as we saw at the outset of our examination of his work, is essentially epistemological.[31] It is a response to the question of how these two proper notions of being are related with regard to the way the human mind can move from knowledge of creatures to knowledge and discussion of divine nature. The connection, according to Henry, could not be the result of a univocal concept common to both. Therefore, it must be through the conception of two distinct concepts together such that they might appear as one. In other words,

> for Henry, a perfection can be abstracted from a creature and conceived with such indeterminacy that it is not just the universal knowledge of a creature but a confused knowledge of *both* God and creature. This exceedingly abstract notion, which Henry calls "analogously common," provides the necessary epistemological bridge from creature to God by constituting a concept of both at once.[32]

Setting the Stage for Scotus

The position of Henry of Ghent will provide the primary impetus and initial context for Scotus's own investigation into the question of how we can claim know or say anything about God. Scotus seeks to show that Henry's position is inherently flawed, for it contains inconsistencies that jeopardize Henry's own analogously common concept, as developed in response to Aristotle and Avicenna. In turn, Scotus sets out to demonstrate that a truly univocal concept of transcendentals does not violate the real transcendence of God. Ultimately, Scotus will posit that analogous concepts necessarily depend on the possibility of concepts predicated univocally. Without

---

31. See Steven Marrone, "Mathew of Aquasparta, Henry of Ghent and Augustinian Epistemology after Bonaventure," *Franziskanische Studien* 65 (1983): 252–90.
32. Dumont, "Henry of Ghent and Duns Scotus," 306.

univocity, one is not left with a choice between analogy and equivocal language, but rather one is left with nothing.

John Duns Scotus and the Univocity of Being

As Robert Prentice puts it well, "Scotus's theory of the univocity of being makes complete sense within his entire system."[33] To clearly understand the philosophical and theological system of John Duns Scotus within the context of the whole, it is imperative that one appreciates his position on the univocal predication of transcendentals, especially being (*ens*). As outlined above, the most proximate source to which the subtle doctor responds is the work of Henry of Ghent. Henry, who had both adopted and adapted the previously held primacy of analogous predication of being, defends his work with arguments that Scotus finds to be inherently problematic and, at times, inexplicable.

Scotus's Epistemological Starting Point and Response to Henry

Scotus deals with the issue of the univocal concept of being in several places within his corpus. This most expansive exploration of this subject appears in his commentary on the *Sentences* of Peter Lombard in the *Ordinatio*.[34] Scotus begins his investigation into the

---

33. Robert Prentice, *The Basic Quidditative Metaphysics of Duns Scotus as Seen in His De Primo Principio*, Spicilegium Pontificii Anthenaei Antoniani 16 (Rome: Edizioni Antonianum, 1997), 24.

34. The critical edition of Scotus's corpus is *Opera Omnia: Studio et Cura Commissionis Scotisticae ad fidem codicum edita*, eds. C. Balíc et al. (Vatican City: Typis Polyglottis Vaticanis, 1950–). The *Ordinatio* is found in vols. 1–7. Further citations of Scotus's work will include the textual citation followed by the edition volume and page numbers in parenthesis.

    For those texts not yet published in critical edition, I will cite the modernized reprint of the Luke Wadding edition: *Opera Omnia: Editio Nova Iuxta Editionem Waddingi XII tomos continentem a Patribus Franciscanis de Observantia Accurante Recognita*, ed. L. Wadding, 26 vols.

question of the nature of our concepts of God (*de natura conceptus nostri Dei*) with this assertion: "I say to begin with, therefore, that it is naturally possible to have not only a concept in which God is known incidentally, for example, in some attribute, but also some concept in which he is conceived *per se* and *quidditatively*."[35] Scotus says this with a deliberate eye toward Henry of Ghent, for whom such a concept of God *per se* and *quidditatively* is not knowable, but only conceived of in a quasi-property (*quasi proprietas*). This *quasi proprietas* is the confused notion or concept of an abstracted and undetermined transcendental that Henry discusses. Scotus therefore asserts that we can have natural concepts by which we conceive of God as such. This is his starting point, and it is an epistemological one. Central to understanding Scotus's theory of the univocity of being is an appreciation for the epistemological question that launches the subtle doctor's investigation. To neglect that Scotus begins his inquiry with a concern about how to *know* God inevitably causes problems with one's understanding of the semantic nature of his theory of univocal predication of some transcendentals, particularly being.

The next move Scotus makes in this section of the *Ordinatio* is greatly important. He begins with the following: "I say that God is thought of not only in some concept analogous to that of a creature, that is, one entirely different from what is predicated of a creature, but also in some concept univocal to himself and to a creature."[36]

(Paris: Vivés, 1891–95). This source will be cited like the critical edition but with the prefatory *Vivés* prior to volume and page number in parenthesis.

35. *Ordinatio* I, dist. 3, pars 1, q. 1–2, no. 25 (Vatican 3:16–17): "Dico ergo primo quod non tantum haberi potest conceptus naturaliter in quo quasi per accidens concipitur Deus, puta in aliquo attributo, sed etiam aliquis conceptus in quo per se et quiditative concipiatur Deus." (English translation: William Frank and Allan Wolter, *Duns Scotus: Metaphysician* [Indiana: Purdue University Press, 1995], 109ff.)

36. *Ordinatio* I, dist. 3, pars 1, q. 1–2, no. 26 (Vatican 3:18): "Dico quod non tantum in conceptu analogo conceptui creaturae concipitur Deus, scilicet qui omnino sit alius ab illo qui de creatura dicitur, sed in conceptu aliquo univoco sibi et creaturae." (English: Frank and Wolter, *Duns Scotus: Metaphysician*, 109). See also Honnefelder, *Johannes Duns Scotus*, 60–63.

Operating beneath the subsequent arguments in support of this position is Scotus's conviction that there is always some univocal notion of being that is present and presupposed in any natural knowledge of God. In other words, theology (literally *God talk*) necessarily requires a univocal concept of being.[37] This stands, as the editors of the critical edition of the *Ordinatio* note, in stark contrast to the position of Henry of Ghent.[38] This aspect of Scotus's motivation will be present throughout his arguments for univocity and against Henry's denial that *only* analogical or equivocal predication are possible.

Throughout his defense of univocity, Scotus frequently singles Henry out for critique. While Scotus sees Henry's greatest transgression as the rejection of a concept that is both common to God and creatures for a confused and conflated notion of undetermined (yet ultimately proper) *being*, the subtle doctor also rejects other positions espoused by Henry. One such example includes Henry's defense of a unique form of Augustinian illumination (the controversial and so-called *lumen theologicum*). Additionally, Scotus has strongly negative feelings about the seemingly Platonic principles that compose Henry's assertion that creatures have *esse essentiae* as divine ideas.[39] Instead of spending any more time focusing on the particular instances of Scotus's rejection of Henry, we will move on to look at Scotus's argument on behalf of univocity, occasionally noting Henry's role in the development of Scotus's thought along the way.[40]

---

37. This is made most explicit in both *Lectura* I, dist. 3, pars 1, q. 1–2, no. 113: "Item, nisi ens importaret unam intentionem, univocam, simpliciter periret theologia" (Vatican 16:266); and *Ordinatio* I, dist. 3, pars 1, q. 3, no. 139: "Sicut argutum est etiam quod Deus non est cognoscibilis a nobis naturaliter nisi ens sit univocum creato et increato, ita potest argui de substantia et accidente" (Vatican 3:86–87).

38. See Henry of Ghent, *Summae quaestionum ordinariarum* a. 21, q. 2.

39. Dumont, "Henry of Ghent and Duns Scotus," 322.

Scotus's Definition of Univocity

In order to defend the claim outlined above that we can say anything meaningful of God—that theology is in fact a real possibility—and that there is a concept univocal to both God and creatures, Scotus must define what he means by univocity. He does this in the *Ordinatio* when he writes,

> And lest there be any contention about the word "univocation," I call that concept univocal that has sufficient unity in itself that to affirm and deny it of the same subject suffices as a contradiction. It also suffices as a syllogistic middle term, so that where two terms are united in a middle term that is one in this fashion, they are inferred without a fallacy of equivocation to be united among themselves.[41]

Richard Cross makes a useful disclaimer about this definition of univocation. He reminds us that Scotus does not consider the satisfaction of these two conditions to be a sufficient proof that the univocity theory is true. On the contrary, Scotus insists that "they merely describe properties that a univocal concept will have."[42] These

---

40. As outlined above, Henry of Ghent serves as the primary dialogue partner and the chief target of Scotus's thought. Because of this, it is only necessary to briefly highlight some of the more prominent themes of departure and rejection, while presupposing Henry's role throughout. See also Timotheus Barth, "Being, Univocity and Analogy According to Duns Scotus," in *John Duns Scotus: 1265–1965*, ed. John Ryan and Bernardine Bonansea (Washington, DC: Catholic University of America Press, 1965), 256–262.

41. *Ordinatio* I, dist. 3, pars 1, q. 1–2, no. 26 (Vatican 3:18): "Et ne fiat contentio de nomine univocationis univocum conceptum dico, qui ita est unus quod eius unitas sufficit ad contradictionem, affirmando et negando ipsum de eodem; sufficit etiam pro medio syllogistico, ut extrema unita in medio sic uno sine fallacia aequivocationis concludantur inter se uniri." (English: Frank and Wolter, *Duns Scotus: Metaphysician*, 109). For the more recent German translation, see Honnefelder, *Johannes Duns Scotus*, 60.

42. Cross, *Duns Scotus*, 37. This is in direct response to the criticism raised by Janice Thomas in her "Univocity and Understanding God's Nature," in *The Philosophical Assessment of Theology: Essays in Honor of Fredrick C. Copleston*, ed. Gerad Hughes (Washington, DC: Georgetown University Press, 1987), 85–100.

---

features are necessary for a univocal concept, but do not necessarily distinguish a univocal concept from an equivocal or analogous one.

It is also important to recall that this is a purely logical exercise, one that deals primarily with concepts in terms of a semantic argument arising from epistemological concerns. In his argumentation, Scotus is acting as a logician and not a metaphysician or natural philosopher (which is one error among others that misguides the Radical Orthodoxy reading of Scotus's work). Univocity, like analogy, has to do with concepts and terms. In this way, Scotus sees the reduction of analogy to equivocation as inescapable without univocity. As Cyril Shircel masterfully puts it,

> To sum up his entire doctrine—as a logician—the subtle doctor concludes that there are some analogous terms which signify many things, and others, again, which signify some common *ratio* which is found variously in various things. Thus *being* designates many things: it designates *being* which is substance and *being* which is accident. And even though in reality *beings* as accident have a relation to substance, yet on part of the signifying term there is no such relation. Hence all such analogies must be reduced to the first mode of equivocation. On the other hand, some analogous terms designate a common *ratio* which is found variously in various things. Thus *healthy* designates a proportion: in animal that proportion is found as in its subject; in pulse it is found as in a sign; and in the diet it is found as conserving that proportion of health. Thus all these analogies are to be reduced to univocation since they designate primarily something in common.[43]

A univocal concept, Scotus asserts, is necessary for syllogistic reasoning. At the heart of Scotus's concern is the validity and veracity of truth claims, particularly those regarding the faith and God. Richard Cross explains this in the following way: "The idea is that, for any concept φ, if we have ground for thinking that '*x* realizes φ'

43. Shircel, *The Univocity of the Concept of Being in the Philosophy of John Duns Scotus* (Washington, DC: Catholic University of America Press, 1942), 28–29.

and 'it is not the case that x realizes φ' are contradictories, then φ is univocal; for any concept ψ, if we have ground for thinking that ψ is the sense of a syllogistic middle term, then ψ is univocal."[44]

Scotus will go on to prove that this understanding of univocation is legitimate through a two-premise argument. The first, or major, premise is that one cannot be both certain and doubtful of the same concept. Therefore, there must be two concepts so related: one about which one is certain that is different from other concepts about which one is doubtful.[45] The second, or minor, premise is influenced by ancient philosophical sources (pre-Socratic thinking) that support the subsequent claim that the first principle was always held to be a being, but what kind was debated. This part of the argument suggests that we can be sure that God is a being, but doubt (like the ancients) whether God is *this* or *that* type of being, infinite or finite, and so on. Scotus claims that this shows that (the concept) *being* is different from (the concepts) *infinite* or *finite*, *this* or *that*, thereby demonstrating being to be a univocal concept because it is predicated of both God and the type.[46] The question that Scotus now addresses is what type of concept should we consider as primary in its predication of both God and creatures.

---

44. Cross, *The Medieval Christian Philosophers*, 174.

45. *Ordinatio* I, dist. 3, pars 1, q. 1–2, no. 27 (Vatican 3:18): "Primo sic: omnis intellectus, certus de uno conceptu et dubius de diversis, habet conceptum de quo est certus alium a conceptibus de quibus est dubius; subiectum includit praedicatum."

46. *Ordinatio* I, dist. 3, pars 1, q. 1–2, no. 27 (Vatican 3:18): "Sed intellectus viatoris potest esse certus de Deo quod sit ens, dubitando de ente finito vel infinito, creato vel increato; ergo conceptus entis de Deo est alius a conceptu isto et illo, et ita neuter ex se et in utroque illorum includitur; igitur univocus."

Concerning *Ordinatio* I, dist. 3, pars 1, q. 1–2, no. 27, Honnefelder writes, "Dieses im Blick auf Heinrichs Position formulierte Argument läßt sich auch—wie in der *Lectura*—als Argument aus der Erfahrung formulieren, das besagt, daß jeder 'bei sich selbst erfärt' (*experitur in se ipso*), daß er 'Seiendes' erkennen kann, ohne unvermeidlich zu den Begriffen von *diesem* order *jenem* Seienden—wie etwa 'teilhabendes Seiendes' (*ens participatum*) oder 'nichtteilhabendes Seiendes' (*ens imparticipatum*)—abzusteigen" (Honnefelder, *Johannes Duns Scotus*, 61). Also, see Cross, *The Medieval Christian Philosophers*, 174–76.

Transcendental Attributes and the Primacy of Being

Scotus believes that we can know something about God apart from or prior to revelation. The process or science by which we are able to come to such knowledge is what Scotus calls *metaphysics*, which is the study of transcendentals.[47] Defined in relationship to Aristotle's understanding of categories, transcendentals are those predicates that defy classification as categories. Examples would include *unity*, *goodness*, and *being*. Most medieval thinkers adopted the Aristotelian list of transcendentals, but Scotus expanded the list to include also those attributes that "can be instantiated by that being that cannot itself be the subject of categorical attributes."[48] Of all the transcendental attributes, Scotus argues for being as the primary and most basic transcendental.[49] The rest of the transcendentals are, in a

47. See *Reportatio* IA, prol., q.3, no. 218: "Dico ergo ad quaestionem quantum pertinet ad istum articulum quod Deus non est subiectum in metaphysica quia, ut supra probatum est in prima quaestione, de Deo tamquam de primo subiecto tantum potest esse una scientia quae non est metaphysica. . .sed primum ens non eest primo notum ex sensibus, sed oportet prius concipere possibilitatem unionis terminorum, et antequam sciamus hanc compositionem esse possibilem oporet quod aliguod ens demonstretur esse primum. Concedo ergo cum Avicenna quod Deus non est subiectum in metaphysica." This edition of *Reportatio* IA is found in John Duns Scotus, *The Examined Report of the Paris Lecture: Reportatio IA*, ed. Allan Wolter and Oleg Bychkov, 2 vols. (St. Bonaventure, NY: Franciscan Institute, 2004–07), 1:76–77. Hereafter cited as Wolter/Bychkov followed by volume and page numbers.   This is not to suggest that Scotus does not believe that the study of transcendental attributes is somehow directly related to God. On the contrary, he writes in *Reportatio* IA, prol., q.3, no. 251 (Wolter/Bychkov 1:88): "Si autem quaeratur utrum theologia sit de omnibus dico quod sic quantum ad aliquas relations reales quas habent omnia ad Deum et econverso Deus ad omnia secundum relationem rationis, ut sunt relations eminentiae et excedentiae secundum triplicem rationem causae efficientis, formalis et finalis, quae fundantur in Deo secundum rationem ut terminat relations excessus ex parte causae effectus, scilicet exemplati et finiti."

48. Cross, *Duns Scotus*, 148.

49. *Ordinatio* I, dist. 8, pars 1, q. 3, no. 115 (Vatican 4:206–7): "Hoc patet ex alio, quia ens non tantum habet passions simplices convertibiles,—sicut unum, verum et bonum—sed habet aliquas passions ubi opposita distinguuntur contra se, sicut necesse-esse vel possibile, actus vel potentia, et huiusmodi. Sicut autem passions convertibiles sunt trancendentes quia consequuntu ens in quantum no determinatur ad aliquod genus, ita passions disiunctae sunt transcendentes, et utrumque membrum illius disiuncti certum genus: et tamen unum membrum illius disiuncti

way, subsumed in being as coextensive with it. Furthermore, being as a transcendental will qualify as, to borrow Cross's term, a "basic common attribute," which is a subset of the transcendentals.[50] Additionally, there are disjunctive attributes that are coextensive with being that are, as Scotus will go on to describe, "formally distinct."[51]

The study of these transcendentals, particularly being as such, will, Scotus posits, allow us to naturally infer the existence of God. However, unlike his predecessors, Scotus does not hold that God should be the starting point of metaphysics, nor does he hold that God is the subject of it. The subject of metaphysics is being as the primary transcendental.[52]

Transcendental Being and Univocity

Having isolated being as the primary and most basic transcendental, and having outlined Scotus's definition for what univocity means, we now move on to elucidate what Scotus means by the *univocity of being*. To begin, there must be a further clarification made. Allan Wolter cautions us to be attentive to the distinction between a "transcendental term" and a "transcendental concept." He writes,

> By transcendental terms we mean those which are used to designate transcendental concepts, such as being, wisdom, truth and so on. Terms may have more than one meaning; concepts, however, can have but

formaliter est speciale, non conveniens nisi uni enti,—sicut necesse-esse in ista divisione 'necesse-esse vel possibile-esse', et infinitum in ista divisione 'finitum vel infinitum', et sic de aliis. Ita etiam potest sapientia esse transcendens, et quodcumque aliud, quod est sommune Deo et creaturae, licet aliquod tale dicatur de solo Deo, aliquod autem de Deo et aliqua creatura. Non oportet autem transcendens, ut transcendens, dici de quocumque ente nisi sit convertibile cum primo transcendente, silicet ente."

50. Cross, *Duns Scotus*, 38. See also Honnefelder, *Johannes Duns Scotus*, 62–63.

51. See *Ordinatio* I, dist. 8, pars 1, q.3, no. 115 (Vatican 4:207) as quoted above in n49.

52. For more see Allan Wolter, *The Transcendentals and Their Function in the Metaphysics of Duns Scotus* (St. Bonaventure, NY: Franciscan Institute, 1946), esp. 1–12. See also Antonie Vos, *The Philosophy of John Duns Scotus* (Edinburgh: Edinburgh University Press, 2006), 289–92.

one. Terms like "being," "unity," and "truth," can be used (whether arbitrarily or by custom) to indicate a common aspect possessed by several different things or they may go further and signify also the distinctive mode of existence that the perfection in question possesses in the respective subject. In the first case, since the meaning of the term remains the same in predication, we have a common univocal concept. In the second instance, there is no common concept at all but as many distinct, but similar, concepts as there are different subjects. The common term in the latter instance is predicated equivocally (according to the logician) or analogously (according to the metaphysician). The example used by Scotus is that of being. When the term designates everything according to the proper *ratio* of each it is predicated analogously or equivocally. Yet it is possible to prescind from all differentiation and to signify by the term merely a common aspect, in which case both the term and the concept are predicated univocally.[53]

This explanation made by Wolter is an important one. What he helps clarify is the distinction between the term and the concept of being as such, and the relationship between the way we use the term *being* and the implications that arise as a result. The last sentence of this quote sets up what Cross will later call "the vicious abstraction" of univocal being.[54] The predicability of a univocal concept of being will depend, as Scotus argues, on a *concept* (i.e., not a *term*) of being that is common to both God and creatures. In other words, this is a semantic theory, one that hinges on the active reflection of a concept or notion, rather than on something bearing an explicitly or primarily ontological character.

Such a concept must be completely simple. Typically, when we think of being, we think of something that is complex, that is, being as applied properly to *either* God *or* creatures. In other words, whether explicitly qualified as such or not, we think of *finite* or *infinite* being, and so forth. Such a concept of being cannot be predicated

---

53. Wolter, *The Transcendentals and Their Function*, 55–56.
54. Richard Cross, "'Where Angels Fear to Tread': Duns Scotus and Radical Orthodoxy," *Antonianum* 76 (2001): 13.

univocally. Scotus believes that one does not at first have a simple concept of being, but rather one can abstract it from a complex and properly applied concept of being. This is, in some sense, a return to the Scotus's earlier assertion related to the question about natural knowledge of God.[55] Drawing on the Aristotelian worldview, albeit a modified one, the subtle doctor believes that we can know something about God from our sense perceptions, which for both Aristotle and Scotus is the necessary starting point for intellection. There is a threefold process that Scotus outlines for conceptualizing transcendental being in such a way as to be able to predicate it univocally of both God and creatures.[56]

First, one takes the complex notion of being as it is properly applied to creatures.[57] Scotus believes that this concept of a creaturely perfection, being, is actually something that includes both the simple and univocally predicable concept of being together with the requisite qualification that this perfection (i.e., "being") is limited or imperfect.[58] Second, one takes that complex notion of being and "removes" the limited imperfection that is proper to creatures. What remains is the simple concept of being that contains no further qualifications or imperfections (as it would apply to creatures). Third, that simple concept devoid of imperfections is considered to the most

---

55. See *Ordinatio* I, dist. 3, pars 1, q. 1–2, nos. 1–68 (Vatican 3:1–48). It begins with the question, "Circa tertiam distinctionem quaero primo de cognoscibilitate Dei; et quaero primo utrum Deus si naturaliter cognoscibilis ab intellectu viatoris," no. 1 (Vatican 3:1). He will ultimately conclude with, "Dico ergo primo quod non tantum haberi potest conceptus naturaliter in quo quasi per accidens concipitur Deus, puta in aliquo attributo, sed etiam aliquis conceptus in quo per se et quiditative concipiatur Deus," no. 25 (Vatican 3:16–17), followed by his proofs for this position.

56. See Ordinatio I, dist. 3, pars 1, q. 1–2, nos. 39–45 (Vatican 3:26–30). See also Ludger Honnefelder, *Scientia Transcendens: Die formale Bestimmung der Seiendeheit und Realität in der Metaphysik des Mittelalters und der Neuzeit* (Hamburg: Felix Meiner, 1990), 189 and passim.

57. This can apply to any creaturely perfection and not just being. Richard Cross uses Scotus's example of wisdom to illustrate this point. I follow his outline below. See Cross, *Duns Scotus*, 38–39.

58. *Ordinatio* I, dist. 3, pars 1, q. 1–2, no. 39 (Vatican 3:26–27).

perfect degree. Scotus believes that this process yields a complex notion of being (or any other transcendental) that can be said to apply properly to God.[59] Returning again to the epistemological starting point that launched Scotus's inquiry, he uses this process to confirm that every investigation concerning God is rooted in the belief that the human intellect has the same univocal concept (i.e., the completely simple and unqualified perfection), which was obtained from sensory and creaturely perceptions.[60]

It is this fundamental and utterly simple concept of being that Scotus asserts can (and must) be predicated univocally of both God and creatures. As noted above, without such a univocal concept, nothing could be known nor said of God. There is an important and subtle distinction that critics of Scotus's argument for univocity of being often overlook. Scotus writes,

> I say that we can arrive at many concepts proper to God in the sense that they do not apply to creatures. Such are the concepts of all the pure perfections when taken in the highest degree. And the most perfect concept of all, by which we know God most perfectly, as it were, in a descriptive sort of way, is obtained by conceiving all the pure perfections and each in the highest degree.[61]

Scotus is very clear here to note that there are concepts *as such* that are proper to God. Such concepts, he argues, are those pure perfections (simple concepts that are said to be applied univocally of both God and creatures) that are considered in the highest degree. What is important to note here is that Scotus then says that these

---

59. Cross, *Duns Scotus*, 38.
60. *Ordinatio* I, dist. 3, pars 1, q. 1–2, no. 39 (Vatican 3:26–27): "Ergo omnis inquisitio de Deo supponit intellectum habere conceptum eundem, univocum, quem accepit ex creatures."
61. *Ordinatio* I, dist. 3, pars 1, q. 1–2, no. 58 (Vatican 3:40): "Dico quod ad multos conceptus proprios Deo possumus pervenire, qui non convenient creatures,—cuiusmodi sunt conceptus omnium perfectionum simpliciter, in summo. Et perfectissimus conceptus, in quo quasi in quadam descriptione perfectissime cognoscimus Deum, est concipiendo omnes perfections simpliciter et in summo."

concepts, as it were, are obtained and therefore applied properly in a "descriptive" sort of way. In other words, as Wolter will go on to suggest, Scotus here is advocating for an *analogous* relationship between the two complex manifestations of the simple concept of being that is univocally predicable.[62] By this, Scotus means that the concept of being properly applied to God (i.e., *conceptus omnium perfectionum simpliciter in summo*) and the concept of being properly applied to creatures are understood as analogous to one another. Scotus anticipates this relationship early on in his argument (another passage often overlooked by critics) when he writes, "I say that God is conceived *not only in a concept analogous* to the concept of a creature, that is, one which is wholly other than that which is predicated of creatures, but even in some concept univocal to Himself and to a creature."[63] Scotus does not substitute univocity for analogy. On the contrary, he makes the claim that one is not simply limited to analogous predication of the concept of being to God and creatures. In fact, in order to say *anything* about God, one must be able to predicate a concept of being univocally to both God and creatures.

The Formal Distinction and Disjunctive Attributes

To understand the relationship between the fundamentally simple and univocally predicable concept of being and its application to both God and creatures, one must sufficiently consider Scotus's formal distinction. As initially noted above, Scotus asserts that the univocally predicable concept of being, as such, is not proper to either God or creatures. Instead, as Cross describes it, such a concept is merely a

---

62. See Wolter, *The Transcendentals and Their Function*, 40–48.
63. *Ordinatio* I, dist. 3, pars 1, q. 1–2, no. 26 (Vatican 3:18), emphasis added. "Dico quod *non tantum in conceptu analogo* conceptui creaturae concipitur Deus, scilicet qui omnio sit alius ab illo qui de creatura dicitur, sed in conceptu aliquo univoco sibi et creaturae."

vicious abstraction from the complex notion of being that is properly applied to creatures or God. The conceptualization of this transcendental notion of being therefore requires a constitutive quality that distinguishes being as properly applied to God from being as properly applied to creatures, for, as Scotus and nearly all of his critics agree, God and creatures do not *actually* share being in common.[64] Scotus posits an intrinsic attribute or something that is really identical to being, yet *formally distinct* from being, that distinguishes the mode thereby constituting being as properly applied to God (infinite being) or properly applied to creatures (imperfect or finite being). In other words, the degree of perfection is a real property and not just a relational quality, as is asserted by someone like Aquinas.[65]

To understand this proposal of a real property we must first recall that, when dealing with the univocal concept of being, Scotus holds that we abstract this concept from a seemingly complex notion of being that is properly applied to creatures or God. This is not to suggest that the complex notion is in any way *really* complex, that is, a substance to which accidents of modification are applied. Scotus clearly rejects this because, in the case of the concept of being predicated properly to God, it would contradict divine simplicity. Instead of accidental or extrinsic qualification, Scotus believes that this viciously abstracted concept of being (or the absolutely simple or "empty" concept of being) is a concept formally distinct from the really unified (nonseparable) being proper to God or creatures. What this really unified being proper to either God or creatures also contains is a formally distinct modal disjunctive attribute.[66]

---

64. See *Ordinatio* I, dist. 8, pars 1, q. 3, no. 139 (Vatican 4:223) and *Ordinatio* I, dist. 8, pars 1, q. 3, no. 153 (Vatican 4:228). Cross does make a nuanced qualification suggesting that Scotus does allow for some unexplained commonality between God and creatures, something which the subtle doctor does not define. See Cross, *Duns Scotus*, 39.

65. See *Quaestiones Quodlibetales* 5, no. 3 (Vivés 12:118).

Cross provides a helpful explanation for what Scotus means when referring to these attributes. Cross writes, "A degree of a perfection belongs to that set of properties labeled 'intrinsic modes.' Such properties are *modes* of some attribute in the sense that they determine the *way* in which that attribute is instantiated."[67] Scotus believes that such modes are intrinsic to the attribute because without the particular mode, the said attribute could never be instantiated. The temptation here is to equate the univocal concept of being with a genus under which both God and creatures could fall and therefore share some sort of common reality. As such, God and creatures would each merely be a species of the genus *being*, resulting in a clearly erroneous position. As Shircel notes, for Scotus, "in no way can God be considered to fall within a genus or category."[68] While Scotus begins *Ordinatio* I, dist. 8, pars 1, q. 3, with the phrase "It seems that God is in a genus," he moves to refute that possibility.[69] This is worth noting, for it appears to be a confusing element for some, which results in a superficial reading of the text. Scotus, perhaps to the surprise of contemporary theologians who have suggested the subtle doctor says the opposite, actually anticipates this critiques and potential misreading of his work. In turn, he offers a preemptive response. The solution, disjunctive attributes, is Scotus's answer to the long-standing problem with the possibility of univocity. It emerges from Scotus's exploration of divine simplicity.[70] Scotus writes,

> It seems that [God is in a genus], because God is formally a being. Being, however, signifies a concept that can be said of God quidditatively (*in quid*). This concept of being is not proper to God, but common to

66. *Ordinatio* I, dist. 2, pars 2, q. 1–4, no. 400 (Vatican 2:355).
67. Cross, *Duns Scotus*, 42. Cross seems to base this summary on Scotus's comments in *Quaestiones Quodlibetales* 5, no. 3 (Vivés 12:118).
68. Shircel, *The Univocity of the Concept of Being in the Philosophy of John Duns Scotus*, 140.
69. For more see Dumont, "Henry of Ghent and Duns Scotus," 316–17.
70. See *Ordinatio* I, dist. 8, pars 1, q. 3, nos. 39–156 (Vatican 4:169–230).

God and creatures, as was said in distinction 3. Therefore, in order for this common concept to become proper it must be determined by some determining concept. That determining concept is related to the concept of being just as a qualitative concept (*quale*) to a quidditative concept (*quid*), and consequently as the concept of a *differentia* to a genus.[71]

Scotus here is making an important move with the admission that the common (univocal) concept of *being* applies to God *in quid* and not just *in quale*. In some sense, this is all presented analogously ("just as"), but there is also a sense in which there is a direct relationship between the common (univocal) concept of being and the mode of being that is proper to God. This common (univocal) concept of being is determined by the disjunctive attributes, such as *infinite/finite*, that result in *being* that is proper to God or creatures, respectively. It is significant that such a notion of being applies to God *quidditatively*, because it is a statement reflecting the "whatness" of God, and not just some accidental (*quale*) characteristic or attribute. This notion of being as applied properly only to God is not divisible or separable, but absolutely simple. At the same time, this disjunctive attribute, *infinitude*, is intrinsically part of and *really* identical to God's essence (*substantia*).

This seems to be impossible, but Scotus introduces perhaps his most original metaphysical contribution to circumvent the apparent problem. Scotus's solution is the formal distinction. Something is formally distinct from, while at the same time really identical or united with, the same thing in an inseparable manner.[72] Put another

---

71. *Ordinatio* I, dist. 8, pars 1, q. 3, no. 39 (Vatican 4:169): "Quod sic: Quia Deus formaliter est ens, ens autem dicit conceptum dictum de Deo in 'quid'—et iste conceptus non est proprius Deo, sed communis sibi et creaturae, sicut dictum est distinctione 3; ergo oportet quod ad hoc quod fiat proprius, quod determinetur per aliquem conceptum determinantem; ille 'determinans' se habet ad conceptum entis sicut conceptus 'qualis' ad conceptum 'quid,' et per consequens ut conceptus differentiae ad conceptum generis." (English translation: Dumont, "Henry of Ghent and Duns Scotus," 315–16).

way, we can imagine something that is an integrated whole divided into distinct parts. Such an exercise results in a mental image of divisibility or consideration of something seemingly integral yet conceivably separate. In the case of something formally distinct, the ability to consider a *particular* dimension of the integrated whole is a feature that is a priori to the mental consideration, resulting, as it were, in the discovery of an extramental distinction. However, because this distinction is such that it is inseparable from the essence (*substantia*) to which it belongs, this attribute is *really identical* with the essence (*substantia*), while at the same time *formally distinct* from it. Such is the case with the modal disjunctive attributes within the *suppositum* that is being properly applied to either God or creatures. It is not a matter of some accidental or extrinsic application of an attribute, but the discovery of an already present, constitutive, intrinsic, formally distinct disjunctive attribute. In the case of God, God has formally distinct properties that can be termed "divine attributes," each of which is *formally distinct* from the divine essence, yet is intrinsic to that essence in such a way as to maintain absolute divine simplicity.[73]

72. See *Ordinatio* I, dist. 8, pars 2, q. 4, no. 193 (Vatican 4:261–62): "Hoc declaro, quia 'includere formaliter' est includere aliquid in ratione sua essentiali, ita quod si definitio includentis assignaretur, inclusum esset definitio vel pars definitionis; sicut autem definitio bonitatis in communi non habet in se sapientiam, ita nec infinita infinitam: est igitur aliqua non-identitas formalis sapientiae et bonitatis, in quantum earum essent distinctae definitions, si essent definibiles. Definitio autem non tantum indicat rationem causatam ab intellectu, sed quiditatem rei: est ergo non-identitas formalis ex parte rei, et intelligo sic, quod intellectus componens istam 'sapientia non est formaliter bonitas,' non causat actu suo collativo veritatem huius compositionis, sed in obiecto invenit extrema, ex quorum compositione fit actus verus."
For more on this subject see Alan Wolter, "The Formal Distinction," in *The Philosophical Theology of John Duns Scotus*, ed. Marilyn McCord Adams (Ithaca: Cornell University Press, 1990), 27–41; and Maurice Grajewski, *The Formal Distinction of Duns Scotus: A Study in Metaphysics* (Washington, DC: Catholic University of America Press, 1944).
73. *Ordinatio* I, dist. 8, pars 1, q. 3, no 148 (Vatican 4:226).

Some Metaphysical Implications of Univocity

While the matter of the metaphysical or ontological implications of Scotus's semantic theory of a univocally predicable *concept* of being are not explicitly drawn out in the subtle doctor's work, it is worth briefly mentioning some such aspects here. This is especially important given the recent trend, inaugurated by the Radical Orthodoxy movement and carried on in the proliferation of their Scotus Story, that relates a narrative that is contrary to the subtle doctor's own work in this respect. Scotus's starting point, as noted clearly above, was epistemological. His elucidation of the question at hand, concerning the possibility of natural knowledge of God, was carried out in a rigorously logical fashion. In the process, Scotus asserts that one can conceive of a concept of being that can be predicated of both God and creatures, not just analogously, but univocally. In fact, to make any validly analogous claim about God, it must be grounded in something univocal or risk the fallacy of equivocity. This univocal concept of being is a vicious abstraction or wholly empty concept that is neither proper to God nor creatures. A concept proper to God or creatures is one in which the univocal concept of being is in some sense modified by an intrinsic disjunctive attribute that is formally distinct from the univocal concept of being yet is also really identical with it.

The assertion of a univocally predicable concept of being is, for Scotus, the condition of the possibility for any theology. All language about God and, therefore, any natural or revealed statements relating to the divine essence necessarily presupposes the univocal predication of some concept. Analogy, Scotus asserts, is simply equivocation without an a priori univocally predicable concept. Again, it is not that Scotus denies the importance and value of analogous language to distinguish between God and creatures, but he is deeply concerned about the validity of such statements in light of a seemingly contradictory claim that *only* analogy is possible.

So while the univocity of being refers primarily and explicitly to the conceptual realm, offering a system of intellection and classification roughly analogous to genera, there are in fact certain metaphysical or ontological implications that naturally arise. One such implication is the possibility of relationality. While the Thomistic metaphysical system posits the foundation of the divine-creaturely relationship as one of participation in or suspension from the divine essence (i.e., *esse* as proper only to God), it lacks an overt commonality or cardinal focus that seems to prohibit any true knowledge of or discourse about God. The apparent suspension of theology is indeed problematic. More specifically, to deny the possibility of univocity of being is to deny natural theology. Without a concept that is abstractable from creation in this world, one is not able to garner terms or concepts of God apart from revelation. Additionally, such a denial presents the problem of exclusive apophaticism and theologically discursive docetism. Apart from revelation, we have no ability to know or say anything about God. Revealed knowledge of God then becomes something that appears without a correlative relationship to reality as such. Univocity, on the other hand, provides both the condition of the possibility for kataphatic theology, while additionally grounding revealed truth in conceptual reality.

Another significant implication arising from univocity is the principle of individuation that Scotus goes on to develop in light of this concept of being. The term commonly used to describe Scotus's theory is *haecceitas* (literally "this-ness"), which is, like our understanding of divine attributes, a formally distinct character of being that is really identical to the same univocal concept. It is what makes a thing (*res*) *this* (*haec*) thing and not *that* thing. Additionally,

Scotus's principle of individuation, *haecceitas*, naturally leads one to consider the relationship between God and creatures in yet another light.[74] The incommunicability and unrepeatability of a given *haecceitas* points to the manifold truth that each instance of creation, or every thing (*res*) that exists, is individually and freely willed into existence by God. Because of the intrinsic and really identical nature of *haecceitas* to the univocal concept of being, each instantiation of creation finds its identity, uniqueness, incommunicability, and intrinsic value in its very existence, not from some accidental or extrinsic quality or attribute.

Members of the Radical Orthodoxy movement, especially John Milbank and Catherine Pickstock, have misunderstood Scotus's univocity of being as essentially ontological or metaphysical.[75] While that interpretation does injustice to the integrity of Scotus's straightforwardly semantic and logical position, there is a shadow of truth latently present in such a misinterpretation. That is, there is indeed metaphysical or ontological significance to a semantic or logical theory of univocity. However, such implications have less to do with *existence* as such and more to do with *relationality*. Scotus's theory of the univocal concept of being does not say anything about the existence of God or creatures any more than we can say (by way of analogy) a genus says anything about a species. Instead, we might best understand Scotus's approach to the univocity of being as anticipating ontological inquiry or metaphysical explication, setting the stage as the foundation and condition for such investigation. To uphold a position that maintains a univocally concept of being that is predicable of both God and creatures says little *in se*, but the system

---

74. For more on this concept in terms of theological anthropology, see Daniel Horan, "Beyond Essentialism and Complementarity: Toward a Theological Anthropology Rooted in *Haecceitas*," *Theological Studies* 75 (March 2014): 94–117.

75. For example see John Milbank, *Theology and Social Theory: Beyond Secular Reason,* 2nd ed. (Oxford: Blackwell, 2006), 302–303.

itself is invaluable when it comes to the development of a theology that might continue to be relevant today.

Conclusion: Reclaiming Scotus

The Possibility of a Postmodern Theology

Radical Orthodox theologians have affirmed the place of narrative in contemporary theological reflection and discourse, along with its significance for accurately conceptualizing the development of the history of theology. Theology, that is *theo-logos*, cannot be separated from the telling of stories, which is an axiom that I believe has been reaffirmed in the preceding chapters, and remains a principle of Radical Orthodoxy to which I am deeply sympathetic. However, there is a problem here. It is not whether or not one engages in a narrative mode to explore and express deeper insights about God and creation, but the problem concerns which stories we tell, how we construct them, and how we express them. The master story or theological metanarrative Radical Orthodoxy tells occupies far too large an intellectual geography to traverse in one small study such as this. However, the Scotus Story, that subnarrative of the Radical Orthodoxy movement, is capable of substantive exploration here. The purpose of this book has been to examine and assess just an aspect of the broader story, a particular narrative that forms one of the foundational legs upon which the larger Radical Orthodoxy master story stands.

As it has become clear by now, it is my contention that Radical Orthodoxy theologians simply have gotten Scotus wrong. Their story is inaccurate and misleading. Whether or not the reception of Scotus's work in the decades following his death led to the emergence of what is now called "modernity" or "the secular" continues to be a debated thesis. However, it has been my intention in the preceding pages, with the assistance of those whose own lifelong work has focused on Scotus and his thought, to highlight just how Scotus's life work is not so easily debatable. Much of what Radical Orthodox theologians assign to Scotus as problematic and varying from the otherwise pristine tradition of Thomas Aquinas cannot actually be found in his work. Instead, a predetermined narrative has been scripted and applied to the subtle doctor in a manner most anachronistic and troublesome to those who see in Scotus's thought the seeds of insight and theological fecundity. And I am, of course, one such person.

I believe another story needs to be told about Scotus, one that neither presumes that modernity is inherently problematic, nor that Scotus is to blame for inaugurating all that will result in the ills of today. Such a story is one that takes Scotus in context and carefully examines what he, his interlocutors, and his followers *actually* say rather than one that treats the medieval Franciscan as a theological puppet, conveniently serving the interests of those contemporary thinkers who need a scapegoat and a simple genealogical starting point for the emergence of modernity. It is my hope that this book has offered a worthwhile prolegomenon to this sort of restorative enterprise. No theologian or philosopher is undeserving of critical engagement, and this is true about Scotus too. Unlike the way that Milbank, Pickstock, and others have discussed Aquinas as if he were the theological panacea to our (post)modern sickness, few Scotists would be so bold as to suggest the subtle doctor has all the answers.

Instead, I believe that Scotus offers contemporary theologians resources for responding to the signs of our times and developing a postmodern theology. Scotus's arguments for supralapsarian Christology, his creative approach to the principle of individuation, his original development of the formal distinction, his views on politics, private property, the Eucharist, and the sacrament of marriage, among other topics, remain subjects in need of further study and contemporary engagement.[1]

The significance of a return to the Scotus Story narrative and the theological and philosophical positions contained therein cannot be overstated. While the importance of the Radical Orthodoxy movement's presentation of Scotus's doctrine of univocity and the implications posited by Milbank, Pickstock, and others in light of that interpretation might at first seem sectarian, the influence of this narrative, as we saw briefly in chapter 2, has been tremendous. The "trickle-down effect" of the Radical Orthodoxy presentation of Scotus has led to popular representations of the Scotus Story that continue to simulate credibility and academic veracity by its repetition. To put it simply, the more people repeat the story and the more hegemonic it becomes, the harder it is to convince others that it is untrue. Fortunately, repeating something does not magically make something true when it isn't, but it can be difficult to speak the truth or challenge the ubiquitous Scotus Story or present an alternative narrative when so many have blindly repeated what has been handed on to them about the subtle doctor. This last comment might be seen as an exaggeration but, as I hoped to have demonstrated in the early

1. Some examples from my own work include Daniel Horan, "Beyond Essentialism and Complementarity: Toward a Theological Anthropology rooted in *Haecceitas*," *Theological Studies* 75 (2014): 94–117.; Horan, "How Original Was Scotus on the Incarnation? Reconsidering the History of the Absolute Predestination of Christ in Light of Robert Grosseteste," *The Heythrop Journal* 52 (2011): 374–91; and Horan, "Thomas Merton the 'Dunce': Identity, Incarnation, and the Not-So-Subtle Influence of John Duns Scotus," *Cistercian Studies Quarterly* 47 (2012): 149–75.

chapters of this book, those who subsequently adopt and adapt the Radical Orthodoxy Scotus Story do so in a largely uncritical manner. Almost no one returns to the primary sources of Scotus, and few consult additional or new secondary sources to support the narrative inherited from the Radical Orthodoxy movement and subsequently represented. Instead, the Scotus Story has become something of an anomalously self-sufficient theory, one that by either the weight of Radical Orthodoxy's influence or the force of its creators has escaped the usual critical view of the academy, save a few Scotists like Richard Cross, Thomas Williams, and Mary Beth Ingham.

The self-referential justification of the Scotus Story has perhaps reached a new level in John Milbank's recent book, *Beyond Secular Order: The Representation of Being and the Representation of the People*. Presented as "a successor volume to *Theology and Social Theory*," this text is the first major project Milbank has published that features a preoccupation with the Scotus Story on par with his work decades earlier.[2] The most fascinating dimension of this book, the arguments about political theory notwithstanding, is that the entire first section is an elaborate representation of the Scotus Story that acknowledges absolutely *none* of the critiques that Scotus scholars have leveled against Milbank's reading of Scotus since *Theology and Social Theory* was published in 1990. Nearly a quarter-century later, little has changed about the Radical Orthodoxy Scotus Story. What is new, however, are the sources Milbank uses to supplement his earlier interpretation. While he does include more citations ostensibly from Scotus's work,[3] the additional references cited throughout

2. Milbank, *Beyond Secular Order: The Representation of Being and the Representation of the People* (Oxford: Wiley-Blackwell, 2014), 1.

3. Although, it must be stated, that his citations of Scotus throughout the first section (1–113) are odd and inconsistent. For example, on the same page Milbank cites in two sequential footnotes what should be the same text, but one that appears under two alternative titles and according to two different citation formats. The first reads, "Duns Scotus, *Opus Oxoniense* IV, dist. 1 q. 1 para. [20]." The second reads, "Duns Scotus, *Ordinatio* I, dist. 32 §23" (Milbank, *Beyond Secular*

concerning Scotus consist primarily of those works by theologians and philosophers presented in chapters 1 and 2 of this book, including Catherine Pickstock, Conor Cunningham, Charles Taylor, Adrian Pabst, and others. What is troubling about this presentation is the overtly circular approach Milbank takes to reinscribing the Scotus Story, drawing heavily from those who support or complement his views on Scotus and the subtle doctor's work, but each of whom had first acquired this Radical Orthodoxy subnarrative from Milbank himself. This latest presentation of the Scotus Story seems to indicate that this particular Radical Orthodoxy narrative is not going away anytime soon, at least if Milbank and his followers have anything to say about it.

In closing, several key points are worth reiterating to further emphasize the meaning and purpose of the subtle doctor's proposition concerning the univocal concept of being. First and foremost, one must always recall the historical and intellectual context within which Scotus was working.[4] It was Henry of Ghent and not Thomas Aquinas to whom Scotus was primarily concerned about responding, a fact too often overlooked in contemporary discussions of analogy and univocity. Second, Scotus does not reject analogy as such, but instead convincingly argues from the vantage point of a logician that a univocal concept of some sort is axiomatically necessary to maintain any analogical discourse. Third, Scotus's starting point is not ontological, but epistemological and semantic. His primary concern is the correlative project that arises from the issue of natural knowledge of God, not establishing or "flattening" an ontological

---

Order, 31nn29–30). Similar inconsistencies and confusing allusions to the works of Scotus as made throughout. It is difficult to know why these references appear this way, but it does make it challenging—if not impossible—to respond to specious interpretations of texts that cannot be easily found. Such citation inconsistencies raise questions about the authenticity of the sourcing throughout *Beyond Secular Order*.

4. This also something argued for in Fergus Kerr, "Why Medievalists Should Talk to Theologians," *New Blackfriars* 80 (2007): 369–75.

order that would place God and creatures under some genus *being*. Finally, the doctrine of univocity is only comprehensible within the context of Scotus's entire system, which takes for granted the formal distinction and Scotus's unique principle of individuation, among other things. To lose sight of the integrated whole of the subtle doctor's project, or to misunderstand any element of this incredibly nuanced system, will inevitably result in a misreading or inaccurate interpretation.

There are indeed metaphysical and other theological implications that arise from a close reading of Scotus's semantic argument that originates from epistemology. However, they are not as disastrous as Radical Orthodoxy would have us believe. For political reasons, in both ecclesiastical and academic terms, Scotus's work has not been appropriated in the same fashion as his medieval contemporaries. At a time in history marked by skepticism about theology and, as Milbank and others emphasize, when the natural and social sciences sovereignly reign within society and the academy, there is an opportunity, if not need, to reconceptualize dogmatic and doctrinal faith claims in a new and intelligible fashion. In subfields ranging from Christology to pastoral theology, there remains ample room for contemporary reappropriation of and engagement with Scotus's insights. Contrary to the position of Radical Orthodoxy theologians, Scotus is not the protomodern antagonist that threatens theology from within, but he is instead an innovative medieval thinker who offers today's church and world a set of philosophical and theological resources, hitherto underutilized, to recast the Christian faith in a relevant, orthodox, and comprehensive manner.

Bibliography

Aertsen, Jan, Kent Emery and Adrian Speer. *Nach der Verurteilung von 1277: Philosophie und Theologie an der Universität von Paris im letzen Viertel des 13. Jahrhunderts*. Studien und Texte. Berlin: Walter de Gruyter, 2000.

Allen, Charles. "Radical Orthodoxy in the Parish or, Postmodern Critical Augustinianism for Dummies." *Encounter* 64 (2003): 219–29.

Alliez, Éric. *Capital Times: Tales from the Conquest of Time*. Translated by Georges Van Den Abbeele. Minneapolis: University of Minnesota Press, 1996.

Alluntis, Felix. "Demonstrability and Demonstration of the Existence of God." In *John Duns Scotus: 1265–1965*, edited by John Ryan and Bernardine Bonansea, 133–70. Washington, DC: Catholic University of America Press, 1965.

Andonegui, Javier. "Escoto en el Punto De Mira." *Antonianum* 76 (2001): 145–91.

Aquinas, Thomas. *Summa Theologica*. Translation by Fathers of the English Dominican Province. 5 volumes. New York: Benzinger Brothers, 1948.

Aristotle. *The Metaphysics*. Translated and edited by Hugh Lawson-Tancred. New York: Penguin, 2009.

Armstrong, Karen. *The Case for God*. New York: Knopf, 2009.

Ashford, Bruce. "Wittgenstein's Theologians? A Survey of Ludwig Wittgenstein's Impact on Theology." *Journal of the Evangelical Theological Society* 50 (2007): 357–75.

Barth, Timotheus. "Being, Univocity, and Analogy According to Duns Scotus." In *John Duns Scotus: 1265–1965*, edited by John Ryan and Bernardine Bonansea, 210–262. Washington, DC: Catholic University of America Press, 1965.

Barron, Robert. *The Priority of Christ: Towards a Postliberal Catholicism*. Grand Rapids: Brazos, 2007.

Bell, Daniel. *Liberation Theology after The End of History: The Refusal to Cease Suffering*. London: Routledge, 2001.

Best, Steven and Douglas Kellner. *The Postmodern Turn*. New York: Guilford, 1997.

Blackburn, Simon. *Oxford Dictionary of Philosophy*. New York: Oxford University Press, 2005.

Blond, Philip, ed. *Post-Secular Philosophy: Between Philosophy and Theology*. London: Routledge, 1998.

Bonansea, B. M. *Man and His Approach to God in John Duns Scotus*. Lanham: University Press of America, 1983.

Boulnois, Olivier. *Duns Scot: Sur la connaissance de Dieu et l'univocité de l'étant*. Paris: P.U.F., 1990.

———. *Etre et representation: Une Genealogie de la Métaphysique Moderne a l'époque de Duns Scot*. Paris: P.U.F., 1999.

———. "Quand commence l'ontothéologie? Aristote, Thomas d'Aquin et Duns Scot." *Revue Thomiste* 95 (1995): 84–108.

Bowlin, John. "Parts, Wholes, and Opposites: John Milbank as Geisteshistoriker." *Journal of Religious Ethics* 32 (2004): 257–69.

Boyle, Nicholas. *Who Are We Now? Christian Humanism and the Global Market from Hegel to Heaney*. Notre Dame: University of Notre Dame Press, 1998.

Brown, Jerome V. "Duns Scotus on Henry of Ghent's Arguments for Divine Illumination: The Statement of the Case." *Vivarium* 14 (1976): 94–113.

Brown, Stephen F. "Avicenna and the Unity of the Concept of Being: The Interpretation of Henry of Ghent, Duns Scotus, Gerard of Bologna, and Peter Aureoli." *Franciscan Studies* 25 (1965): 117–50.

————— "The Intellectual Context of Later Medieval Philosophy: Universities, Aristotle, Arts, Theology." In *Medieval Philosophy*, edited by John Marenbon, 188–203. London: Routledge, 2004.

———. "Peter of Candia's Hundred-Year 'History' of the Theologian's Role." *Medieval Philosophy and Theology* 1 (1991): 156–90.

Burrell, David. "Analogy and Philosophical Language." PhD diss, Yale University, 1973.

———. *Aquinas: God and Action.* Notre Dame: University of Notre Dame Press, 1979.

———. *Knowing the Unknowable God: Ibn-Sina, Maimonides, Aquinas.* Notre Dame: University of Notre Dame Press, 1986.

Caputo, John. *Deconstruction in a Nutshell: A Conversation with Jacques Derrida.* New York: Fordham University Press, 1997.

———. *The Prayers and Tears of Jacques Derrida.* Bloomington: Indiana University Press, 1997.

———. *The Weakness of God: A Theology of the Event.* Bloomington: Indiana University Press, 2006.

———. *What Would Jesus Deconstruct? The Good News of Postmodernism for the Church.* Grand Rapids: Baker Academic, 2007.

Caputo, John, Mark Dooley, and Michael Scanlon, eds. *Questioning God.* Bloomington: Indiana University Press, 2001.

Caputo, John and Michael Scanlon, eds. *God, The Gift and Postmodernism.* Bloomington: Indiana University Press, 1999.

Clarke, W. Norris. *Explorations in Metaphysics: Being, God and Person.* Notre Dame: University of Notre Dame Press, 1994.

Courtine, J. F. *Suarez et le systéme de la métaphysique.* Paris: P.U.F., 1990.

Cox, Harvey. *The Secular City.* London: SCM Press, 1967.

Cross, Richard. *Duns Scotus.* New York: Oxford University Press, 1999.

———. *The Medieval Christian Philosophers: An Introduction.* New York: I. B. Tauris, 2013.

———. *The Metaphysics of the Incarnation: From Aquinas to Scotus.* New York: Oxford University Press, 2002.

———. "Scotus and Suárez at the Origins of Modernity." In Hankey and Hedley, *Deconstructing Radical Orthodoxy: Postmodern Theology, Rhetoric and Truth*, 65–80.

———. "'Where Angels Fear to Tread': Duns Scotus and Radical Orthodoxy." *Antonianum*76 (2001): 7–41.

Cunningham, Conor. "The Difference *of* Theology and Some Philosophies of Nothing." *Modern Theology* 17 (2001): 289–312.

———. *Genealogy of Nihilism: Philosophies of Nothing and the Difference of Theology.* London: Routledge, 2002.

———. "Philosophies of Nothing: Reconstructing Metaphysics." PhD diss, University of Cambridge, 2000.

De Saint-Maurice, Bérard. *John Duns Scotus: A Teacher for Our Times.* St. Bonaventure, NY: Franciscan Institute, 1955.

DeHart, Paul. *Aquinas and Radical Orthodoxy: A Critical Inquiry.* London: Routledge, 2012.

Deleuze, Gilles. *Difference & Repetition.* Translated by Paul Patton. New York: Columbia University Press, 1994.

Derrida, Jacques. *Margins of Philosophy.* Translated by Alan Bass. Chicago: University of Chicago Press, 1982.

———. *Of Grammatology.* Translated by Gayatri Chakravorty Spivak. Baltimore: Johns Hopkins University Press, 1997.

———. *Writing and Difference.* Translated by Alan Bass. Chicago: University of Chicago Press, 1980.

Doak, Mary. "The Politics of Radical Orthodoxy: A Catholic Critique." *Theological Studies* 68 (2007): 368–93.

Dumont, Stephen. "Henry of Ghent and Duns Scotus." In *Medieval Philosophy*, edited by John Marenbon, 291–328. London: Routledge, 2004.

Duns Scotus, John. *Opera Omnia*. Edited by L. Vivés. 26 volumes. Paris: 1891–95. (Revised Luke Wadding edition).

———. *Opera Omnia: Studio et Cura Commissionis Scotisticae ad fidem codicum edita*. Edited by Carlo Balíc et al. 21 volumes. Vatican City: Typis Polyglottis Vaticanis, 1950–.

———. *Opera Philosophica*. Edited by Girard Etzkorn, Romuald Green, and Timothy Noone. 5 volumes. St. Bonaventure, NY: Franciscan Institute, 1997–2006.

———. *Philosophical Writings*. Edited and translated by Allan Wolter. Indianapolis: Hackett, 1987.

———. *Quaestiones Quodlibetales*. Edited and translated by Allan Wolter and Felix Alluntis. Princeton: Princeton University Press, 1975.

———. *Reportatio IA*. Edited and translated by Allan Wolter and Oleg Bychkov. 2 volumes. St. Bonaventure, NY: Franciscan Institute, 2005–08.

Dupré, Louis. *Passage to Modernity: An Essay in the Hermeneutics of Nature and Culture*. New Haven: Yale University Press, 1993.

Eagleton, Terry. *The Event of Literature*. New Haven: Yale University Press, 2012.

———. *The Illusions of Postmodernism*. Oxford: Blackwell, 1996.

Exposito, C. *Introduzione a Suarez: Meditazioni metafische*. Milan: Rusioni, 1996.

Fiorenza, Francis Schüssler. "The New Theology and Transcendental Thomism." In *Modern Christian Thought: The Twentieth Century* edited by James Livingston and Francis Schüssler Firoenza, 197–232. 2nd ed. Minneapolis: Fortress Press, 2006.

Ford, David. "Radical Orthodoxy and the Future of British Theology." *Scottish Journal of Theology* 54 (2001): 385–404.

Frank, William and Allan Wolter. *Duns Scotus: Metaphysician*. Indiana: Purdue University Press, 1995.

Funkenstein, Amos. *Theology and the Scientific Imagination*. Princeton: Princeton University Press, 1989.

Gadamer, Hans-Georg. *Truth and Method*. Translated by Joel Weinsheimer. New York: Continuum, 1975.

George, Francis Cardinal. *The Difference God Makes: A Catholic Vision of Faith, Communion, and Culture*. New York: Herder and Herder, 2009.

Ghent, Henry of. *Quodlibeta Magistri Genrici Goethals a Gandavo Doctoris Solemnis*. Edited by I. Badius. 2 Volumes. Louivain: Bibliothéque SJ, 1961.

———. *Summae quaestionum ordinariarum*. Edited by Stephen Brown. St. Bonaventure, NY: Franciscan Institute, 1953.

Gibson, Arthur. *Metaphysics and Transcendence*. London: Routledge, 2003.

Gillespie, Michael Allen. *The Theological Origins of Modernity*. Chicago: Chicago University Press, 2008.

Gilson, Etienne. *Études sur le role de la pensée médiévale dans la formation du systéme Cartésien*. Paris: Vrin, 1930.

———. *Jean Duns Scot*. Paris: Vrin, 1952.

———. "Les seize premiers Theoremata et la pensée de Duns Scot." *Archives d'histoire doctrinale et litteraire de Moyen Age* 12–13 (1937–38): 5–86.

Grajewski, Maurice. *The Formal Distinction of Duns Scotus: A Study in Metaphysics*. Washington, DC: Catholic University of America Press, 1944.

Grant, Edward. *God & Reason in the Middle Ages*. New York: Cambridge University Press, 2001.

Gregory, Brad. *The Unintended Reformation: How a Religious Revolution Secularized Society*. Cambridge: Harvard University Press, 2012.

Griffiths, Paul. "Either/Or: A Review of *The Monstrosity of Christ.*" *Commonweal* 136 (June 19, 2009): 22–24.

Guarino, Thomas. *Foundations of Systematic Theology.* New York: T & T Clark, 2005.

Haldane, John. "Analytical Thomism: A Prefatory Note." *The Monist* 80 (1997): 485–86.

Hall, Alexander W. "Confused Univocity?" *Proceedings of the Society for Medieval Logic and Metaphysics* 7 (2007): 18–31.

———. *Thomas Aquinas and John Duns Scotus: Natural Theology in the High Middle Ages.* London: Continuum, 2007.

Hankey, Wayne. "Radical Orthodoxy's *Poiēsis:* Ideological Historiography and Anti-Modern Polemic." *American Catholic Philosophical Quarterly* 80 (2006): 1–21.

Hankey, Wayne and Douglas Hedley, eds. *Deconstructing Radical Orthodoxy: Postmodern Theology, Rhetoric and Truth.* Burlington: Ashgate, 2005.

Harris, C. R. S. *Duns Scotus: The Philosophical Doctrines of Duns Scotus.* 2 volumes. Oxford: Clarendon, 1927.

Hauerwas, Stanley. *A Better Hope: Resources for a Church Confronting Capitalism, Democracy, and Postmodernity.* Grand Rapids: Brazos, 2000.

———. *A Community of Character: Toward a Constructive Christian Social Ethics.* Notre Dame: University of Notre Dame Press, 1981.

———. *The Peaceable Kingdom: A Primer in Christian Ethics.* Notre Dame: University of Notre Dame Press, 1983.

———. *With the Grain of the Universe: The Church's Witness and Natural Theology.* Grand Rapids: Baker Academic, 2001.

Heidegger, Martin. *Being and Time.* Translated by John Macquarrie and Edward Robinson. San Francisco: HarperCollins, 2008.

———. *Die Kategorien- und Bedeutungslehre des Duns Scotus.* Tübingen: Mohr-Siebeck, 1916.

Helmer, Christine. Review of *Truth in Aquinas*, by John Milbank and Catherine Pickstock. *International Journal of Systematic Theology* 5 (2003): 93–95.

Hemming, Laurence Paul. "*Quod Impossibile Est!* Aquinas and Radical Orthodoxy." In *Radical Orthodoxy? A Catholic Inquiry*, edited by Laurence Paul Hemming, 76–93. London: Ashgate, 2000.

Honnefelder, Ludger. *Johannes Duns Scotus*. München: C. H. Beck, 2005.

———. *Scientia Transcendens: Die Formale Bestimmung der Seiendheit et Realität in der Metaphysik der Mittelalters und der Neuzeit*. Paradeigmata 9. Hamburg: Fleix Meiner, 1990.

Horan, Daniel. "Beyond Essentialism and Complementarity: Toward a Theological Anthropology Rooted in *Haecceitas*." *Theological Studies* 75 (2014): 94–117.

———— "How Original Was Scotus on the Incarnation? Reconsidering the History of the Absolute Predestination of Christ in Light of Robert Grosseteste." *Heythrop Journal* 52 (2011): 374–391.

———— "Praying With the Subtle Doctor: Toward a Contemporary Scotistic Spirituality." *The Cord* 58 (2008): 235–238.

———. "A Rahnerian Theological Response to Charles Taylor's *A Secular Age*." *New Blackfriars* 95 (2014): 21–42.

———— "Thomas Merton the 'Dunce': Identity, Incarnation, and the Not-So-Subtle Influence of John Duns Scotus." *Cistercian Studies Quarterly* 47 (2012):149–75.

Hyman, Gavin. *The Predicament of Postmodern Theology: Radical Orthodoxy or Nihilist Textualism?* Louisville: Westminster John Knox, 2001.

Ingham, Mary Beth. "John Duns Scotus: An Integrated Vision." In *The History of Franciscan Theology*, edited by Kenan Osborne, 185–230. St. Bonaventure, NY: Franciscan Institute, 1994.

———. "Re-Situating Scotist Thought." *Modern Theology* 21 (2005): 609–18.

———. *Scotus for Dunces: An Introduction to the Subtle Doctor.* St. Bonaventure, NY: Franciscan Institute, 2003.

Ingham, Mary Beth and Mechthild Dreyer. *The Philosophical Vision of John Duns Scotus.* Washington, DC: Catholic University of America Press, 2004.

Inglis, John. "Philosophical Autonomy and the Historiography of Medieval Philosophy." *Journal of the History of Philosophy* 5 (1997): 21–53.

———. *Spheres of Philosophical Inquiry and the Historiography of Mediaeval Philosophy.* Leiden: Brill, 1998.

Janz, Paul. "Radical Orthodoxy and the New Culture of Obscurantism." *Modern Theology* 20 (2004): 363–405.

Kallenberg, Brad. *Ethics as Grammar.* Notre Dame: University of Notre Dame Press, 2001.

Kent, Bonnie. *Virtues of the Will: The Transformation of Ethics in the Late Thirteenth Century.* Washington, DC: Catholic University of America Press, 1995.

Kerr, Fergus. *After Aquinas: Versions of Thomism.* Oxford: Blackwell, 2002.

———. *Theology After Wittgenstein.* Oxford: Blackwell, 1986.

Kilby, Karen. "Karl Rahner." In *The Modern Theologians: An Introduction to Christian Theology since 1918*, edited by David Ford, 92–105. 3rd ed. Oxford: Blackwell, 2005.

King, Peter. "Scotus on Metaphysics." In *The Cambridge Companion to Duns Scotus*, edited by Thomas Williams, 15–68. New York: Cambridge University Press, 2003.

Klein, Terrance. *How Things Are in the World: Metaphysics and Theology in Wittgenstein and Rahner.* Milwaukee: Marquette University Press, 2003.

———. *Wittgenstein and the Metaphysics of Grace.* New York: Oxford University Press, 2007.

Long, D. Stephen. *Divine Economy: Theology and the Market.* London: Routledge, 2000.

———. "Radical Orthodoxy." In *The Cambridge Companion to Postmodern Theology*, edited by Kevin Vanhoozer, 126–45. New York: Cambridge University Press, 2003.

Lyotard, Jean-François. *The Postmodern Condition: A Report on Knowledge.* Translated by Geoff Bennington and Brian Massumi. Minneapolis: University of Minnesota Press, 1984.

MacDougall, Scott. "Scapegoating the Secular: The Irony of Mimetic Violence in the Social Theology of John Milbank." In *Violence, Transformation, and the Sacred: "They Shall Be Called Children of God,"* edited by Margaret Pfeil and Tobias Winright, 85–98. Maryknoll, NY: Orbis, 2012.

MacIntyre, Alasdair. *After Virtue: A Study in Moral Theory.* 3rd edition. Notre Dame: University of Notre Dame Press, 2007.

Macken, Raymond. "La théorie de l'illumination divine dans la philosophie d'Henri de Gand." *Reserches de théologie ancienne et medieval* 39 (1972): 82–112.

Mann, William. "Augustine on Evil and Original Sin." In *The Cambridge Companion to Augustine*, edited by Eleonore Stump and Norman Kretzmann, 40–48. New York: Cambridge University Press, 2001.

Manzano, Isidoro. "Individuo Y Sociedad en Duns Escoto." *Antonianum* 76 (2001): 43–78.

Marenbon, John. "Aquinas, Radical Orthodoxy and the Importance of Truth." In Hankey and Hedley, *Deconstructing Radical Orthodoxy: Postmodern Theology, Rhetoric and Truth*, 49–63.

Marrone, Steven. "Henry of Ghent and Duns Scotus on the Knowledge of Being." *Speculum* 63 (1988): 22–57.

———. "Mathew of Aquasparta, Henry of Ghent and Augustinian Epistemology after Bonaventure." *Franziskanische Studien* 65 (1983): 252–90.

———. "The Notion of Univocity in Duns Scotus's Early Works." *Franciscan Studies* 43 (1983): 347–95.

McCord Adams, Marilyn. "The Metaphysics of the Trinity in Some Fourteenth Century Franciscans." *Franciscan Studies* 66 (2008): 101–68.

McGrath, Sean. *The Early Heidegger and Medieval Philosophy: Phenomenology for the Godforsaken*. Washington, DC: Catholic University of America Press, 2006.

Milbank, John. *Beyond Secular Order: The Representation of Being and the Representation of the People*. Oxford: Wiley-Blackwell, 2014.

———. "The Grandeur of Reason and the Perversity of Rationalism: Radical Orthodoxy's First Decade." In *The Radical Orthodoxy Reader*, edited by John Milbank and Simon Oliver. London: Routledge, 2009.

———. "On Theological Transgression." In *The Future of Love: Essays in Political Theology*, 145–74. Eugene, OR: Wipf and Stock, 2009.

———. *Theology and Social Theory: Beyond Secular Reason*. Second edition. Oxford: Blackwell, 2006.

———. *The Word Made Strange: Theology, Language, Culture*. Oxford: Blackwell, 1997.

Milbank, John and Simon Oliver, eds. *The Radical Orthodoxy Reader*. London: Routledge, 2009.

Milbank, John and Catherine Pickstock. *Truth in Aquinas*. London: Routledge, 2001.

Milbank, John, Catherine Pickstock, and Graham Ward. "Introduction: Suspending the Material: The Turn of Radical Orthodoxy." In *Radical Orthodoxy: A New Theology*, edited by John Milbank, Catherine Pickstock, and Graham Ward, 1–20. London: Routledge, 1999.

Möhle, H. *Ethik als Scientia Practica nach Johannes Duns Scotus: Eine Philosophische Grundlegung*. Münster: Aschendorff, 1999.

Newell, Christopher. "Communities of Faith, Desire, and Resistance: A Response to Radical Orthodoxy's *Ecclesia*." In *The Poverty of Radical*

Orthodoxy, edited by Lisa Isherwood and Marko Zlomislić, 178–95. Eugene, OR: Pickwick, 2012.

Nichols, Aidan. *The Shape of Catholic Theology*. Collegeville, MN: Liturgical, 1991.

Nietzsche, Friedrich. *On The Genealogy of Morals: A Polemic*. Translated by Douglas Smith. New York: Oxford University Press, 2009.

Noone, Timothy. "Scholasticism." In *The Cambridge Companion to Philosophy in the Middle Ages*, edited by Jorge Gracia and Timothy Noone, 55–64. Oxford: Blackwell, 2006.

———. "Universals and Individuation." In *The Cambridge Companion to Duns Scotus*, edited by Thomas Williams, 100–28. New York: Cambridge University Press, 2003.

Oliver, Simon. "Introducing Radical Orthodoxy: From Participation to Late Modernity." In *The Radical Orthodoxy Reader*, ed. John Milbank and Simon Oliver. London: Routledge, 2009.

———. *Philosophy, God and Motion*. London: Routledge, 2005.

Pabst, Adrian. *Metaphysics: The Creation of Hierarchy*. Grand Rapids: Eerdmans, 2012.

Paterson, Craig and Matthew Pugh, eds. *Analytical Thomism: Traditions in Dialogue*. London: Ashgate, 2006.

Perrier, Emmanuel. "Duns Scotus Facing Reality: Between Absolute Contingency and Unquestionable Consistency." *Modern Theology* 21 (2005): 619–43.

Pickstock, Catherine. *After Writing: On the Liturgical Consummation of Philosophy*. Oxford: Blackwell, 1998.

———. "Duns Scotus: His Historical and Contemporary Significance." *Modern Theology* 21 (2005): 543–74.

———. "Modernity and Scholasticism: A Critique of Recent Invocations of Univocity." *Antonianum* 78 (2003): 3–47.

———. "Postmodernism." In *The Blackwell Companion to Political Theology*, edited by Peter Scott and William Cavanaugh. Oxford: Blackwell, 2004.

———. *Repetition and Identity: The Literary Agenda*. New York: Oxford University Press, 2013.

———. "The Univocalist Mode of Production." In *Theology and the Political*, edited by John Milbank, Slavoj Zizek, and Creston Davis, 281–325. Durham: Duke University Press, 2005.

Prentice, Robert. *The Basic Quidditative Metaphysics of Duns Scotus as Seen in His De Primo Principio*. Rome: Edizioni Antonianum, 1997.

Puntel, Bruno. *Analogie und Geschichtlichkeit*. Fribourg: Herder, 1969.

Rahner, Karl. *Foundations of Christian Faith: An Introduction to the Idea of Christianity*. Translated by William Dych. New York: Crossroads, 2002.

———. "Philosophy and Theology." In *Theological Investigations*. Translated by David Bourke. Vol. 13. New York: Crossroads, 1975.

Reno, R. R. "The Radical Orthodoxy Project." *First Things* 100 (February 2000): 37–44.

Reuther, Rosemary Radford. "The Postmodern as Premodern: The Theology of D. Stephen Long." In *Interpreting the Postmodern: Responses to "Radical Orthodoxy*," edited by Rosemary Radford Reuther and Marion Grau. New York: T & T Clark, 2006.

Ricoeur, Paul. ———. *Freud and Philosophy: An Essay in Interpretation*. Translated by Dennis Savage. New Haven: Yale University Press, 1970.

———. *Interpretation Theory: Discourse and Surplus of Meaning*. Fort Worth: Texas Christian University Press, 1976.

———. *The Rule of Metaphor: Multi-Disciplinary Studies of the Creation of Meaning in Language*. Translated by Robert Czerny. Toronto: University of Toronto Press, 1977.

Roland, Tracey. *Culture and the Thomist Tradition: After Vatican II*. London: Routledge, 2003.

Rose, Gillian. *Dialectic of Nihilism: Post-Structuralism and Law.* Oxford: Blackwell, 1984.

Roseman, Philip. *Peter Lombard.* New York: Oxford University Press, 2004.

Shakespeare, Steven. *Radical Orthodoxy: A Critical Introduction.* London: SPCK, 2007.

Shircel, Cyril. *The Univocity of the Concept of Being in the Philosophy of John Duns Scotus.* Washington, DC: Catholic University of America Press, 1942.

Smith, James K. A. *Introducing Radical Orthodoxy: Mapping a Post-Secular Theology.* Grand Rapids: Baker Academic, 2004.

"A Little Story About Metanarratives: Lyotard, Religion, and Postmodernism Revisited." *Faith and Philosophy* 18 (2001): 353–68.

———. *Speech and Theology: Language and the Logic of Incarnation.* London: Routledge, 2002.

———. *Who's Afraid of Postmodernism? Taking Derrida, Lyotard and Foucault to Church.* Grand Rapids: Baker Academic, 2006.

Stiver, Dan. "Theological Method." In *The Cambridge Companion to Postmodern Theology,* edited by Kevin Vanhoozer, 170–85. New York: Cambridge University Press, 2003.

Stone, M. W. F. "Scholastic Schools and Early Modern Philosophy." In *The Cambridge Companion to Early Modern Philosophy,* edited by Donald Rutherford, 299–327. New York: Cambridge University Press, 2006.

Taylor, Charles. *A Secular Age.* Cambridge: Belknap, 2007.

Thiemann, Ronald. *Revelation and Theology: The Gospel as Narrated Promise.* Notre Dame: University of Notre Dame Press, 1985.

Thijssen, J. M. M. *Censure and Heresy at the University of Paris 1200–1400.* Philadelphia: University of Pennsylvania Press, 1998.

Thomas, Janice. "Univocity and Understanding God's Nature." In *The Philosophical Assessment of Theology: Essays in Honor of Fredrick C.*

Copleston, edited by Gerard Hughes, 85–100. Washington, DC: Georgetown University Press, 1987.

Todisco, Orlando. "L'Univocita Scoista Dell'Ente E La Svolta Moderna." *Antonianum* 76 (2001): 79–110.

Tonner, Philip. "Duns Scotus's Concept of the Univocity of Being: Another Look." *Pli* 18 (2007): 129–46.

Vos, Antonie. *The Philosophy of John Duns Scotus*. Edinburgh: Edinburgh University Press, 2006.

Ward, Graham. *Cities of God*. London: Routledge, 1998.

———. *Cultural Transformation and Religious Practice*. Cambridge: Cambridge University Press, 2005.

———. "Introduction, or, A Guide to Theological Thinking in Cyberspace." In *The Postmodern God: A Theological Reader*, edited by Graham Ward, xv–xlvii. Oxford: Blackwell, 1997.

———. "Introduction: 'Where We Stand.'" In *The Blackwell Companion to Postmodern Theology*, edited by Graham Ward, xii–xxvii. Oxford: Blackwell, 2001.

———. *Politics of Discipleship: Becoming Postmodern Citizens*. Grand Rapids: Baker Academic, 2009.

———. "Radical Orthodoxy and/as Cultural Politics." In *Radical Orthodoxy? A Catholic Enquiry*, edited by Laurence Paul Hemming, 97–111. Burlington: Ashgate, 2000.

———. "Suffering and Incarnation." In *The Blackwell Companion to Postmodern Theology*, edited by Graham Ward, 192–208. Oxford: Blackwell, 2001.

Werpehoski, William. "Ad Hoc Apologetics." *Journal of Religion* 66 (1986): 282–301.

Williams, Thomas. "The Doctrine of Univocity is True and Salutary." *Modern Theology* 21 (2005): 575–85.

————. "Introduction: The Life and Works of John Duns the Scot." In *The Cambridge Companion to Duns Scotus,* edited by Thomas Williams, 1–14. New York: Cambridge University Press, 2003.

————. "Radical Orthodoxy, Univocity and the New Apophaticism." Paper presented at the International Congress for Medieval Studies, Kalamazoo, MI, 2006.

Wippel, John. *Metaphysical Themes in Thomas Aquinas.* Washington, DC: Catholic University of America Press, 1984.

————. "The Parisian Condemnations of 1270 and 1277." In *A Companion to Philosophy in the Middle Ages*, edited by Jorge Gracia and Timothy Noone, 65–73. Oxford: Blackwell, 2006.

Wolter, Allan. "The Formal Distinction." In *The Philosophical Theology of John Duns Scotus.* Edited by Marilyn McCord Adams, 27–41. Ithaca: Cornell University Press, 1990.

————. "The 'Theologism' of Duns Scotus." In *The Philosophical Theology of John Duns Scotus.* Edited by Marilyn McCord Adams. Ithaca: Cornell University Press, 1990.

————. *Transcendentals and Their Function in the Metaphysics of Duns Scotus.* St. Bonaventure, NY: Franciscan Institute, 1946.

Index

Kallenberg, Brad, 138n104

Kant, Immanuel, 3, 22, 27, 47, 49,
  57, 69, 137

Neo-Kantian, 28

Kataphaticism, 126-7, 186

Kerr, Fergus, 78, 138, 138n104,
  140

Klein, Terrance, 138n104

Leo XIII (pope) 136

Locke, John, 22, 23

Lombard, Peter, 169

Lonergan, Bernard, 137

Long, D. Stephen, 19, 21,
  140n110

Lumen theologicum, see
  Illumination

Luther, Martin, 69

MacDougall, Scott, 11n12

MacIntyre, Alasdair, 78, 139

Manzano, Isidoro, 100

Marrone, Steven, 160

McCabe, Herbert, 138n104

McClendon Jr., James Wm.,
  138n104

McKinnon, Donald, 138n104

Metanarrative, 2, 8, 10, 76, 77, 83,
  103, 189

Metaphysics, 25, 27, 38, 40, 43, 46,
  47, 50, 51, 51n114, 55, 64, 67,

69, 70, 71, 72, 77, 88, 93, 94,
  108, 119, 136, 141, 143,
  143n115, 148, 151, 166, 175,
  176; Implications of univocity
  for, 185-8; Milbank's critique
  of Scotus's view of, 29-33

Methexis, 37

Milbank, John: *Beyond Secular
  Order*, 16n2, 17n3, 35n61, 192,
  192n3; as a contributor to the
  Scotus Story, 15-34; as founder
  of Radical Orthodoxy, 1-6;
  *Philosophy: A Theological
  Critique*, 17n3; *Radical
  Orthodoxy: A New Theology*,
  59, 153; *The Radical Orthodoxy
  Reader*, 59-60; *Theology and
  Social Theory*, 1, 17n3, 20-34,
  35, 66n13, 81, 85, 143, 192;
  Truth in Aquinas, 9-10, 20,
  31n43, 36; *The Word Made
  Strange*, 34, 35

Modernity: as theological
  problem, 1-3, 22-23, 25;
  origins of, 20-26; *see also*
  Scotus Story, Secular

Modus significandi, 109

Neoplatonism, 70, 71, 153

Newell, Christopher, 154, 155

Newton, Isaac, 25

Nietzsche, Friedrich, 26-27, 29, 32, 34, 80, 81, 141

Nihilism, 15, 18, 19, 21, 24, 26, 27, 29n38, 30, 33, 38, 48, 63, 64, 71, 129, 141; Scotus as nihilist, 49-52, 55

Nominalism, 16, 18, 24, 66, 69, 75n32, 78-82, 88; Pickstock on, 38-39; Scotus as nominalist, 16n2

Nominalism-voluntarism, 23-24, 39

Nouvelle théologie, 137

Occam, *See* William of Ockham

Oliver, Simon, 19, 32n50, 59

Ontology, 29, 32, 32n49, 37, 38, 46, 47, 51, 52, 71, 119, 122, 123; *Communio*, 94; Individualistic, 69; Meo-, 49, 51; Non-, 23; Participatory, 29, 34; of violence, 26-27, 29, 68, 81

Ontotheology, 30, 30n52, 117, 118n54

Pabst, Adrian, 12, 17n3, 61, 62, 75, 80, 40, 89, 96, 193; as a contributor to the Scotus Story, 70-74

Perrier, Emmanuel, 154

Pickstock, Catherine, 11; *After Writing*, 20, 36, 36n64, 39, 65, 68n15, 116n50, 118, 144, 149; as a contributor to the Scotus Story, 16, 34-48; on formal distinction, 41-48; Milbank's influence on, 35-39; misinterpretation of formal distinction, 118-9; on Scotus's univocal predication of being, 39-48; *Truth in Aquinas*, 9-10, 20, 31n43, 36

Plato, 21, 37, 171

Postmodern: Hauerwas's critique of, 62-64; Radical Orthodoxy as, 2; theology, 189-94

Power, 22-23, 25-26, 74, 81, 91

Preller, Victor, 138n104

Prentice, Robert, 169

Protomodernity, 3, 13, 15, 35, 46, 47, 53, 54, 57, 72, 86, 97, 194

Quiddity, 170, 182-3

Quasi-property, 170

Radical Orthodoxy: history of, 1-4; presentation of Scotus in, 15-58; methodological presuppositions of, 104-8; misinterpretation of Scotus's semantic argument, 108-13;

175-6; being, 176-80; Thomism, 137

University of Paris, 161
Univocity, 6, 8, 11, 12, 16, 20, 25, 26, 33, 36n64, 37n66, 39-47, 49, 50, 51, 52, 55, 57, 58, 73, 81, 82, 85, 58, 66, 73, 81, 82, 85, 86, 86n57, 89, 90, 91, 98, 99, 102, 108, 110, 111, 112, 113, 114, 144, 144n119, 146, 147, 150, 151, 151n136, 152, 154, 155, 155n148, 156, 191, 193, 194; Cross defends Scotus's view of, 116-8; Scotus's definition of, 172-4; Scotus's view of, 157-84; Williams defends Scotus's view of, 121-33; metaphysical implications of, 185-8; *see also* Univocal concept of being
Univocal concept of being, 7, 10, 54, 66, 77, 87, 88, 94, 111n35, 169, 171, 177, 181-3, 185, 187, 193; *see also* Univocity
Univocal mode of predication, 42

Vicious abstraction, 109, 111, 113, 114, 117, 180, 185
Voluntarism, 38, 39, 132, 144; *see also* Nominalism-voluntarism
Vos, Antonie, 80n40, 158

Ward, Graham, 12, 19, 21, 48, 48n103, 54, 55, 56, 62, 85; as a contributor to the Scotus Story, 18, 52-53
William of Ockham, 16n2, 38, 49, 75n32, 76, 78, 88; as an heir to Scotus, 18, 51, 68-69, 73-74, 79, 88, 150; *see also* Occam
Williams, Thomas, 9, 12, 98, 99, 102, 121-33, 136n97, 151, 155, 156, 157, 192; on Scotus's doctrine of the univocity of being, 121-33
Williams, Rowan, 138n104
Wittgenstein, Ludwig, 138-40, 138n104
Wolter, Allan, 107, 108, 114n43, 148, 152, 158, 176, 177, 180

Zwingli, Ulrich, 89

CPSIA information can be obtained at www.ICGtesting.com
Printed in the USA
LVOW05s0234151114

413847LV00006B/10/P